FINDING GOD AMONG OUR NEIGHBORS, VOLUME 2

FINDING GOD AMONG OUR NEIGHBORS, VOLUME 2

AN INTERFAITH SYSTEMATIC THEOLOGY

KRISTIN JOHNSTON LARGEN

Fortress Press

Minneapolis

FINDING GOD AMONG OUR NEIGHBORS, VOLUME 2
An Interfaith Systematic Theology

Cover image: Peeling paint worn tree © iStockphoto.com / John_Woodcock
Cover design: Tory Herman

Print ISBN: 978-1-4514-8801-2
eBook ISBN: 978-1-5064-2330-2

The paper used in this publication meets the minimum requirements of American National Standard for Information Sciences — Permanence of Paper for Printed Library Materials, ANSI Z329.48-1984.

Manufactured in the U.S.A.

This book was produced using Pressbooks.com, and PDF rendering was done by PrinceXML.

To the faculty, staff, and students of the Lutheran Theological Seminary at Gettysburg, in gratitude for all that has been, and in hope for all that will be.

And to Gettysburg Seminary President Michael Cooper-White, for being a trusted compass, steady pilot, and wise friend.

CONTENTS

Acknowledgments   ix
Introduction   xi
1.   A Brief Introduction to Indigenous Religions   1
2.   A Brief Introduction to Sikhism   33
3.   A Brief Introduction to Confucianism   61
4.   A Brief Introduction to Daoism   89
5.   Life, Death, and What Comes After   117
6.   Trinitarian, Troubling, Tangible Spirit   159
7.   A Relevant, Vibrant Church for the Twenty-First Century   185

Conclusion: An Ending Is Always a Beginning   219
Bibliography   223
Index   235

Acknowledgments

I have many people to thank for their support and assistance during the research and writing of this book. First and foremost, I would like to thank Will Bergkamp and Lisa Gruenisen at Fortress Press. They are both excellent to work with, and I am grateful for their guidance, attention, and encouragement.

I am deeply appreciative of my colleagues and friends who read and commented on sections of specific chapters; their suggestions were very helpful. Any errors or misrepresentations that remain are my responsibility alone. Specifically, I want to thank Rick Carlson, Vince Evener, Mark Vitalis Hoffman, Louis Komjathy, Leo Lefebure, Derek Nelson, Mark Oldenburg, and Richard Payne for their insight and wisdom.

In addition, I discussed material from chapters 5 and 6 in several of my classes, and many student comments helped me clarify my arguments. I am particularly grateful to students Melissa Woeppel and Erika Tobin for reading and commenting on a draft of chapter 5.

Different versions of chapter 6 were presented in several contexts: at the 2015 Fall Academy at Gettysburg Seminary (subsequently published in *Seminary Ridge Review*, Spring 2016) and at the Religious Life and Public Space in Asia Conference sponsored by the Lutheran World Federation, which occurred in Hong Kong, September 2015. A very early version of chapter 5 was presented at the Parliament of the World's Religions in Salt Lake City, Utah, in October 2015.

Finally, and as always, my husband John read the last three chapters very carefully, and his wise comments and excellent proofreading skills were invaluable.

Introduction

This book continues the work of volume 1, which I described as an attempt to do systematic theology in a new way by considering interreligious engagement as part of the foundation of Christian theology, rather than its decoration. There, I used the metaphor of building a house, arguing that interreligious engagement needs to be included in the very foundation of the house itself, not merely its use as ornamentation. I am committed to the idea that conversation with the religious "other" has much to teach Christians about our own beliefs and practices and that, in fact, there is insight and wisdom in those conversations that simply cannot be found anywhere else. The Christian tradition as a whole, and Christian theology in particular, is poorer without interreligious engagement.

In particular, let me lift up three critical arguments that support this comparative work. First, in light of the deep interconnectedness of the whole human family, it is incumbent upon Christian theology to engage non-Christian religious traditions for the sake of the neighbor, whom Christians are called not only to refrain from bearing false witness against but, even more, to love. Second, Christian theology can and should expect to learn something about God in the course of that engagement based on God's own universal self-revelation. Finally, Christian theology can and should expect that it will be stretched and challenged but at the same time deepened and strengthened through this engagement, with wonderful, unpredictable results. Though it sometimes feels uncomfortable and risky, this process can transform and nurture the whole Christian community, empowering not only our witness to the gospel but also our relationships with non-Christian communities all over the world, with whom we must partner in the work of justice and peace. It is my hope that all three of these commitments are demonstrated in the chapters that follow.

As in the previous volume, what this means in the context of this book is that in the articulation of a Christian doctrine of salvation, for example, I include for consideration the concept of immortality in Daoism, and in the construction of a Christian understanding of the Holy Spirit, I discuss the way Sikhs view their holy book, the Guru Granth Sahib, as the embodiment of the divine spirit shared by all the previous ten human gurus. In this way, I am attempting to incorporate some general methods and commitments of comparative theology into the basic practice of Christian systematic theology itself, such that the task of defining and interpreting Christian doctrine inherently includes the task of interpreting that doctrine in conversation with specific practices and beliefs of non-Christian religious traditions.

Introduction to Part 1

As in the previous volume, part 1 consists of four chapters, each of which seeks to introduce Christians to a different religious tradition, with the exception of chapter 1. The subject of chapter 1 is indigenous religions, and in that chapter, while a general introduction to the category is provided and some basic characteristics of indigenous religions are described, more detailed examination is limited to the Ainu of Japan, the Aboriginal people of Australia, and the Yoruba of Africa. Chapter 2 focuses on Sikhism, chapter 3 is on Confucianism, and chapter 4 discusses Daoism. These four chapters are meant to supplement and complement the first four chapters of volume 1, which examine Hinduism, Judaism, Buddhism, and Islam.

Here as there, it is important to note that the introductions to these religions are intended specifically for Christians, particularly those who are in seminary and preparing for careers in public ministry. This means that I have chosen and organized the material for these chapters into categories that make sense for Christians, anticipating the questions Christians will ask and the specific things Christians will want to know. Therefore, the chapter on Daoism, for example, is structured differently than an introductory text written by a Daoist for a more general audience.

One final point of clarification needs mentioning here as well. As in volume 1, throughout the book, I have chosen not to use the diacritical marks needed to accurately transliterate foreign words into English. These marks are used to indicate pronunciation, vowel placement, and inflection, among other things. Obviously, they are very important for those who know the languages. However, for those who do not, they are meaningless and confusing, and because this book is not designed for specialists, I have chosen to omit them primarily to avoid bogging down the general reader. Those who know the words in the original languages will mentally supply them and those who do not will not miss them.

Introduction to Part 2

In part two, the explicitly comparative theological part of the book, I treat three different Christian theological loci: soteriology, pneumatology, and ecclesiology. Again, these chapters supplement and complement the chapters in volume 1: doctrine of God, doctrine of creation, and anthropology. The narrative thread of each chapter winds through core Christian claims in each of these areas, and as in the previous volume, these claims are enhanced by and juxtaposed with relevant claims from different indigenous traditions, Sikhism, Confucianism, and Daoism. Through this juxtaposition, the chapters seek to nuance and deepen an understanding of Christian theology, helping the reader see familiar territory in new ways and gain a fresh perspective on traditional faith claims.

The quote from Francis Clooney, which was also included in the previous volume, is worth repeating here as well, as it gets at the heart of what the chapters in part 2 are attempting. In his book *Comparative Theology: Deep Learning Across Religious Borders*, Clooney writes: "If [comparative theology] does not disrespect doctrinal expressions of truth, neither does it merely repeat doctrinal statements as if nothing is learned from comparative reflection. Rarely, if ever, will comparative theology produce new truths, but it can make possible fresh insights into familiar and revered truths, and new ways of receiving those truths."[1] This, then, is the overarching goal of the book: creating for the Christian reader in particular the possibility of fresh insights and new ways of understanding and articulating those insights—not only for one's own theological edification but for the sake of the church as a whole and the presentation of the gospel.

As in volume 1, no specific conclusions are drawn from the interreligious interludes in this second section of the book. Instead, I have left the specific interpretation to the reader, inviting you to make connections for yourself in the hope that you will draw your own insights, thus contributing to the theological conversation in your own way from your own theological context and tradition. However, to facilitate these connections, there are questions at the end of each chapter, inviting reflection on specific points of comparison between Christianity and the different traditions.

I close this introduction on the same note that concluded the introduction to volume 1. The principal theological conviction that grounds this particular book and the comparative method that shapes it is my belief that theology matters: it matters for one's individual life in the world and it matters for the human community as a whole. It is my strong conviction that Christian theology can and should positively inform and transform the way Christians think and live in such a way that not only are their lives richer and more meaningful but also that they, in turn, through the power of the Holy Spirit, are inspired to create richer and more meaningful societies. But this can only happen if Christian theology meets people where they are and speaks to the situations in which they find themselves.

The context in which Christianity finds itself in the twenty-first century is a global, plural one, and if Christian theology has nothing to say about the millions and millions of people with vibrant, diverse, passionately held religious beliefs and practices, it risks relegating itself to a position of irrelevancy and indifference. In today's context, Christian theology requires not only fidelity to the gospel and a healthy respect for the tradition but also intellectual courage, daring, and innovation. It requires seeking God where God is found, loving the

1. Francis X. Clooney, *Comparative Theology: Deep Learning Across Religious Borders* (Malden, MA: Wiley-Blackwell, 2010), 112.

neighbor God has placed in front of us, and trusting that God is always there, guiding us down paths as yet untrodden, where an as-yet-unimagined future awaits. This is the spirit in which this book was written. I hope that it is also the spirit in which it is read.

A Brief Introduction to Indigenous Religions

As a person of European descent, I begin this chapter with some trepidation. Almost without exception—perhaps, indeed, completely without exception—when Europeans and their descendants have encountered indigenous populations, there have been terrible, terrifying consequences for those indigenous people. It is a grim history of systematic genocide, played out over and over again in diverse countries and contexts all over the world, and it is only in the past few decades that there have been national and international responses of apology and reparation.[1] Particularly when it comes to the category of religion—about which more will be said in the following pages—it is impossible to ignore the fact that the very meaning of religion in indigenous cultures historically has been misunderstood and distorted by colonial powers, to say nothing of how it has been demonized and dismissed. Alternatively—albeit with no less distortion—it also has been appropriated and mainstreamed, which has its own serious problems and challenges. With all this in the background, what can, or better, what should, an outsider like myself say?

In spite of all the challenges and concerns, there are many reasons a chapter on indigenous religions is extremely important in a book such as this. Two of these should be mentioned at the outset as they have particular relevance for Christians in the Global North—and even more specifically, for Christians in the United States. The first is the easy and careless borrowing of what is described as "Native American Spirituality" by many US nonnative people without any understanding or respect for the different native communities and their uniqueness. For example, the dreamcatcher craze seems to be mostly over, but bundled sage (often referred to as "smudge sticks") still can be found in New Age bookstores and continues to be used in nonnative home blessings. One can book a spiritual retreat that will include a sweat lodge or sometimes even a vision quest without ever realizing that what one experiences has been

---

1. As one example, see the United Nations Declaration on the Rights of Indigenous Peoples, adopted by the General Assembly on September 13, 2007, http://tinyurl.com/jv4cvbv.

tailor-made for a European American audience and bears little resemblance to its original form and meaning.

Figure 1. Chief Seattle, photograph taken in 1864.

Another example of this is the way in which Native Americans are often extoled for their care of the earth and appreciation of the deep relationality of all creation. This can result in a caricature being co-opted by individuals and organizations to further their own ends—problematic even when those ends are noble. If you are of a certain age, you remember the "crying Indian" commercial that came out in the 1970s: a "Native American" (the actor himself was not Native American, although he often played one on TV) canoes through a polluted city and sheds one tear as trash is thrown at his feet.[2] It was a Keep America Beautiful public service announcement against pollution.

Similarly, there are few people who have not seen a poster or bumper sticker with some poignant environmental message attributed to Chief Seattle (or Chief Sealth, as he is also known). Some of these bon mots include, "Earth does not belong to us, we belong to the earth," "Take only memories, leave only footprints," and "Man did not weave the web of life, he is merely a strand in it. Whatever he does to the web, he does to himself." The vast majority of these quotes come from a speech he made in either 1854 or 1855, which was published in 1887 and translated by Henry Smith.[3] It has been reprinted and altered multiple times since then—most famously as the children's book *Brother Eagle, Sister Sky* in 1991—and Seattle himself and the words attributed to him have attained cult-like status. The fact that the veracity of the words is impossible to verify, and that embellishment and even fabrication by his European interpreters clearly has occurred over time is irrelevant: he is a symbol of Native American wisdom that transcends time and place, and his specific historical, tribal location is immaterial to his message. Denise Low notes how problematic this is: "Written reproductions of orally performed Native American literatures omit the performative context and distances texts from historical and cultural contexts. . . . With Seattle's speech, this historic specificity is crucial."[4]

While it is undeniable that ecological sensibilities are manifest in a myriad of different beliefs and practices in a wide variety of indigenous peoples, as John Grim and others have noted, "idealized conceptions of the ecologically friendly native fail to represent the reality of indigenous peoples throughout the world."[5] As is true for all peoples, communities, and societies:

> Human culture is fluid and constantly subjected to change occasioned by natural and human factors. War, commerce, famine,

2. "Keep America Beautiful – (Crying Indian) – 70s PSA Commercial," YouTube video, 1:06, posted by "Justin Engelhaupt," December 31, 2010, http://tinyurl.com/qaa7gsl.

3. Arnold Krupat, "Chief Seattle's Speech Revisited," *American Indian Quarterly* 35, no. 2 (Spring 2011): 193.

4. Denise Low, "Contemporary Reinvention of Chief Seattle: Variant Texts of Chief Seattle's 1854 Speech," *American Indian Quarterly* 19, no. 3 (Summer 1995): 407.

5. Joseph Witt and David Wiles, "Nature in Asian Indigenous Traditions: A Survey Article," *Worldviews* 10, no. 1 (2006): 43.

and other natural factors often engender human migration, which result in changes in culture, as a result of inter and intra-cultural interactions. In the process of these interactions the pristine character of any culture is impacted. In view of this, different cultures respond in a variety of ways to outside influences.[6]

The word that is important here is "pristine." Outsiders sometimes construct a pure version of indigenous life that they imagine to have existed in some idyllic past before native communities were "corrupted" by European ideals and practices (one hears Rousseau's championing of "man in his primitive state" in the background). This creates a paralyzing Procrustean bed on which indigenous peoples are forced to lie, denying indigenous communities the right to develop, change, and grow organically according to both the external and internal factors that shape their lives on a daily basis.

Instead, as should not be surprising, there is no one "native," nor one simple model of indigenous engagement with the environment. Rather, there are important distinctions between the way native peoples view the world and their relationship with it, and generalizations across continents can only be made with great care—particularly generalizations across Asia, which stretches from Siberia down through Indonesia. It may be true that "much can be learned from the religious relationships between indigenous peoples and the natural world that could facilitate less ecological degradation and thus a healthier, more sustainable lifeway for the rest of humanity."[7] Nevertheless, the best way to do this is not through adopting feel-good platitudes and romanticized images but rather through serious engagement with and study of particular ways of being in specific religious communities.

The point in these examples is that without a better understanding of indigenous peoples and religions in general, this kind of exploitation and misrepresentation will simply continue, fueling misunderstandings and ongoing relationships of ignorant arrogation. This chapter is only the most basic and tentative beginning to such an understanding, but it is a beginning nonetheless.

The second reason why some knowledge of indigenous religious traditions is of increasing importance for Western Christians is less about historical (and ongoing) racism and oppression and more about contemporary practical numerical realities: that is, the rapidly growing population of Christians in the Global South. As of 2015, one out of every four Christians now lives in Africa, where Christian belief and practice is deeply marked by and infused with aspects of indigenous cultural and religion. This fact is changing the face of Christianity everywhere thanks to immigration and travel patterns, and no amount of denial will halt the process.

6. Adekunle Oyinloye Dada, "Old Wine in New Bottle: Elements of Yoruba Culture in Aladura Christianity," *Black Theology* 12, no. 1 (April 2014): 19.

7. Ibid.

This is related to another practical fact, which has to do with the number of distinct religions worldwide. When taken together, "indigenous religions are the majority of the world's religions."[8] What that means, of course, is not that any one particular indigenous religion or community has as many adherents as Islam or Christianity, for example—some indigenous religions exist only in one small community—but instead that when viewed as a group (which some might view as problematic), the sheer number of indigenous religious traditions around the world dwarfs any other single religion and/or category of religion. This statistic is important because it brings into view people who are often overlooked and ignored by those who focus exclusively on what are considered world religions—and again, let me note that the whole categorization of religion is a matter of some dispute.[9] There may be only relatively small numbers of Ainu in Japan or Sami in Sweden or Aboriginal people in Australia, but when taken together, these traditions constitute the majority of religions in the world.

With that as background, this chapter proceeds as follows. I begin with some general definitions and continuing issues in the study of indigenous religions. I then share some general characteristics that are in evidence, in one form or another, in most indigenous traditions. Finally, I conclude the chapter with three case studies—brief introductions to three specific indigenous traditions as a way of rooting and exemplifying the more general information in a specific context.

INDIGENOUS RELIGIONS: AN INTRODUCTION

WHAT IS RELIGION?

A definition of religion is crucial because the way religion is defined naturally determines who is classified as religious: that is, any particular definition of religion serves both to include and exclude different people, depending on whether their practices and/or beliefs fit the definition. Tony Swain notes why this is of particular importance when considering indigenous religions:

> From the time of the Deists, the implicit definitions of religion were largely those which Lord Herbert of Cherbury had pronounced universal human "common notions"—the belief in a Supreme Being, the worship of that Being, the moral orientation of worship, the sense of sin that can be expiated, and the belief in a retributive after life. And it was because Aborigines lacked such beliefs that they were, until the 1870s, said to be totally devoid of a religious life.[10]

8. Graham Harvey, ed., *Indigenous Religions: A Companion* (London: Cassell, 2000), 3.

9. See, for example, the excellent analysis in Tomoko Masuzawa, *The Invention of World Religions: Or, How European Universalism Was Preserved in the Language of Pluralism* (Chicago: University of Chicago Press, 2005). See also Harvey, *Indigenous Religions*, 6.

What was true for Aborigines was true for other indigenous peoples as well. Because they often lacked words for concepts Europeans deemed critical for religious belief, and because their practices often did not follow the patterns of worship and social engagement found in Christianity in particular, they were deemed "heathen" and considered to be subhuman or worse. In this way, religion provided a justification for a wide variety of abuses by colonizing powers.

However, Lord Herbert's definition of religion is not the only one. Graham Harvey writes, "Health, wealth and the pursuit of happiness are central concerns of religions. . . . Religions are structured, orderly, socially sanctioned ways of reaching out to those things, or that thing, which people most want."[11] Note that in this definition, what is important is not abstract concepts or philosophical ideas but concrete realities that have a profound impact on one's physical, material, emotional, and economic life in the here-and-now. When religion is defined according to those terms, there is no question that indigenous peoples have robust religious beliefs and practices that, in contrast to many Europeans, pervade every aspect of their lives. Ironically, it is the comprehensive nature of their religious life that makes it hard to talk about indigenous religions as a separate category. In many indigenous communities, it is not so much that a person has this or that religious belief or practice, but rather that he or she simply is religious—and almost all aspects of life are shaped by that worldview. Indeed, as Harvey notes, "most languages have no word for 'religion.' Most people do not separate bits of their lives into neat boxes which can be labeled 'religion,' 'politics,' or 'catering.'"[12]

WHO IS INDIGENOUS?

Some reflection on the whole category of "indigenous religions" is necessary here, because even though the term clearly functions—and if we follow Ludwig Wittgenstein and his conviction that the meaning of words/language comes in their use, then we can concede that the term does have meaning for us—at the same time, it is important to recognize the problematic generalizations that it also fosters. Again, Harvey notes that "just as there is no single reality (apart from that of stereotypical racist clichés) that is identifiable as 'the native American,' there is no single 'Native American religion.'"[13] Following his reasoning here, even less is there anything that could be called a single indigenous religion. Instead, there are vast differences between groups, both those in close proximity to one another and those separated by oceans and continents. Therefore, there is no one single checklist against which one might

10. Tony Swain, *Aboriginal Religions in Australia: A Bibliographic Survey* (New York: Greenwood Press, 1991), 26.

11. Harvey, *Indigenous Religions*, 1.

12. Ibid., 2.

13. Ibid., 6.

measure a tradition and call it "indigenous"—simply put, the term is somewhat of an artificial one, generated by academics.

Harvey observes that "the academic Study of Religions has adopted three broad categories for religions": world religions, new religious movements, and indigenous religions.[14] Furthermore, that third category has only recently been developed in any serious way; the academic study of indigenous religions previously had been primarily the purview of anthropologists.[15] Nor do these distinctions exhaust the challenges around naming. Mary MacDonald notes three different terms that are used by different populations to describe indigenous peoples and their cultures. She writes, "Primitive, primal, indigenous—three ways of naming, the first employed by colonizers, the second by scholars, and the third by native peoples who suffered in the dislocations of the colonial era and are today reconstructing their identities."[16] Of course, even this last term raises questions: How long must a people live in a place to be considered indigenous? And what does the word mean for diasporic peoples who still cling strongly to that self-identification, even when they are far removed from its geographical location? Other terms that are occasionally used are "animist," "traditional," and "local" religious traditions.

However, the challenges around naming and the multitude of differences between peoples does not mean that nothing at all can be said about indigenous religions in general. Returning to Wittgenstein for a moment, his category of family resemblances is helpful here: there may not be one single feature that is common to all indigenous religions, but there are multiple overlapping characteristics that serve to unite them in one family. Let me offer here a compelling example of the way in which differences between peoples can be recognized and honored while still allowing the umbrella term "indigenous religions" to function. This is how Nomalungelo Goduka introduces the edited volume *Indigenous Peoples' Power and Wisdom*:

> As is customary in Indigenous communities when one embarks on a spiritual journey, I will follow the protocol of invoking our ancestors and those of the contributors. I will also call upon *oo-khoko*—the elders from our villages and communities to provide us with the healing powers and humbling wisdoms to guide us as we remember the past, engage with the present, and predict a future built on inclusive paradigms and ways of knowing. In the process of paving the way for the contributors to tell these "cultural truths" as these truths were told to them, I am also calling upon their ancestors to support and sustain our contributors with spiritual wisdoms so they can have a clear heart and mind to capture and

14. Ibid.

15. Mary MacDonald, "The Primitive, the Primal, and the Indigenous in the Study of Religion," *Journal of the American Academy of Religion* 79, no. 4 (December 2011): 821.

16. Ibid., 819.

narrate these knowledges the best way they know how. During my brief visits to the various continents, countries, and villages to engage in conversations and listen to stories as they were told to me, I made every effort, in the early hours of the day or after sunset to jog, walk, and wander for spiritual revival, and to connect with the ancestors of each contributor.[17]

She then goes on to introduce herself, which she does not by answering the questions "Who are you? What is your address and phone number?" but rather by locating herself "within the spiritual and cultural contexts, which is the accepted and appropriate procedure for the *ama-Xhosa* of South Africa, the group to which [she belongs]."[18] In order to do that, these are the questions she must answer:

Uyintombi kabana – Who are you a daughter of?
Iphi inkaba yakho – Where was your umbilical cord buried?
Ngokwesiduko Ningamani – What are your panegyric legends?[19]

She explains the reason for these questions as follows: "Responses to these questions provide a holistic identification grounding the individual in spiritual and cultural contexts. These contexts form deep roots for Indigenous peoples that do not only connect us to one another in our villages and communities, but also to the land."[20] While these particular questions may be unique to one specific religion (or group of religions), it is likely that other indigenous peoples would recognize the spirit behind them and relate them to their own specific practices that serve a similar function.

To conclude this section of the chapter, I want to mention just two of these characteristic features that, in one way or another, play an important role in most (if not all) indigenous religions: land and personhood.

LAND

Marcia Langton has a helpful description of "place," which, though focused particularly on Aboriginal religion, is more broadly applicable. She first quotes philosopher Edward Casey, who writes, "Human beings—along with other entities on earth—are ineluctably place-bound. More than earthlings, we are placelings, and our very perceptual apparatus, our sensing body, reflects the kinds of places we inhabit."[21] She then goes on to say, "Aboriginal concepts of

---

17. Julian E. Kunnie and Nomalungelo I. Goduka, eds., *Indigenous Peoples' Wisdom and Power: Affirming Our Knowledge Through Narratives* (Aldershot, UK: Ashgate, 2006), x.

18. Ibid.

19. Ibid.

20. Ibid.

21. Marcia Langton, "Sacred Geography," in *Aboriginal Religions in Australia: An Anthology of Recent*

land estates refer simultaneously to social, physical and metaphysical matters. . . . The meanings of social responsibility—the bonds of being related to one another—are expressed through the rituals and ideas of the sacred landscape, through symbols of the past and present (the living and the dead) embodied in particular places. These places are themselves part of the fabric of relatedness in Aboriginal life in the desert."[22]

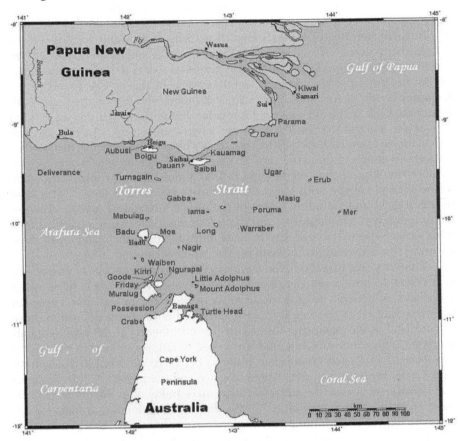

Figure 2: A Map of the Torres Strait Islands, in between the northern tip of Australia and Papua New Guinea.

The inherent and inextricable nature of the relationship between indigenous peoples and the specific geographical places they inhabit can hardly be overstated. Identity is essentially related to land: specific rock formations,

Writings, ed. Max Charlesworth, Françoise Dussart, and Howard Morphy (Aldershot, UK: Ashgate, 2005), 134.
   22. Ibid., 135.

particular bodies of water and their animal/plant inhabitants, and especially sacred thin places where spirits draw near and communication with divinities and ancestors is facilitated. The various stories of community, clan, and family origins are all nested in particular places, and people take as totems particular animals that are also nested in these places.

Mary MacDonald identifies three "facts of life" that "inform the perspectives of indigenous communities": concern with the land itself, relationships of the inhabitants of the earth to each other, and fertility—fertility of the earth, fertility of animals (for those who hunt), and fertility of the people themselves.[23] All of these characteristics are interrelated, and all are nontransferable, grounded in precise geographical spaces that for the most part cannot be replicated elsewhere. A good example of this can be found in the Saltwater People of Australia, Torres Strait Islanders who live on the Cape York Peninsula. One of the elders states his relationship with the sea this way: "I am part of the sea and the sea is part of me when I am on it."[24] In this way, he articulates an essential reality that characterizes his people—and also many other indigenous peoples around the world: "The essence of being a 'Saltwater' person is more ontological than technological. It is about how you spiritually relate to the sea and engage with spiritual forces that create it and you."[25] This kind of ontological understanding is one of the most foundational aspects of life in many indigenous communities, and these communities are thus governed by a wide variety of rituals that seek to manage, nurture, strengthen, and repair these all-important relationships between people, land, and animals.

The last point that should be mentioned here is the concept of possession, as it relates to how nonnative human beings typically view their relationship with land in general. It is an accurate generalization to say that European societies, marked as they are by Christianity and concepts of dominion, have viewed land as an inanimate object that has no inherent rights and demands no moral obligation. As Chris Budden writes, to talk about land in the typical discourse of European colonialism leads to conversation around concepts of "real estate, economic worth, measured space and ownership. It is a discourse that stands over against the metaphors that mark Indigenous discourse; such as, 'mother earth,' 'place,' or 'home.'"[26] Whether building homes, drilling for oil, constructing roads, damming rivers, or commercially fishing, best practices are governed overwhelmingly and almost exclusively by their impact on human beings—either aesthetic, economic, or physical. There is little, if any, consideration for what is best for the land itself (or the sea, or whether or not something violates the integrity of the soil, mountains, rivers, etc.). Even

23. MacDonald, "Primitive, Primal, Indigenous," 824.

24. As cited in Ian J. McNiven, "Saltwater People: Spiritscapes, Maritime Rituals and the Archaeology of Australian Indigenous Seascapes," *World Archaeology* 35, no. 3 (December 2003): 329.

25. Ibid., 330.

26. Chris Budden, "Exploring Contextual Theology in Australia in Dialogue with Indigenous People," *International Journal of Public Theology* 2, no. 3 (2008): 295.

though environmental concerns are pushing those questions to the forefront more and more, it is still true that even environmental concerns are framed primarily as human concerns: What is air pollution doing to our health? Will our children have enough water? Will we be able to grow enough food for the increasing population?

By contrast, "For Indigenous peoples, land cannot be owned, bought, or sold. She does not belong to us, we belong to her. We are born out of this land; we spend our lives on this land as her guests; and after death we go back to that same land."[27] This attitude is typified by a more reciprocal relationship between human beings and their larger environment, a stronger sense of responsibility toward it, and a recognition of its own integrity and intrinsic value. It is a radically different worldview that displaces humans from the top of the creation pyramid and instead places them in an interconnected web where all beings—sentient and insentient—have value. Different communities live out this conviction in a wide variety of ways, including ceremonies around hunting and gathering, celebrations that mark changing seasons, and various types of sacrifices offered to mark different times and events. These practices themselves are organically related to the spaces and places different indigenous peoples inhabit, which is why they resist easy generalization. This is demonstrated in the three case studies that conclude the chapter.

PERSONHOOD

A second feature of most indigenous religions I want to mention here is what might be called "personhood." In most Western cultures—and certainly in Christianity—the category of person has been restricted to human beings and sometimes to only very specific human beings. In various times and places, full personhood was granted only to those of the right race, the right gender, and the right mental/physical abilities. (Many would argue that this question of full personhood continues today around issues of sexual orientation, for example, and disability.) In any case, it is only in rare instances where any being other than a human is granted the status of person.

By contrast, in most indigenous communities, the category of person is very broad, transcending boundaries of both time and species. Indeed, generally in an indigenous worldview, the world is heavily populated by spirits, ancestors, animals, humans, gods, and natural powers—all of whom impact life on a daily basis and all of whom are deeply interconnected. One's own personhood, then, is always understood in the larger context of these various persons that constitute any individual identity. In this way, then, the very concept of an individual is radically different in indigenous societies than in a typical European framework. At the same time, however, it must be remembered that the relationships and interactions between these "persons" vary greatly among peoples, and not all religions use the language of personhood in the same way.

27. Kunnie and Goduka, *Wisdom and Power*, xi.

Of the many possible examples of this kind of personhood, I mention just two: ancestors and animals.

Ancestors in Africa

While ancestors play an active role in many indigenous religious traditions, they are particularly important in traditional African societies. However, here again, the nature and dynamic of the actual lived relationship between ancestors and their (living) descendants is different from place to place. For example, the Yoruba, who will be discussed in more detail later in the chapter, have two different categories of ancestors. Those who have led a good life, died a good death (typically at an old age), and left faithful descendants who will carry on their memory and respect them are considered to be *orun rere*, which literally means "being in the 'good heaven.'"[28] It is believed that these ancestors in particular have the power to influence and be involved in the life of the family and the society and can be embodied by a medium (*egungun*), particularly during festivals and celebrations.

Another specific example can be found in the Ohafia people of Nigeria. There (as in many places), shrines to one's ancestors are established and maintained on a regular basis, and indeed, this ritual maintenance is an important aspect of daily life. John McCall, in his fieldwork in Nigeria, emphasizes the variety and complexity of the whole notion of an ancestor. He writes:

> I found that ancestors do not occupy a single "position" in a structural sense but are embodied in a number of different ways in a wide range of activities and material culture. . . . It was this *multivalent pervasiveness* and the particular way that Ohafia people engaged with the socially constructed experience of it, that constituted an ancestral presence in Ohafia life; a presence that, immanent in the landscape itself, was attested to by the shrine found at every turn and the offerings of kola and palm wine that punctuated the daily flow of life.[29]

The term "multivalent pervasiveness" is particularly helpful and apt here, reminding us how difficult it is to categorize the role of ancestors in even one specific indigenous community, let alone more broadly. At the same time, the basic conviction undergirding the relationship one has with the ancestors is the same: an individual's particular identity is fundamentally communal and thus cannot be fully understood or realized without a lived relationship to one's ancestors.

There is one specific practice of the Ohafia that illustrates this conviction

---

28. E. Thomas Lawson, *Religions of Africa* (San Francisco: Harper & Row, 1984), 63.

29. John C. McCall, "Rethinking Ancestors in Africa," *Africa* 65, no. 2 (1995): 258; italics mine.

well, which relates to the paternal compounds of familial groups. McCall notes that members of a specific lineage are often referred to by the name of their common ancestor (in this case, Ndi Kalu [people of Kalu]), and the houses of the various descendants of Kalu are all located in the compound, the grave of each man being located under the house he built. The specific room that stands over the grave, then, becomes a room of central importance.

> The sons of the compound use the room over the grave as a meeting place where matters of family interest are discussed. When libations are poured the ancestors invoked are the founder of the compound in which the gathering is taking place and his descendants. Before any living man may drink, a portion is poured into a small hole in the floor which is said to lead to the mouth of the founder himself.[30]

There are different but similar rituals for female ancestors, who are remembered with pots (*ududu*) that are kept in the kitchen hearth.[31]

Animals in America

The other example worth mentioning is the role of animals in many Native American communities. In most if not all Native American traditions, animals play a central role, and the relationship between humans and animals is critical to the life and well-being of the whole community. Animals also play a role in most creation stories. They have an ability to affect life both positively and negatively, depending on how they are treated, and, as noted above, they are endowed with personhood. Dave Aftandilian notes in his work with Creek and Cherokee peoples how in this specific case, animals possess sentience, exercise agency, and are also believed to have a soul and an afterlife.[32]

Thus there is a deep kinship between humans and animals, and great care is taken in the maintenance of the relationships between them. So, for example, Aftandilian observes that because of the power animals possess—more power even than humans have—they must be respected. If they are not—if they are overhunted, for example, or if their bodies are mistreated—they can and will retaliate: "animals have the spiritual power to punish offenses against them."[33] By the same token, when they are cared for and treated well, they also reward humans for kindness and respect; this is attested to in many different Creek and Cherokee stories.

Not surprisingly then, there are a variety of rituals that the Creek and Cherokee perform to strengthen and nurture these relationships. One of the

---

30. Ibid., 260.
31. Ibid.
32. Dave Aftandilian, "Toward a Native American Theology of Animals: Creek and Cherokee Perspectives," *Cross Currents* 61, no. 2 (June 2011): 197.
33. Ibid., 198.

most important of these is the Green Corn ceremony, a form of "world renewal" ceremony that is performed on behalf of all living beings.[34] This ceremony involves a variety of ritual practices, including prayer, fasting, dancing, and sacrifice, among others. The larger purpose behind it is reciprocity—that is, giving back to the universe the energy that has been taken out of it, like when a hunter kills an animal for food. This is one way that the personhood of animals can be seen in Native American religious practice and the relationality—indeed, familial kinship—between humans and animals is experienced.

In this section, I hope to have demonstrated both some of the challenges inherent in the category of indigenous religions, and also certain ways in which this category can function well to help outsiders understand some of the core convictions and traditional values of indigenous peoples. At the very least, I hope to have invited more caution in the use of the term and more respect for the uniqueness of indigenous peoples and the need to appreciate their particularities, as well as their similarities. In service of that last goal, I now turn to three specific communities, describing each of them in more detail.

THREE BRIEF CASE STUDIES

It has become more commonplace in chapters on indigenous religions to offer case studies of specific indigenous communities, recognizing the inherent problems with relying exclusively on generalizations. While certainly there are similarities between different peoples, traditions, and nations, it is of crucial importance to allow each community to stand independently and speak with its own voice. So in the rest of the chapter, I offer a brief introduction to three different indigenous traditions, using as a lens one key practice that is both characteristic and important for understanding that particular community.

AUSTRALIAN ABORIGINAL PEOPLES: THE DREAMING

There is a great deal of literature on Australian aboriginal peoples, much of it stemming from the catastrophic history of British colonization, which is ongoing. As in other countries, the history of European contact and engagement with the indigenous peoples of Australia is sordid and shameful, and the legacy of this history still lingers today in many different ways. Janneke Hut notes that the colonial era began in Australia with the coming of James Cook in April 1770. Even though he was charged with getting the consent of the natives as he took possession of the land, he violated that charge by reinterpreting the doctrine of *terra nullius*. Originally intended to describe land completely uninhabited by human beings, he interpreted it as "'a land which was inhabited but which the inhabitants could not possess' either due to incapability of the inhabitants derived from the concept of the 'primitiveness'

34. Ibid., 200.

Figure 3: Map of Australia.

of the Indigenous population or to the lack of sophisticated titles or legal documents to the land."[35] She goes on to say, "And thus all right 'to land which had been occupied for *40,000 years, for 1,600 generations and more*' had in a single instant been wiped out. The indigenous peoples of Australia had now become subject to British law."[36]

Tony Swain offers a similar view in his brief history of the study of Aboriginal religions in Australia. There he recounts the purely pejorative responses by sailors and explorers who described the indigenous peoples as

---

35. Janneke Hut, "In Search of Affirmed Aboriginality as Christian: 'If you do not walk on the tracks of your grandparents, you will get lost . . .'" *Exchange* 41, no. 1 (2012): 22.

36. Ibid.; italics original.

"more like monsters than human beings," "savage, cruel, black barbarians," and "the most miserable people on earth."[37]

Swain notes that as time passed, attitudes changed—albeit slowly—until finally, from the 1960s on, Aboriginal peoples themselves began to contribute to the study of their culture and spiritual life. He concludes with the following assessment:

> The history of the study of Aboriginal religions can be seen as a gradual, faltering progress towards the simple realization that Aboriginal Australians are human beings, who, like us, try to give significance to their life. The questions Western writers have asked about Aborigines and their religions have been, in order, as follows:
> *Do they exist?
> *Are they monsters?
> *Do they have a religion to make them human?
> *Are their beliefs the most primitive of all human notions?
> *What possible function might their religion have?
> *What does their religious life mean?
> With the emergence of Aborigines writing about their own traditions and their experience of colonization we are, after two hundred years, only now perhaps ready for the next question:
> *What are we going to say to one another?[38]

One of the most well-known (albeit misunderstood) concepts coming out of Aboriginal religions is that of "The Dreaming" or "Dreamtime." The concept itself does not have one single definition and instead means different things to different Aboriginal peoples. It suffers from what justifiably can be called a mistranslation into English—more about that in a moment.[39] Even in light of both indeterminacy and misunderstanding, the importance of this idea for Aboriginal religion cannot be overstated. Lynne Hume writes, "The central feature of Aboriginal cosmology and epistemology that is reiterated throughout Australia, despite regional variations and the vastness of the continent, is The Dreaming and its integral link between humans, land, and all that lives on the land."[40]

The Dreaming refers to a timeless reality that connects the creation of the world by the ancestors to the present moment and infuses the present with the sacred power of that creation. This reality is still accessible today,

37. Swain, *Aboriginal Religions in Australia*, 4–5.

38. Ibid., 22–23.

39. For an excellent introduction to this concept of the "Dreaming," and Aboriginal spirituality in general, see the website for the Australian museum: http://australianmuseum.net.au/Indigenous-Australia-Spirituality.

40. Lynne Hume, "Accessing the Eternal: Dreaming 'The Dreaming' and Ceremonial Performance," *Zygon* 39, no. 1 (March 2004): 237.

primarily through dreams and certain ritual performances, and so it transcends the categories of past, present, and future. It encapsulates all time in itself. Hume describes this creative reality this way:

> In the creative period Dreaming ancestors rose up from beneath the earth to give shape to an existing, yet amorphous, world. . . . As they traveled over the land they left tangible expressions of their essence in the shape of some site or rocky outcrop, tree or water hole, metamorphosing a part of themselves into some feature of the environment or imprinting themselves onto cave walls or into ritual objects. Where the ancestors bled, ochre deposits were created; where they dug in the ground, water flowed and springs formed; where they cut down trees, valleys were formed. Not only did they put form to the formless, but also they instituted tribal laws, customs, and rites and left an essential part of themselves, an essence, in certain places and in ritual objects. When their work was done, they returned to where they had emerged. Their power, however, was not diminished. The ancestors were and continue to be an intrinsic part of the land over which they moved. The two are inseparable. Almost everywhere across the continent of Australia, the land is crisscrossed with a network of tracks along which these beings journeyed. Because all things are imbued with the Dreaming ancestors' spiritual essence, all share a common life force that is sacred.[41]

Thus The Dreaming refers not only to that time of genesis, but also to the power of those creative ancestors, the natural laws of creation they founded, and the connections that bind every single being to both the ancestors and the land still today.

The Dreaming is an English translation of *altjiranga ngambakala*, a term in the Arrernte dialect group of the Aranda people, who traditionally lived in Central Australia, around Alice Springs. Early missionaries noted the difficulty of translating the root word, *altjira* (or *alchera*), recognizing that it seemed to encompass many different complex but related ideas. In the late nineteenth century, the phrase "dream time" was finally used, because, to outside observers, the word "seemed to indicate a past period of a vague and 'dreamy' nature"—and because in daily use, *alchera* was used for "dream."[42] However, it is in some ways unfortunate because it suggests something insubstantial and illusory when compared to waking time or what we call reality. This dichotomy does not exist for the Aboriginal people themselves.

One of the most important realities conveyed by The Dreaming is the

41. Ibid., 238.
42. Ibid., 240.

sacred character of all life, particularly of the land itself. As one author notes, "In this sense everything of importance in Aboriginal life has a religious or sacred dimension and we cannot easily separate, as Emile Durkheim wished to do, a realm of the 'sacred' from a realm of the 'profane' in Aboriginal cultures."[43] However, this idea requires nuance. To be precise, it is not simply that "the land is sacred" in some general, abstract sort of way. Instead, particular places and geographical features have specific connections with specific ancestors, and thus their sacred nature is of a unique and precise character. John Morton writes, "If a totemic being is said to have created a particular place, that place, or 'sacred site,' cannot be separated from the ancestor, and people refer to it in personal terms as 'him' or 'her.' Clusters of such sites coalesce to form estates or 'countries' held by particular family groups who likewise see themselves as consubstantial with the ancestors. Hence there is a threefold identity between people, places, and ancestors."[44] This means that the connections between people and places are not easily transferable; rather, the concrete connection between a specific place and a specific person/people is very strong and irreplaceable.

Another aspect of The Dreaming that should be mentioned is the various ways in which this reality is accessed. One important feature of The Dreaming is the power of out-of-body travel that it can convey: it is believed that healers in particular can leave their bodies and travel to different realms while in a trance state. Some Aboriginal people describe traveling back to their homelands while dreaming, and this becomes a way for people to remain connected to their land regardless of where they are living at any given time.[45]

An additional way of accessing Dreamtime is through various rituals of music and dance. Hume notes how only specific individuals can perform certain dances because in so doing, they are channeling particular ancestors to whom they are related. In many cases, in the process of the dance, they actually embody that ancestor, "giving birth" to him or her in the dancer's own body, linking the past to the present. Hume writes that music and dance "aid in the transformation of a Dreaming event into a now event, of Dreaming ancestor into a living human descendant, the reincarnation of the never-dying spirit part of an ancestor."[46] Eric Venbrux notes a similar phenomenon in the Tiwi Aborigines' mortuary rituals, which are used to guide the deceased along the way to their resting place. Venbrux writes that "in mortuary ritual, the performers are as close to the Dreamtime as they can get," as they reenact an ancient ceremony, inviting the presence of ancestral spirits in a creative performance that recalls the original creative acts of the ancestors.[47]

---

43. Charlesworth, Dussart, and Morphy, *Aboriginal Religions in Australia*, 9.

44. John Morton, "Aboriginal Religion Today," in Charlesworth, Dussart, and Morphy, *Aboriginal Religions in Australia*, 198.

45. Hume, "Accessing the Eternal," 248.

46. Ibid., 250.

47. Eric Venbrux, "Social Life and the Dreamtime: Clues to Creation Myths as Rhetorical Devices in Tiwi Mortuary Ritual," *Religion and the Arts* 13, no. 4 (2009): 470.

This same dynamic is also present with maritime Aboriginal peoples. Ian McNiven has observed a connection between what he calls "seascapes" and "spiritscapes"—physical spaces and geographical features that are infused with spiritual meaning through a variety of rituals. He writes, "Seascapes are animated spiritscapes because ancestor spirits—both creator beings and the 'Old People'—imbue seas with spiritual energies, fecundity and sentience."[48] And, as on land, the connections people have with places are very specific and intimate, related to specific Dreaming creator beings. This is why another name for The Dreaming is "The Law."

The connections different individuals and clans have with particular areas of the sea and land have been legitimized and validated through generations of inheritance that connect back to specific Dreaming ancestors. McNiven writes, "Dreaming cosmologies spiritually link people, places and animals, and in the process imbue clans with sacred law. This law maintains 'cosmological order,' is legitimated 'in and by the Dreaming' and is operationalized through inherited and inalienable possessory *right, rules* and *responsibilities*."[49] People engage in specific rites and rituals in order to substantiate those connections, both particularly and in general, and also to mediate between the past and the present: the dead ancestors and their living relatives whose lives overlap in their connections to the land and sea.

The concept of The Dreaming provides one powerful explanation for why specific places, geographical features, and landscapes are of such critical importance to Aboriginal identity. One's existence, one's very being, is constituted through the relationships one has to family and clan, which are themselves fundamentally connected to The Dreaming ancestors and the specific places infused with their spirits. "This is why the land is so important to Aborigines. It connects them, via their own thoughts and actions, stories and mythologies, to the eternal, ever-present Dreaming, a reality that exists alongside that of mundane, everyday reality."[50]

THE AINU: SPIRIT-SENDING CEREMONIES

Many different indigenous peoples simply use their word for "people" to describe themselves, and the Ainu fall into this category. The word itself means "human," and it is meant specifically to contrast with *kamui*, "a word that designates the male and female gods who dwell in the spirit world."[51] Like many indigenous peoples, the history of the Ainu is complicated and not easily charted. From the picture below, the proximity to Russia of the northern islands of Japan, including Hokkaido, the traditional home of the Ainu, is evident.

---

48. McNiven, "Saltwater People," 332.

49. Ibid., 335.

50. Hume, "Accessing the Eternal," 256.

51. Honda Katsuichi, *Harukor: An Ainu Woman's Tale*, trans. Kyoko Selden (Berkeley: University of California Press, 2000), 11.

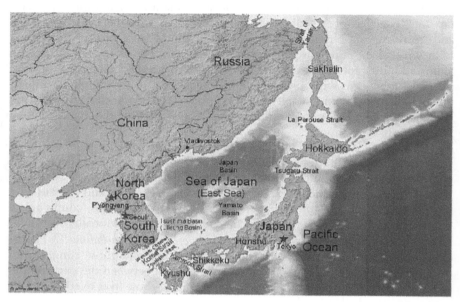

Figure 4: Map of Japan.

Looking at the small size of the straits that separate them, it is not hard to imagine a time when land travel would have been possible all the way up and down the Japanese peninsula over to the Russian mainland. This certainty of prehistoric migration makes it almost impossible to definitively establish geographic or chronological origins of the Ainu people as a whole.[52] However, what is known for sure is that the predecessors to the contemporary Ainu people were established in Hokkaido and the other northern islands at least twenty thousand years ago. Archeological discoveries have revealed settlements dating back that far, although, again, the connection between those settlers and the current Ainu is not entirely clear.[53]

Up until the mid-nineteenth century, Hokkaido was not considered part of Japan, which meant the Ainu were neither citizens of Japan nor of Russia, and they lived autonomously. Their homeland, which they called *Ainu mosir* (the world of humans), was extensive, stretching all the way up to the southern tip of the Kamchatka peninsula and all the way down onto the northern part of the Japanese main island of Honshu.[54] Now their territory has been reduced primarily to the island of Hokkaido.

52. Richard Siddle, "Ainu History: An Overview," in *Ainu: Spirit of a Northern People*, ed. William W. Fitzhugh and Chisato O. Dubreuil (Washington, DC: Arctic Studies Center, National Museum of Natural History, 1999), 67.

53. Yugo Ono, "Ainu Homelands: Natural History from Ice Age to Modern Times," in Fitzhugh and Dubreuil, *Ainu*, 32–38.

54. William W. Fitzhugh, "Ainu Ethnicity: A History," in Fitzhugh and Dubreuil, *Ainu*, 10.

The period of the Meiji Restoration (1868–1912) was particularly difficult for the Ainu. The Meiji Restoration consolidated Japan under imperial control and is considered to have brought Japan into the modern industrial age. The entire country saw dramatic changes, including the Ainu territory. This is when Hokkaido received its name—formerly it had been known as Ezochi—and a settlement plan for the island was implemented, which included relocation and resettlement of Ainu communities in order to better exploit Hokkaido's environmental riches. By the end of the nineteenth century, the 17,000 Ainu left on Hokkaido accounted for only 2 percent of the island population.[55] During this time, the Ainu were classified as Japanese and forced to assimilate: they were not allowed to speak their own language, even in their own homes, and they were not allowed to practice their traditional ceremonies.[56] Currently the total Ainu population is listed at around 25,000 out of a total Japanese population of roughly 126 million.[57]

There has been a great effort in the past few decades to establish some protections for the Ainu people and restore some of their traditional rights. In 1997, the Japanese government passed the *Ainu Shinpo* (Ainu New Law) aimed at protecting and promoting Ainu culture, but its implementation has been mixed at best. Perhaps more promising is the United Nations Declaration on the Rights of Indigenous Peoples, adopted in 2007, which Japan endorsed, although much more work remains to be done. There are political ramifications with Russia related to what are called the Northern Territories, and there also continues to be a strong negative cultural and racial bias in Japanese society. Currently the Ainu Association of Hokkaido is the largest Ainu association, attempting to safeguard Ainu culture, but there is an increasing number of grassroots organizations and individuals assisting in this work as well.[58]

THE AINU AND THE LAND

It is important to say something about Hokkaido's natural environment, as the Ainu are integrally related to their natural surroundings. Of particular importance are Hokkaido's forests, lush and vast up until the Meiji Restoration, which, as noted above, brought intensive agricultural development and both lumber and fishing industries. Until that time, however, it was said that the trees formed a "sea of foliage,"[59] and these forests not only provided wood but also supported a flourishing habitat for a wide variety of animals, several of which are of particular importance—both physically and spiritually—to the Ainu.

---

55. Siddle, "Ainu History," 72.

56. Jiro Sasamura, "Beyond the Ainu Shinpo: An Ainu View," in Fitzhugh and Dubreuil, *Ainu*, 369.

57. Crystal Porter, "After the Ainu Shinpō: The United Nations and the Indigenous People of Japan," *New Voices* 2 (December 2008): 214.

58. "Where, Since When and How Have the Ainu People Existed," the Ainu Association of Hokkaido, accessed Nov. 14, 2014, http://tinyurl.com/hnwbk8s. See also Kelly L. Dietz, "Ainu in the International Arena," in Fitzhugh and Dubreuil, *Ainu*, 359–65.

59. Katsuichi, *Harukor*, 18.

Of these, three are worth noting in particular. Perhaps the most important is the brown bear, about which more will be said below in conjunction with "spirit sending" ceremonies. In addition, however, are deer and salmon. Fish always have been a central part of the Ainu diet, and salmon will are of critical importance; the word for fish in the Ainu language actually means "salmon."[60] There are over a dozen major rivers in Hokkaido, and the long fishing season, which lasts from early spring into winter, traditionally provided the Ainu with one of their major food sources.[61] Various kinds of deer were also plentiful on Hokkaido and the other islands, and these, too, were hunted throughout the year.

As with other indigenous people, there are important rites and rituals that relate directly to hunting: "Correct behavior toward animals, regarded as visitors from their heavenly abode, made sure that they returned to earth again and again to make themselves available as food and useful materials."[62] In addition, there are special ceremonies involving sacrifices meant to protect the hunters, particularly in the context of bear hunting, and sacrifices also are made before each season to ensure that enough of the animals would come.

THE AINU AND THE GODS

The world of the Ainu is heavily populated with gods; they are everywhere, and can take physical form in almost anything, including what we would consider both animate and inanimate objects. The word for god and the word for spirit are the same—*kamuy*—"a generic term for both physical and immaterial entities on the earth who possess abilities superior to those of [a hu]man. Specifically, gods can be animals, plants, minerals, or other geographical and natural phenomena that have a place on earth."[63] Even more unusual to a Western mindset, spirits also can inhabit human-made things, such as tools, kitchen utensils, and hunting instruments.[64] In short, according to Ainu belief, almost everything in the universe has a spirit. These spirits typically live in their own realm, but they can come into the human realm disguised in whatever form they choose—and they readily and often do so.[65] For the Ainu, animal spirits are the most significant and therefore, they are treated with great respect, especially the spirits of the bear and the fish owl—these are the two most important.[66] Asian brown bears are considered to be mountain gods (*kimun-kamuy*) in disguise. Ironically to Western sensibilities, the way the Ainu welcome these gods who visit in animal form is to hunt them and then send

---

60. Ibid., 26.

61. Hans Dieter Ölschlieger, "Technology, Settlement, and Hunting Ritual," in Fitzhugh and Dubreuil, *Ainu*, 210–11.

62. Ibid., 219.

63. Hisakazu Fujimura, "*Kamuy*: Gods You Can Argue With," in Fitzhugh and Dubreuil, *Ainu*, 193.

64. Ibid., 193.

65. Hiroshui Utagawa, "The Archaeology of *Iyomante*," in Fitzhugh and Dubreuil, *Ainu*, 256.

66. Shigeki Akino, "Spirit-Sending Ceremonies," in Fitzhugh and Dubreuil, *Ainu*, 249.

them back to the spirit world with a sending ceremony. Part of the purpose of this ritual is to demonstrate that nothing is wasted, so the bones and food remains are "sent back" with respect and gifts.

This understanding of *kamuy* has important ramifications for how the physical world in general is viewed, including the human body. The spirit of any being is what is most real and what endures; it is the spirit that is immortal while the body is merely temporary and disposable. "The Ainu people believe that one's flesh and bones are nothing but the container of the spirit, which exists for the purpose of living one's life and will be abandoned after this use."[67] What this also presumes is a belief in reincarnation. Once a person dies, their soul—assuming it is free of attachments and unresolved feelings—departs for the next world immediately, leaving the body from the heart, where it resides, and then on through the mouth, nose, anus, ears, eyes, or navel. When it arrives in the next world, it is guided to the proper womb, where it will be reborn. This process continues indefinitely, and the same process occurs with all spirits and with all bodies, with some restrictions.[68]

> Humans and animals die; plants wither; rivers and lakes dry up; volcanoes go extinct; and things end their life cycles. At this stage, their spirits leave their containers. In the case of a human being at death, the soul departs from the body, yet the soul is considered immortal even after flesh decays and bones return to the soil. The spirits are thought to repeat themselves and reincarnate according to their specific species and gender, so for instance, a man will always return as a man and a female cat as a female cat.[69]

Finally, given the close proximity of the gods who are dwelling in the human realm and their importance in the daily life of the Ainu, there is a robust give-and-take relationship between humanity and the gods. Gods can be argued with, challenged, and even required to apologize for not providing protection that a specific offering should have guaranteed.[70] There are expectations on both sides, and when those expectations are violated by either one, compensation can be demanded.

THE IYOMANTE CEREMONY

All of this forms the necessary backdrop for understanding the *iyomante* ceremony, one of the central defining practices of the Ainu. All through the twentieth century, they were pressured to stop it; however, with the increased recognition and autonomy that has come in the past decade, it has been

67. Fujimura, "*Kamuy*," 197.
68. Ibid.
69. Ibid., 193.
70. Ibid., 196.

reinstated. In its broadest meaning, *iyomante* (thing/send, thing/let go, sending back spirits[71]) can refer to any of the spirit-sending ceremonies that can be performed with animals, tools, or plants: "Instead of keeping . . . spirits in the human world after they have been caught or 'used up' (as in the case of spent or broken [hu]man-made objects), the Ainu return them to the spirit world with elaborate 'sending' ceremonies."[72] However, typically *iyomante* refers more specifically to the bear-sending ceremony, the most important of the sending rituals—although it also can refer to another important sending ceremony, that of the fish owl, which is the *kamuy* associated with protecting the community. Another word that is sometimes used is *opunire*, which is the word for animal-sending ceremonies in general—including those for foxes and raccoon dogs—however, the terminology is not consistent and varies from place to place.[73]

There are several important convictions underlying this practice. First, of course, is the idea of the interconnectedness between humanity and the other beings and objects that make up our world. Life is deeply interrelated, and one's actions have important ramifications that ripple out and affect the rest of the community. Therefore, care and respect must be shown in all aspects of life in order to ensure continued harmony and survival. Humans, then, have a responsibility to the rest of creation: "The *iyomante* expresses the belief that life and nature can be renewed continuously as long as there is human commitment to reciprocity with nature: what is taken must also be given back in equal measure, and with reverence."[74]

The *iyomante* ceremony typically occurs with adult bears hunted in the wild, although a similar ceremony can take place with cubs reared in captivity as well. The ceremony unfolds as follows:[75] Preparations begin weeks in advance, including the cooking of food offerings and rice wine. The day of the ceremony, the bear is brought out of his cage and allowed to exercise and run around. Then he is ceremonially "shot" with blunt arrows, and then he is strangled. Once dead, the bear is skinned and his head is removed—this is believed to separate the spirit from the body. Food and wine are shared with the bear's spirit, which is believed to still be present, over two nights, and then it is encouraged to be on its way back to the realm of the gods. The point of the feast is to send the spirit back to the world of the gods with many gifts, which the Ainu hope will encourage other gods to visit them as well, bringing them the gifts of bear skin, claws, and so on. It must be emphasized that this practice not only has value for the human community, it has value for the gods as well. "It is said that gods achieve ever higher rank in the god world by their repeated

71. Utagawa, "Archaeology of *Iyomante*," 256.

72. Akino, "Spirit-Sending Ceremonies," 249.

73. Ibid., 251–52.

74. Fitzhugh, "Ainu Ethnicity," 26.

75. The description is taken from Akino, "Spirit-Sending Ceremonies," 248–55.

visits to earth. . . . In this way the *iyomante* becomes the forum representing the symbiotic relationship among animals, humans and the spirit world and provides a mechanism for influencing earthly events: it signifies and validates the relationship between humans and gods."[76]

THE YORUBA: DIVINATION

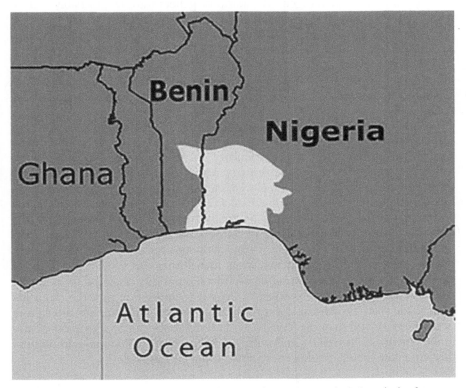

Figure 5: Yorubaland, the traditional home of the Yoruba people, is in the lighter shade of gray.

The Yoruba are an ethnic group located primarily in the Southwest region of Nigeria, but they are also found in parts of Benin and Togo. The name used to designate this cultural area is Yorubaland (depicted in light gray above). The total Yoruba population is currently estimated at roughly 35 million. The umbrella term Yoruba is widely used, both to describe the people themselves and the religion. However, caution with the term also should be shown: "Scholars investigating Yoruba ethnic identity have justifiably argued that until the nineteenth century the people now called Yoruba, despite their cultural affinities, belonged to multiple ethnicities,"[77] including Akoko, Bunu, Awori,

---

76. Ibid., 250.

Ife, Oyo, and many more—and many of these were also subdivided into smaller groups as well. However, in the diaspora, Yoruba peoples found it advantageous to come together: "They needed each other for spiritual guidance, marriages and other measures to combat life in exile."[78] It should also be noted that the Yoruba religion actually has many traditional expressions, and the religion is also generally known as Orisha-Ifa.

Not unlike other indigenous traditions, generalizations justifiably can be made, but they must be made with care. Anthony Buckley writes that "the overwhelming problem in Yoruba religious studies is complexity."[79] Festivals, rituals, and beliefs all vary from region to region—and even town to town, such that in almost every aspect of the religion, "regional variation and individual idiosyncrasy abound."[80] So while the broad outlines of what follows are accurate, it must be remembered that both belief and practice differ contextually.

Finally, let me note the importance of the Yoruba religion for Western readers specifically, not only because of its influence in Africa as one of the largest indigenous traditions—particularly in West Africa—but also for its influence in the Americas. The primary reason for this influence is the slave trade and the role West Africa played in that trade during the seventeenth through the nineteenth centuries. Paul Lovejoy notes that the West Central region of Africa was the source of the majority of slaves exported to the Americas up until the last quarter of the seventeenth century, and during the whole period from 1600 to 1800, it played a dominant role in the African slave trade in general.[81] It is significant, then, that during this time, "The Bight of Benin . . . was the only exporting region that temporarily displaced west-central Africa as the largest single supplier."[82] As a consequence of this, the claim has been made that "no African group has had a greater influence on the culture of the New World than the Yoruba."[83] This influence can be seen most clearly in the practice of Santería, Candomblé, and even perhaps Vodoun—although in this latter case there are other more direct influences as well.

---

77. Olatunji Ojo, "'Heepa' (Hail) Òrìṣà: The Òrìṣà Factor in the Birth of Yoruba Identity," *Journal of Religion in Africa* 39, no. 1 (2009): 31.

78. Ibid.

79. Anthony D. Buckley, "The God of Smallpox: Aspects of Yoruba Religious Knowledge," *Africa* 55, no. 2 (1985): 187.

80. Ibid., 188.

81. Paul E. Lovejoy, *Transformations in Slavery: A History of Slavery in Africa* (Cambridge: Cambridge University Press, 1983), 52.

82. Ibid., 54.

83. J. Omosade Awolalu, "A Review of Scholars' Views on the Yoruba Concept of God," *Journal of Religious Thought* 31, no. 2 (Fall–Winter 1974–75): 5.

ORISHA

The Yoruba religion describes a Supreme God and also a variety of other divinities who mediate between this God and creation. When it comes to the divinities themselves, the word one most often sees is *orisha*. The word actually refers to a spirit or divinity that embodies or reflects one aspect of the Supreme God in the Yoruba religious system. (The word also is spelled *orisa* or *orixa*.) The *orisha* function in conjunction with—and in a mediating role with—that God. Olodumare (or Olorun) is the name of the Supreme Being in Yoruba theology, and he is considered to be the creator of the world. He is remote, distant, and almost never directly approached—the chasm is simply too great. For this reason, then, images are never made of Olodumare, nor are there shrines to him or sacrifices made to him directly: "he is considered to be too vast, too sacred, to be concretized. The images which the Yoruba make of their *Orisa* are, therefore, intended to reflect an aspect of the thought processes and the values of Olodumare, their High God."[84]

There are a wide variety of *orisha*—the number cannot be fixed exactly, and some of them are found only in very localized contexts while others have a much wider influence. These divinities are of particular importance given the fact that Olodumare is understood to be removed from the daily activities and events in the world and thus is not consulted or appealed to directly by humans. Jacob Olupọna describes it this way:

> Olódùmarè created the entire universe but operates on it somewhat removed, in a way that is reminiscent of Western Deist theology of God as a clockmaker. When it came time to actually create life on Earth, Olódùmarè directed the council of divine spirits called òrìṣà to descend to earth under the leadership of the eldest òrìṣà Ọbàtálá. Olódùmarè gave to Ọbàtálá all of the tools they would need to create land and life but did not participate in the act of creation itself. Although the course of fate ultimately lies in the hands of Olódùmarè, he (or she, or it, or they) do not directly intervene in the course of events. Therefore, adherents of Yoruba traditional religion address their supplications and prayers to the òrìṣà who brought life to the earth and continue to be invested in what happens there.[85]

Of all the divinities, a particularly significant place is given to Orunmila, the divinity associated with salvation. Orunmila is the one who mediates the will of Olodumare and hence is the "mouthpiece of all the divinities."[86] In this role, Orunmila is associated with wisdom and is believed to know all things,

---

84. Wande Abimbola, "Aspects of Yoruba Images of the Divine: Ifa Divination Artifacts," *Dialogue & Alliance* 3, no. 2 (Summer 1989): 24–25.

85. Jacob K. Olupọna, *African Religions: A Very Short Introduction* (Oxford: Oxford University Press, 2014), 27–28.

including all periods of time and all actions and desires of human beings: "It was Orunmila's special privilege to know about the beginning and the end of all things, including the origin of the divinities, the things they love and hate."[87]

It is said that Olodumare wanted an emissary on the earth, someone who could mediate his will and also facilitate communication between human beings and himself. In order to decide who would fill that role, he devised a test. Olodumare feigned confusion over a certain matter and asked the other divinities for their insight. They all failed in their counsel, with the sole exception of Orunmila. "Olodumare then appointed Orunmila as his deputy and the great consultant for all on earth."[88]

DIVINATION

The way in which the divinities are contacted and engaged is primarily through various rituals involving divination and sacrifice, and these two religious activities almost always go together. In English, the word "divination" is a Latin cognate with "divine," and it refers to the means by which one discovers and consults the gods (or God) for guidance and insight into a problem or question. Many different cultures have rituals for this process, although the means by which such knowledge is obtained vary greatly. In the Yoruba traditions, divination has been understood as "a way of exploring the unknown in order to elicit oracular answers to questions beyond the range of ordinary human understanding."[89]

One of the most important and complex divination systems in Yoruba religions is *Ifa*.[90] *Ifa* can be translated literally as "that which draws or make[s] everything come together,"[91] and Charles Obafemi Jegede asserts that "the Ifa divination system is the *logos* through which everything came into being."[92] (However, *Ifa* is also used as a name for Orunmila, the divinity who governs this practice.) It is practiced regularly, and certainly when any individual, or group of individuals, has to make an important decision.

There are several different components of *Ifa*. First and foremost are the *Babalawo*, the *Ifa* priests. (Women can also be priests—they are called *Iyanifa*—although not all Yoruba traditions recognize them.) The job of the priest is to interpret the divination, particularly the *Odu*, the body of sacred literature that is used to explain and convey the will of the gods. The corpus

---

86. Charles Obafemi Jegede, "An Exploration into Soteriology in Ifa: Oral and Intangible Heritage for Humanity," *Black Theology* 11, no. 2 (2013): 211.

87. Ibid., 212.

88. Ibid., 213.

89. Ibid., 203.

90. See "The Ifa Divination System," YouTube video, 3:06, uploaded by "UNESCO," September 28, 2009, http://tinyurl.com/z3je669.

91. Jegede, "Exploration into Soteriology," 204.

92. Ibid.

consists of a total of 256 *Odu*—that same word also refers to the individual chapters that are then subdivided into smaller verses, called *Ese*. There are sixteen major *Odu*, and the remaining 240 are considered minor *Odu*. The training of the *Babalawo* is extensive—sixteen or more years—in order to memorize the long corpus of complex and esoteric verses that make up the *Odu*.[93] Each *Odu* has its particular divination sign drawn in sand or powder on the divination tray.

Figure 6: A mask representing Esu.

93. Abimbola, "Aspects of Yoruba Images," 25.

In addition to the priests, there are several key objects used in divination. First is the *Ikin*, a set of sixteen sacred palm kernels that are the primary divining objects (although sometimes a divining chain or cord is used). "Used to provide answers to all human and divine problems, *Ikin* cease to be regarded as ordinary palm kernels. They become sacred, and are seen as the earthly and physical symbol of Orunmila's virtually unlimited wisdom."[94] The *Ikin* are interpreted on the *Opon*, which is the divination tray/board, carved in wood and usually carved with faces representing the face of Esu, the trickster divinity. He is a complex and contrary divinity, containing elements of both good and evil, and this "boundary" identity is part of what makes him such an ideal mediator between heaven and earth. Even though Esu has no shrines dedicated to him exclusively, because of his important mediating role, all sacrifices are indirectly related to and directed toward him. "So important is his role and influence in successful divination, that Ifa often prescribes the offering of sacrifices to him to ensure his cooperation."[95] Finally, the *Agere-Ifa* is the carved container that holds the *Ikin*. There are always carved figures that hold up the bowl: these are human beings, not divinities, and they are meant to be shown as dancing, offering sacrifices, or expressing gratitude in some other way, symbolizing a positive outcome to the divination.

To begin the divination, the priest taps on the tray with a specialized instrument, called the *Iroke Ifa*, to invite the divine spirits to be present. Then the priest cups the *Ikin* in his hands, shifting them from one hand to another, and, depending on how many and which *Ikin* are left in his hand, he makes a mark on the tray. This continues until there are a total of two columns, each having four sets of marks.[96] Together, these marks correspond to specific *Odu*, which are then recited and interpreted as an answer to the question or problem that necessitated the divination in the first place.

The obvious next question is, "What then?" What happens after the divination occurs? Almost always, the answer is sacrifice. Jegede describes the relationship between divination and sacrifice very well. He writes, "While divination is a diagnostic device, ritual is a way of solving problems. Ritual is the method that Orunmila uses to save his people. Everything in nature can be offered for sacrifice depending on the odu. It can be an animal of any kind, especially domestic animals, or birds, food, cloth, honey, palm oil, and many other items."[97]

There is the general belief in the Yoruba religions that in order to appease the divinities and to keep order and balance in the many relationships that characterize life, sacrifices have to be made: giving to receive, making an offering to bring peace. As Buckley notes, "Nearly every verse of Ifá chanted

94. Ibid., 26.
95. Ibid., 25.
96. Lawson, *Religions of Africa*, 68.
97. Jegede, "Exploration into Soteriology," 214.

Figure 7: An Ifa divination tray with Ikin.

in divination demands that a sacrifice be made. Not every sacrifice consists of a letting of blood. But nevertheless the message of each Ifá verse is that the only way in which a supplicant can avoid disaster is by making an appropriate sacrifice."[98]

In this way, the dynamic, fluid, and active relationship between humanity and the divinities is evident, and it touches and influences all aspects of human life. Like many other indigenous religions, the Yoruba operate out of a deeply relational understanding of the cosmos, which includes various layers of the spiritual and the material, beings both living and beyond death, and a wide variety of divinities. As such, one must always be asking after the relevant forces that are influencing one's circumstances and seek to pacify them. As Adekunle Oyinloye Dada writes, "the conception of reality among the Yoruba is holistic. . . . For the people, reality is a unified whole."[99] Both divination and sacrifice are a means by which one can learn what is required in any given situation to receive health, success, and wholeness by addressing the larger context in which one lives.

98. Buckley, "God of Smallpox," 192.
99. Dada, "Old Wine," 21.

CONCLUSION

This chapter has only skimmed the surface of the vast ocean that is indigenous religious traditions. Each tradition is an entity unto itself, and yet together, they play a central role in understanding the overarching function and place of religion in the world today. Even more critically, for a Western Christian audience in particular, it is necessary to become aware of the ongoing dynamic adaptations different peoples are making (and being forced to make) in light of both globalization and technological modernization. Few if any indigenous cultures exist that are entirely isolated from the modern world, and thanks to both population growth and climate change, this isolation is increasingly impossible to maintain. For example, native peoples in the Amazon of Brazil—which is home to the greatest number of "uncontacted" native peoples—are being invaded by loggers and ranchers and are at serious risk from disease.[100] This contact naturally affects religious beliefs and practices as well.

The simple fact is that life for all of us is rapidly changing, perhaps for indigenous peoples most of all. For centuries, they have been on the losing end of that change and have suffered the most. Learning more about who they are, what they value, and how they see the world is one important way to respect and support their continued thriving and the protection of their homes, and also open up the possibility of transformation in one's own understanding of and relationship to indigenous religions themselves.

---

100. See the website of Survival, http://www.survivalinternational.org/, accessed June 9, 2016.

A Brief Introduction to Sikhism

INTRODUCTION

My first visit to a Sikh *gurdwara* took place in New Delhi, India, where I visited the Gurdwara Bangla Sahib. It is a beautiful building, noted for its connection to the eighth guru, Guru Har Krishnan, and for its expansive *sarovar* (sacred pool). Guru Har Krishnan lived in a house on the location, and when a smallpox/cholera epidemic developed in the city, he left the safety of the house, going out to serve the sick and give them fresh water from a small well nearby. The young guru eventually died from smallpox himself. The well was enlarged to today's pool, and still today the water is considered holy, having healing powers.

There, as in other *gurdwaras*, the stranger is made to feel welcome, greeted warmly regardless of one's religious affiliation. There, as in other *gurdwaras*, one hears the sounds of the *kirtan*, the singing of hymns from the sacred text, the Guru Granth Sahib. There, as in other *gurdwaras*, there is a generous *langar*, a free vegetarian meal served to all who are present, all of whom eat together side by side on the floor, a symbol of their spiritual equality before God. There, as in other *gurdwaras*, both women and men cover their heads, remove their shoes, and gather around the Guru Granth Sahib. Many, though not all, wear the five signs of the *Khalsa*, the community of the initiated who have committed to a life of discipline and purity, on their way to becoming a *gurumukh*. It was both familiar and strange to me, and in the years since, I have grown to appreciate my experience there even more.

Sikhism is one of the youngest of the so-called "world religions," but it is rapidly growing and continuing to expand outside its homeland of India, although the Indian state of Punjab remains the spiritual and physical heartland of Sikhism. Currently, there are roughly 25 million Sikhs around the world, with the vast majority living in India. The largest diaspora population outside India is in Great Britain.[1] The word *Sikh* is a Punjabi word and means "learner"

---

1. "The Global Religious Landscape: Other Religions," *Religion and Public Life*, Pew Research Center, published December 18, 2012, http://tinyurl.com/j58e79d.

Figure 8. Gurdwara Bangla Sahib, New Delhi, India (author's photo).

or "disciple," thus a Sikh is a disciple of the guru. (Although most English speakers pronounce it as *seek*, in Punjabi it is pronounced with a short *i*, more like *sick*.) However, a clarifying word around terminology is important here. Similar to Hinduism, Sikhism is a Western construct, not first used by the community itself but imposed upon it from outside by Westerners who had a Christian background and were therefore working out of an alien paradigm.[2] Thus, even though it has been widely adopted by the global Sikh community today, the origins of the category should be noted.

Sikhs themselves refer to their path as *Sikhi* and *Gursikhi*, and also *Gurmat* (the gurus' doctrine). They refer to the Sikh community as the *Panth*.[3] This language was first used by those who heard the message of Guru Nanak and began to follow his teachings, and continues to be used today for the community that believes in one God and follows the gurus who reveal the true teachings of this God. *Guru*, of course, is a word common in the Indian context, and in many places today the word defines a person of authority and wisdom. However, for the Sikh community, the word is quite specific and refers first to God (the *Sat Guru*, the true teacher), then the ten human gurus (beginning with the first, Guru Nanak), and then finally the sacred text, the Guru Granth Sahib—the embodiment of truth serves as the final guru.

There are different definitions that attempt to respond to the question "Who is a Sikh?" but one definition includes the following components. A Sikh is any person who faithfully believes in the following five sources of authority and who does not adhere to any other religious tradition:

- One immortal Being
- Ten human Gurus, from Guru Nanak to Guru Gobind Singh
- The Guru Granth Sahib
- The teachings of the ten Gurus
- The water initiation ceremony instituted by Guru Gobind Singh[4]

Origins

A comparison that one sometimes sees in surveys of Sikhism brings together Guru Nanak and Martin Luther. They lived at roughly the same time, and it is typically said that both were engaged in a kind of reform movement. While aspects of this comparison might illuminate Sikhism for Western readers, obviously there are vast differences that must be kept in mind between the European Roman Catholic context of Luther's day and the Hindu/Muslim context of northern India. Yet, certainly an argument can be made that both men had experienced a different way of relating to God (as each understood the Divine) than what was typical at the time, and both challenged the notion that the performance of external rites and rituals was the best way to maintain this relationship. Both won many followers, and both inaugurated a new form of religious practice and belief.

2. See Eleanor Nesbitt, "Issues in Writing 'Introductions' to 'Sikhism,'" *Religions of South Asia* 1, no. 1 (2007): 47–63.

3. Ibid., 3.

4. Ibid., 2.

Figure 9: A fresco of Guru Nanak.

Guru Nanak is considered the founder of Sikhism. He was born to an upper-caste *Khatri* Hindu family in 1469 in the village of Talwandi (now called Nankana) in what is modern-day Punjab. At this time, northern India was under Muslim rule, and this continued as the Mughal Empire came to power. There also was a historic Hindu presence in the north, and in addition, there were multiple Hindu kingdoms in the central and southern parts of the country. Thus Guru Nanak would have been exposed to both Hinduism and Islam from an early age. There were tensions between the two faith traditions, but there were also those who sought harmony through and beyond them, focusing on love of God and the oneness of the Divine. Guru Nanak was influenced by these voices and had a personal experience of God that convinced him of God's unity and sovereignty. This was the core of the message he taught until his death.

We have few historical details about his life. However, a century or so after his death, various stories and legends were collected and circulated in a corpus of literature called the *Janamsakhi* stories.[5] As is typical in this form of hagiographic biography, Guru Nanak is given mythic stature, and his life is characterized by a variety of miraculous accounts, including supernatural abilities to control nature and communicate with animals, who seek to protect him. More important, however, is Guru Nanak's message about equality before God: "From his birth to his death, the Janamsakhis portray Nanak as rejecting the prevalent confines of caste, gender, religion, and ethnicity only to underscore that all human beings are equal."[6] The stories emphasize that he had both Hindu and Muslim friends and also was concerned about the welfare of women, speaking out against the traditional practices that discriminated against them.

The traditional story of his life tells that in 1499, while he was bathing in the Bein River, he had a mystical experience and received a call from God. In the *Janamsakhi* accounts, the story of his transformative revelation is described this way:

> As the Primal Being willed, Nanak the devotee was ushered into the Divine Presence. Then a cup filled with *amrit* (nectar) was given him with the command, "Nanak, this is the cup of Name-adoration (*naam piala*). Drink it. . . . I am with you and I do bless and exalt you. Whoever remembers you will have my favour. Go, rejoice, in My Name and teach others to do so. I have bestowed upon you the gift of my Name. Let this be your calling." Nanak offered his salutations and stood up.[7]

Nanak reappeared after three days, declaring, "There is neither Hindu nor Muslim," and he began to travel, teaching his message and accepting disciples. The tradition states that he settled in Kartarpur, in Punjab, where he died in 1539. Before he died, he designated one of his followers to be his successor, and this began the succession of gurus that continued until final teaching authority was bestowed upon the sacred text, the Guru Granth Sahib.

The traditional image of Guru Nanak is standardized and hardly varies. He is typically depicted with a long white beard, which symbolizes his wisdom and also conforms with the Sikh commitment to uncut hair. He is usually shown seated and sometimes there is a mark on the sole of his bare foot, which is meant to symbolize his enlightened spiritual status. His eyes are usually slightly

5. There is a wonderful volume of *Janamsakhi* paintings, originally from the eighteenth century, that illustrate a wide variety of events (including many miracles) from Guru Nanak's life. A helpful introduction is also included. Surjit Hans, ed., *B-40 Janamsakhi Guru Baba Nanak Paintings* (Amritsar: Guru Nanak Dev University, 1987).

6. Nikky-Guninder Kaur Singh and Todd Curcuru, "Sikhism," in *Religions of the World*, ed. Lawrence E. Sullivan (Minneapolis: Fortress Press, 2013), 115.

7. Nikky-Guninder Kaur Singh, trans., *The Name of My Beloved: Verses of the Sikh Gurus* (San Francisco: HarperSanFrancisco, 1995), 18.

hooded, illustrating "the divine intoxication of mystical meditation."[8] He wears a saffron robe and cloak, and a beaded necklace, all of which signal his status as a sage. He is typically shown with his prayer beads. Finally, his head is haloed, and he is wearing a turban—sometimes white, sometimes saffron. His right hand is often raised in a gesture of blessing.

THE TEN HUMAN GURUS

There are a total of ten human Gurus in Sikhism, beginning with Guru Nanak, who always has pride of place. It is believed, however, that God is the original and true guru who inspires all those who follow with divine wisdom. The ten gurus are believed to share the same spirit, and the unity of their message is always emphasized. Thus Sikhism makes a distinction between the spirit of the teaching, which is one, and the different physical "encasements" of that teaching, which are distinct from one another and temporary. This is true for the physical bodies of the human gurus and also the textual body of the Guru Granth Sahib: both equally "encapsulate and mediate divinely inspired words."[9]

In brief, the order of the Gurus is as follows: Guru Nanak (1469–1539) is first. He chose Guru Angad, a nonrelative, as his successor, thus establishing a spiritual leadership that is not tied to family or blood relationships. (However, many subsequent gurus did choose family members as their successors.) Guru Angad (1504–52) was followed by Guru Amar Das (1479–1574), who became guru at the age of seventy-three. (All of the gurus, with the exception of the ninth, became guru immediately following the death of the previous guru. In some cases, the next guru was named shortly before the death of the previous guru.) Guru Amar Das was responsible for instituting some of the distinctive Sikh rituals around birth and death and differentiating them from similar Hindu rituals. He is also known for a collection of hymns called the *Anand Sahib*, which are still a part of Sikh daily ritual today. He died at the age of ninety-five and appointed his son-in-law as his successor. Guru Ram Das (1534–81) is most famous for founding Amritsar, the sacred city of the Sikhs, and excavating the large lake, also known as the Amritsar, which surrounds the Golden Temple.

The fifth guru, Guru Arjan (1563–1606), is best known for compiling the Adi Granth, bringing together hymns from the previous four gurus as well as his own compositions. In addition, he built the Harmandir Sahib (the Golden Temple) and installed the sacred text inside it. Guru Arjan was the first Sikh martyr, tortured and executed by the Mughal emperor Jahangir. The sixth guru was Guru Hargobind (1595–1644), the son of Guru Arjan. It was under his leadership that the Sikhs armed themselves and became a powerful military force, frequently clashing with the Mughal emperor Shah Jahan. He is noted

---

8. John Bowker, *World Religions* (London: DK Publications, 2006), 87.

9. Kristina Myrvold, "Making the Scripture a Person: Reinventing Death Rituals of Guru Granth Sahib in Sikhism," in *The Death of Sacred Texts: Ritual Disposal and Renovation of Texts in World Religions*, ed. Kristina Myrvold (Burlington, VT: Ashgate, 2010), 128.

for wearing two swords, one symbolizing his temporal authority (*miri*) and the other his spiritual authority (*piri*). These two swords form the emblem on the Khanda, the flag indicating the presence of the Khalsa.

Guru Har Rai (1630–61) was the seventh guru—the grandson of Guru Hargobind. Before his death at age thirty-one, he appointed his younger son guru. Guru Har Krishan (1656–64) became the eighth guru when he was just five years old. After helping heal many people who were suffering from a raging smallpox epidemic in Delhi, he himself died of the disease when he was eight years old. The Bangla Sahib, mentioned previously, was built on the site where Guru Har Krishan served and ultimately died. The ninth guru was Guru Tegh Bahadur (1621–75), grand-uncle of Guru Har Krishan. Guru Tegh Bahadur is most famous for protecting both Hindus and Sikhs from forced conversion by the Mughals, who eventually imprisoned, tortured, and executed him. The tenth and last human guru was Guru Gobind Singh, son of Guru Bahadur.

Guru Gobind Singh (1666–1708) became guru when he was only nine years old and is widely revered as the second most important guru, after Guru Nanak, in terms of his service to the Sikh community. Guru Gobind Singh is considered to have embodied the Sikh ideal of a warrior-scholar, a religious and a political leader who exemplified both military and spiritual strength and discipline. Of his many accomplishments, two are most important. First, he instituted the Khalsa, about which more will be said shortly. Second, before his death, he invested the sacred text, the Adi Granth, with the personhood of the guru. That is, he designated the text as the final guru: the "body" of the text is literally the "body" of the guru. This text, from then on known as the Guru Granth Sahib, would stand in perpetuity as the definitive guide for the Sikh community. This is why the book itself is treated with such respect and venerated so highly.

THE GURU GRANTH SAHIB

Beginning with Guru Nanak, the gurus had written poetic hymns praising God and extoling the virtues of discipleship. These were called *gurbani* (inspired writings of the guru). The disciples of the gurus began writing these down, of course, and so collections quickly began to form. In 1603, Guru Arjan took it upon himself to collect those hymns and begin compiling a sacred text. (The word *granth* is a Sanskrit word that means "book.") Part of the reason for his action was that the Sikh community was growing in number and spreading geographically, and he felt it was necessary to authenticate the hymns that could actually be attributed to the gurus and weed out the false texts. He went away to a secluded place near Amritsar, which has become the pilgrimage site of Ramsar, and there compiled the Adi Granth (Original/First Book).

Sikh tradition holds that the text was completed on August 30, 1604, and it was installed at the Harmandir Sahib (the Golden Temple) on September 1, 1604. A century later, the tenth guru, Guru Gobind Singh, added some further

Figure 10: The Guru Granth Sahib, Khalsa Diwan Sikh Temple, Hong Kong (author's photo).

hymns to the text and then closed the canon. This final version of what would come to be called the Guru Granth Sahib was installed in the temple on October 20, 1708. The name Guru Granth Sahib is typically used by Sikhs to affirm the text as guru. The modern version of the text we have today was standardized for printing in Punjab in the nineteenth century. In most *gurdwaras*, the text is still read and sung in Punjabi, although in many diaspora *gurdwaras* vernacular translations are often projected simultaneously. Nevertheless, privilege is still given to the original text, and technically the title "Guru Granth Sahib" refers only to the text written in *gurmukhi*, not a translation.

The importance of the Guru Granth Sahib cannot be overstated for the Sikh community: "Almost every Sikh ceremony is conducted in the presence of the physical book and the living performance traditions of reciting, singing, and expounding the sacred hymns cast a haze of quotations over the whole of Sikh life."[10] This book is considered to be the embodiment of all the wisdom of the ten human gurus, and it is the center of Sikh life. Every morning, a hymn from the Guru Granth Sahib, the daily *hukamnama*, is read from the Harmandir Sahib in Amritsar and delivered via mobile technology all around the world. And as with so many other things, there is even an app for that whereby one immediately receives the daily passage, which functions as a guide for that day.

Even though the Guru Granth Sahib can be read, it is really meant to be sung, and the practice of communal singing of the hymns, called *kirtan*, is a central devotional practice of Sikhism. This activity is meant to focus the community on God and, indeed, facilitate one's immersion in God. For this reason, many people surround themselves with the music of the text throughout the day, a practice made much easier by computers and cell phones: "The ideal Sikh should thus read, recite, sing, listen, and continually dwell on the context of Guru Granth Sahib so as to develop understanding of the Guru's guidance within the text and implement the teaching in everyday life."[11]

Unlike many other sacred texts, the Guru Granth Sahib contains no historical narrative and no ritual instruction. Rather, the entire text is composed only of hymns (*shabads*): spiritual poetry that expresses the individual's acute longing for God. The emphasis on the musical aspect of the hymns is seen in the structure of the text itself. The text is organized into three main sections. The first is an introductory section containing three liturgies: one for the morning (the *Jap*), one for evening, and one for bedtime. The third is the shortest by far and concludes with Guru Arjan's *Mundavani* and a final string of melodies called the *Ragmala*. The second is the longest section.[12] The hymns in that section are organized according to their musical composition in a total of thirty-one sections. Within each section, the hymns are further divided by author, following the chronological order of the gurus. The gurus are not named specifically, however. Instead, they are called *Mahalla* 1, *Mahalla* 2, and so on.

Another notable feature of the text is that it includes hymns written by Muslim and Hindu poets as well. This marks it as a truly inclusive and universal

---

10. Myrvold, "Making Scripture a Person," 126.

11. Ibid., 129.

12. Pashaura Singh, "The Guru Granth Sahib," in *The Oxford Handbook of Sikh Studies*, ed. Pashaura Singh and Louis E. Fenech (Oxford: Oxford University Press, 2014), 131.

text, and vividly illustrates one of the key characteristics of Sikh identity. A related characteristic that signals its universality is that unlike many other sacred scriptures of the time, the text was not written in the languages of the cultural elite—Sanskrit or Arabic—but rather uses various vernaculars in order to be more accessible to a wider variety of people, including the lower castes and classes.

The book itself is an aesthetic delight, and before talking in more depth about its contents, let me describe the visual appearance of the text and the specifics of its veneration. The text itself is written in *gurmukhi* script, and most editions of the text are beautifully ornamented. The book itself is large: the standard length is 1,430 pages, and it is quite imposing when compiled in one volume. Typically, a family does not have a complete granth at home; instead, they have a smaller volume that contains the most-sung hymns for daily use. By contrast, all *gurdwaras* have a copy of the full text—indeed, the definition of a *gurdwara* (guru's door) is the place where the sacred scripture is housed and read from daily.

There are important rituals that are performed not only when a text is installed in a new *gurdwara* but also before and after it is read. In the morning, there is a special ceremony in which the text is opened—called the *prakash*—and another ceremonial closing at night—the *sikhasan*—before the text is taken away to rest for the evening. When not in use, it is covered with fine, richly covered cloths (*rumalas*) and sometimes garlands as well. It is placed on an elevated platform, also covered in cloths, so it does not touch the ground, and a whisk (*chauri*) is waved over the book while it is being read. Anytime it is moved, it is carried on someone's head, and when devotees come into its presence, they prostrate themselves before it. Both men and women also must cover their heads and take off their shoes. Finally, there are also death rituals for a text that has become worn-out, and they parallel almost exactly the cremation rituals for a person. These rituals have become formalized and institutionalized in modern times, and there are now designated sites and days for cremations. Interestingly enough, some of these sites also provide this service for the sacred texts of other religious traditions, including the Bible, the Bhagavad Gita, and the Qur'an.[13]

Fitting with the Sikh emphasis on equality, however, anyone can read the book publicly—both men and women can read and officiate at Sikh services. There is no trained or ordained priesthood in Sikhism; the only requirement for leadership is faithful lifestyle and discipleship. In the context of a corporate service, the text is always read in Punjabi, even though there are translations available for personal or private use. Given the poetic nature of the hymns, as well as the musical component of the text, translation is very difficult and often does not capture the original meaning. This is especially true in English, with

---

13. For more on these rituals and their contemporary forms, see Myrvold, "Making Scripture a Person."

many scholars noting that English translations typically impose a male gender and male imagery on the divine that is absent in the original Punjabi.[14]

Let me close this section with some examples of hymns from the text itself. First and foremost, of course, are the hymns written by the gurus. And of these, the first that should be mentioned is the *Jap*. This is the most well known of Sikh hymns. Chanted daily, it is the text that begins the book. Nikky-Guninder Kaur Singh describes it this way: "It is recited at the break of dawn when the mind is fresh and the atmosphere is serene. Described as the ambrosial hour in the Jap, dawn is considered most conducive to grasping the divine Word."[15] The opening words of this hymn serve as a summation of Sikh belief as a whole, and as such, they will be discussed a bit later in the chapter. Instead, here are two verses of the hymn—one from the beginning and one from the end—that also provide insight into Sikh belief:

> The True Sovereign, Truth by Name,
>   infinite love the language.
> Seekers forever seek gifts
>   and the Giver gives more and more.
> What can we offer for a glimpse of the Court?
> What can we say to win divine love?
> In the ambrosial hour, exalt and reflect upon the True Name.
> Through actions each is dressed in a body,
>   but liberation comes only from the Gaze of grace.
> Says Nanak, know the Absolute thus.

> Let continence be your smithy, and patience your goldsmith.
> Let wisdom be your anvil, and knowledge your hammer.
> Let awe be the bellows, and inner control the blazing fire.
> In the circle of love, let the ambrosia flow,
> In this true mind, forge the Word,
> Such fulfilment comes to those blessed with the Gaze.
> Says Nanak, happy are they who are gazed upon.[16]

Another important section of the Adi Granth is the *Rahiras*. This is a collection of hymns from various gurus that comprises part of the evening recitation. The last hymn of that section (before the final concluding couplet) is another very popular hymn, written by Guru Arjan. It is said to contain the whole

---

14. As one example, in their translation of selected hymns, Christopher Shackle and Arvind-pal Singh Mandair describe the translation problem and explain their choice of masculine pronouns by deferring to "the Gurus' own usage and their preference for masculine epithets like 'Lord' or 'Master.'" *Teachings of the Sikh Gurus: Selections from the Sikh Scriptures* (London: Routledge, 2005), 1. But clearly this is a debatable solution.

15. N. Singh, *Name of My Beloved*, 45.

16. Ibid., 48, 62.

Adi Granth in miniature and uses an image that has become a popular one for describing the text: a plate offering savory food that sustains the devotees on the path to the Divine. It is described this way: "Sikh Scripture begins with Guru Nanak's celebration of the infinite one . . . and ends with Guru Arjan's analogy of the text as a platter that holds three dishes: truth (*sat*), contentment (*santokh*), and reflection (*vicar*). . . . The ingredients were to be savored and absorbed—not merely swallowed—so that their literary nutrients would create a peaceful mode of existence for his community and for future generations."[17] The hymn reads as follows:

> In the platter, three things lie:
> truth, contentment, contemplation.
> They contain the ambrosial name,
> by which we are all sustained.
> They who eat, they who savour,
>   they are liberated.
> This thing must not be abandoned;
> ever and ever, keep it in your heart.
> The dark ocean can be crossed
> if we take hold of the Guru's feet.
> Says Nanak, this vastness is the Creator's handiwork.[18]

The final text I want to share is from the *Lavan*, the hymn that is recited at wedding ceremonies. It was written by Guru Ram Das and has four stanzas, each of which describes higher levels of "circles" into which the couple will pass in their life together. As each stanza is sung, the couple circumambulates the Guru Granth Sahib, along with their relatives. This is the first verse:

> Creator, as we revolve in the first divine circle,
>   we resolve to return to the world of action.
> As we resolve to act rightfully, and make Your Word
>   our god and scripture, our misdeeds are dispelled.
> Scriptures steadfastly urge us to act righteously
>   and contemplate Your Name.
> By remembering the True Guru,
>   all our misdeeds and offences are dispelled.
> Bliss is ours at once, we are blessed with great fortune,
>   and the Divine tastes so very sweet.
> Nanak the slave says, in the first circle
>   the wedding ceremony is begun.[19]

17. N. Singh and Curcuru, "Sikhism," 120.
18. N. Singh, *Name of My Beloved*, 128.
19. Ibid., 147.

Another important part of the Adi Granth is the texts that were written by fifteen pre-Nanak Muslim and Hindu saints, notable for their inclusion: the early Sikh community clearly believed that even though they were not Sikh, they had something beneficial to teach about God. Further, these texts root Sikh belief in a longer historical tradition, providing a link with the divine revelation that came before. Thus Nirmal Dass notes that these texts are neither a footnote to the hymns by the gurus, nor are they only marginally important. Instead, "they are the intertextual ground from which Sikh piety itself springs—for prehistory implies continuity. In brief, the words of the gurus complete the utterances of the various saints: the old flows into the new, and the new encompasses the old; both receive and perfect each other."[20] Several of these hymns follow.

The first selection is by Namdeva, about whom little is known for certain. It is believed that he came from a low-caste Shudra family and lived sometime in the late thirteenth- to mid-fourteenth century. His hymns reference Hindu deities.

> The guru made my life fruitful;
> I forgot suffering and gained peace.
>
> The guru put wisdom's kohl in my eyes;
> without Ram's name life and heart are empty. (Rest)
>
> Namdeva perceived Him through meditation,
> and now my soul has blended with His soul.[21]

Another lowly Hindu poet is Ravidas—a cobbler who lived in Varanasi sometime in the fifteenth century.

> Like a well filled with frogs
> that know nothing of other lands,
> so my heart,
> rapt with worldly delight,
> knows nothing of this world
> or the next.
>
> O Lord of all creation,
> Show Yourself for an instant. (Rest)
>
> My mind is sullied, O Madho;
> I cannot grasp the substance

---

20. Nirmal Dass, trans., *Songs of the Saints from the Adi Granth* (Albany: State University of New York Press, 2000), 1.

21. Ibid., 45.

of Your reality.
Have mercy and lift my confusion.
Grant me wisdom
that I may come to understand.

Even great yogis
cannot begin to describe
all Your virtues.
I want to love You
and worship You,
so says Ravi Dass the cobbler.[22]

Punjab, Partition, and Political Upheaval

Before moving to a discussion of Sikh beliefs and practices, a brief word about modern Sikh history is helpful. Even though Sikhs are now found throughout the world, the homeland of the majority of Sikhs is the Indian state of Punjab, located in the upper northwest corner of India. All of the ten human gurus came from Punjab, and still today, being Sikh is closely linked to being Punjabi. The name Punjab refers to the five rivers—in fact, tributaries of the Indus river—that flow through this region, making it such rich land for agriculture.

The Sikh community carries with it a sense of strength and perseverance in the face of struggle, born of a long history of conflict in India. In the first few centuries of its life, the Sikh community lived mostly peaceably with other religions, although there was some persecution under the Mughal rulers. In what is sometimes thought of as the height of political Sikhism, a Sikh state was established for a brief period in the early nineteenth century. In 1799, Ranjit Singh was able to seize control of Lahore in a bloodless coup and formed a state by joining twelve different Sikh groups into one. He was crowned Maharaja in 1801 and ruled for forty years, expanding his territory to include the area of Kashmir, among others. His state was characterized by great opulence; Singh, for example, wore the world's largest diamond on his right arm.[23] Still today, Ranjit Singh is valorized as "the Lion of Punjab," and this period in Sikh history is remembered with pride.

However, this period did not last. Not quite ten years after Singh's death, the Sikhs lost their state to the British. They were defeated in 1849, and the British took over as rulers of the region. Ranjit Singh's wife, Maharani Jindan, served as regent for a time, but eventually she was imprisoned and her son Dalip was exiled to England and converted to Christianity. In a symbolically important move, the great diamond was cut down to fit into Queen Victoria's crown.[24] Even in defeat, however, the British respected the Sikhs as soldiers

---

22. Ibid., 90.
23. N. Singh and Curcuru, "Sikhism," 118.

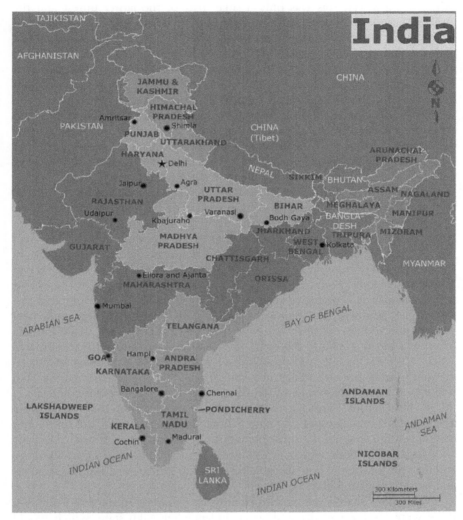

Figure 11: Map of India with the state of Punjab in the upper left corner of the country, on the border with Pakistan.

and encouraged their distinctive identity and traditions. In this way, somewhat ironically, the presence of the British actually strengthened Sikh culture and fortified the Khalsa. Sikhs served valorously in the British army and were an important part of the British forces in WWI.

Fast forward to 1947. There was agitation all over India in the years leading up to partition, and in the Punjab there were conflicts between Sikhs and

24. Ibid.

Muslims. However, this was only a small part of the larger unrest and the escalating violence between Muslims and Hindus as different groups jockeyed for position and demanded power. Finally, in 1947, the British voted to end their rule in India, leaving Louis Mountbatten, who had been appointed the last viceroy of India, to come up with a transition plan. Wanting to avoid a civil war, Mountbatten sped up the initial timeline and very quickly resigned himself to the need for dividing the country and giving Muslims a country of their own, which would be called Pakistan. However, during this process, India's 6 million Sikhs were marginalized, and without an astute leader who could advocate for them, their voices and concerns went largely unheeded. The new countries came into being August 14 and 15, 1947, and the violence started immediately as hundreds of thousands of people went on the move.

It should be noted that the partition of India did not geographically disrupt the entire country equally; rather, the partition itself affected just two provinces: Bengal in the east and Punjab in the northwest. When Pakistan came into being, Punjabi territory was divided into west and east regions, and over half the land became part of Pakistan. This was a terrible time for India. In Punjab, like all of the border regions, there was a horrific frenzy of violence as people desperately crisscrossed the new border—either willingly or out of fear or compulsion. It is estimated that in all, over 14 million people migrated one direction or another. At that time, most Sikhs who found themselves in the new country of Pakistan crossed back into India with the Hindus, while Punjabi Muslims crossed over into Pakistan. The death toll of partition was estimated at half a million people, and thousands of women were kidnapped and raped as well. One of the end results of partition was that it concentrated the Sikh population in the Indian state of Punjab, giving them more power politically.

A few decades later, in response to the demands of those who were agitating for a Punjabi-speaking state, Punjab was again divided, this time along language lines, creating the three Indian provinces as they exist today: Haryana and Himachal Pradesh, which are populated primarily by native Hindi speakers, and the current state of Punjab, which is made up primarily of Punjabi speakers and has a dominant Sikh majority.

One more chapter in this history must be recorded. In the 1970s and 80s, there were loud voices demanding an independent Sikh state, which would be known as Khalistan (the land of the Khalsa). This agitation increased the violence in Punjab, which culminated in a dreadful atrocity called Operation Blue Star. It happened in 1984, in early June, when the Sikh community was celebrating the martyrdom of Guru Arjan. The Golden Temple complex was packed with pilgrims when the Indian government sent in troops and tanks to remove Jarnail Singh Bhindranwale, a Sikh leader who had been opposing Prime Minister Indira Gandhi and arguing for greater Sikh autonomy. He had moved into the Harmandir Sahib in 1982. Thousands were killed both in the complex itself and in the surrounding countryside, including Bhindranwale himself, and many historical treasures—including sacred Sikh manuscripts—were destroyed. In addition, the Akal Takhat (the administrative building in the complex and the highest seat of Sikh religious authority) was damaged so badly that it had to be rebuilt.

This was, of course, a public relations nightmare for Gandhi, and it was deeply offensive to the Sikh community around the world. And, tragically, it did not go unanswered. Four months after Operation Blue Star, on October 31, 1984, Indira Gandhi was assassinated by two of her Sikh bodyguards. In response, retribution was swift and terrible. There were massive anti-Sikh riots all over the country in which thousands were killed, most of whom were in Delhi. This continues to be an open wound in India, as none have been punished for the killings and there is widespread belief in government complicity in the massacre. The Sikh authorities have called this a genocide. In India, both Sikhs and Hindus have, for the most part, put this incident behind them, but it is certainly not forgotten.

God, Humanity, and Faithful Living

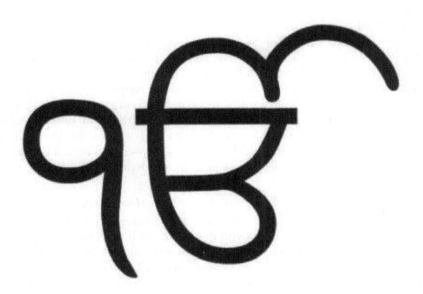

Figure 12: The ek onkar (Ik oankar) is the symbol that represents the one supreme reality.

The first twelve words that open the Guru Granth Sahib are the most widely known and professed by Sikhs, and they sum up well the heart of Sikhism. The first two words are *ik oankar*, which can be translated in a variety of ways: "One reality is," "This being is one," or "There is one god."[25] This opening statement affirms that Sikhism is a monotheistic religion whose adherents worship one god who is both universal and particular—the one revealed in the many. However, it should be noted that in spite of many English translations that reinforce the image of a male deity, God is viewed much more mystically than in most of Western monotheism and is not worshipped as embodied at all. Therefore, most Sikh art is aniconic. The symbol above, which represents the *ik oankar*, is the most well-known Sikh symbol and used extensively in a wide variety of contexts. It symbolizes both the oneness and the limitlessness of the divine: "Without confining the divine in any way, the rhythmic unity sustained by the numeral 1, the syllabic oan, and the unending geometric arc launches the spectator toward an all-encompassing infinity."[26]

The remaining ten opening words are as follows: "truth by name, the creator, without fear, without hate, timeless in form, beyond birth, self existent, (known by) the grace of the Guru."[27] Eleanor Nesbitt notes that in English translations, a pronoun is often substituted at the beginning of each quality, e.g., "He is the creator." This implies a gendering of God that is not actually present in the text itself and facilitates a specific image of God that Sikhism expressly avoids.[28] Taken together, these twelve words are called the *mul mantar* (root mantra). This designation indicates that these words contain the heart of Sikh belief and the core of Sikh theology.

One can say, then, that Sikhism confesses a transcendent Divine, who has graciously communicated the true path to insight and unity to the gurus and who can be experienced in this life. Focusing on the divine reality and orienting one's whole life to the Divine leads to happiness and contentment and also motivates one to live justly and purely, serving others with kindness and generosity. There is less emphasis on the afterlife and more emphasis on one's life in the here-and-now. Sikhism also stresses the good of the community—indeed, the good of the whole society—and so ethical behavior is seen as a critical aspect of one's relationship to the Divine.

THE EQUALITY OF THE WHOLE HUMAN FAMILY

The consequence of this belief is that one's relationship with God is not separable from one's relationship with the rest of the human family. In order to honor and worship God, one must honor and serve all one's brothers and sisters without distinction because before God, all humans are equal. This equality of every human being is a foundational conviction of Sikhism. This belief comes out of its origins and directly relates to Guru Nanak's rejection of the caste system of fifteenth-century India and his rejection of religious divisions. For

25. Nesbitt, "Issues in Writing 'Introductions,'" 22–23.
26. N. Singh and Curcuru, "Sikhism," 112.
27. Nesbitt, "Issues in Writing 'Introductions,'" 24.
28. Ibid.

Sikhs, all individuals have the Divine within themselves, and all are equal before God. Therefore, all are deserving of respect and care.

Sikhs believe in an individual's own ability to determine his or her destiny, and it is up to each individual, with the support of God and the aid of the community, to mold one's own life faithfully and seek union with God. The spiritual goal in Sikhism is *mukti* (liberation), which in Sikhism means to escape from the cycle of reincarnation and to reunite the soul with God. (It is believed that the body is finite; only the soul is immortal.) The way this happens is not through renunciation or asceticism but rather through active engagement in family and community life, and active service to those in need. Thus Sikhism is about living in the real world: "Morality is not fostered in some distant cave or once a week in a religious space; rather, it is practiced in everyday nitty-gritty acts, within the immediate world of family, classes, sports and profession."[29]

There is no sense in Sikhism that there is a higher reality in some alternate dimension that must be sought through special rituals, nor is the religious path described as one away from or out of this world. Instead, the emphasis is on realizing and experience truth in the present reality, in one's present circumstances. As noted above, this demands an ethical life that includes not only a relationship with the Divine but service and kindness to others as well. An important means of supporting a faithful life is by immersing oneself in the words of the Guru Granth Sahib as often as possible.

There are two important anthropological concepts in Sikhism that directly relate to the path of liberation. Sikhism describes the religious path as moving from being a *manmukh* (being devoted to oneself) to being a *gurumukh* (being devoted to the guru). The life of a *manmukh* is characterized by what are called the five robbers—lust, anger, greed, attachment, and pride. Their root cause is self-absorption and selfishness—a turning into oneself—which creates separation and division between oneself and others, and oneself and the Divine (including one's own divine core). These robbers can be guarded against by constantly focusing on the One—the divine that links all humanity and all creation together and fosters love within us. Opening ourselves to that One, that love, inspires us to live rightly with care and responsibility toward the larger human community and the world as a whole. Guru Nanak did not challenge the karmic system of Hinduism, but he did teach that God's love could break into that system and help form the individual into a *gurumukh*, such that they could even attain *mukti*—the highest stage of union with God—before death.

THE KHALSA

It is impossible to talk about the Sikh community without mentioning the Khalsa, one of the most important, visible signs of Sikhism. This is an exemplary

---

29. N. Singh and Curcuru, "Sikhism," 120.

Figure 13: The Khanda, the symbol of the Khalsa.

community of Sikhs (Khalsa is typically translated as "pure") that embodies the heart of Sikhism and is its most visible presence in the world. It requires a water ritual of initiation and carries with it particular signs of membership and also a specific code of conduct. Not all Sikhs are members of the Khalsa—in fact, the majority of Sikhs are not.[30] The Khalsa was created by the tenth and last guru, Gobind Singh, and the story of its inauguration is powerful and dramatic.

The setting was the new year celebration that was held in 1699 in Anandpur Sahib (the second-holiest city in Sikhism). Throngs of people attended, and when everyone was gathered, Guru Gobind Singh called out for a volunteer who was willing to sacrifice his head. A man came forward, and the guru took him inside his tent and then came out alone with a bloody sword. He repeated this four times. The fifth time, however, the five men all came out with Guru Gobind Singh and showed that they were unharmed. These five men who demonstrated that they were willing to give their lives for the guru were called the *panj pyare*—the five beloved ones. The guru then poured water into an iron bowl and stirred it with his sword. His wife, Mata Jitoji, added some

---

30. One article suggests that the number of Khalsa Sikhs is around 15 percent of the total Sikh population. Hew McLeod, "The Five Ks of the Khalsa Sikhs," *Journal of the American Oriental Society* 128, no. 2 (2008): 327.

sugar to the water—thereby mixing the strength of steel with the sweetness of sugar. The resultant drink is known as *amrit* (nectar).

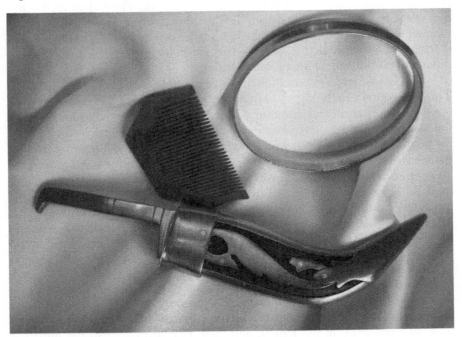

Figure 14: Three of the five Ks: the kangha (comb), the kirpan (ceremonial sword), and the kara (steel bangle).

Each of the five men drank from the bowl, and the water also was sprinkled on them. This ritual symbolized their fellowship, which would transcend all other allegiances, including class, caste, and geographical affiliation. Each man received the title *Singh* (lion), which was meant to signify a new family lineage; subsequently, the women would receive the title *Kaur* (prince or princess). After the first five disciples completed the ritual, thousands of others followed, receiving a new identity that was reinforced by five external signs of membership, often called the five Ks: *kesha, kangha, kirpan, kara,* and *kaccha.* The traditional view as to the origin of these signs is that Guru Gobind Singh desired that each member of the Khalsa should "proclaim to the world" his or her unique religious identity by having a clearly visible "uniform" that would distinguish them from everyone else. Others argue for a longer development that did not take its final form until the end of the nineteenth century.[31] Members of the Khalsa are called *Amritdhari* Sikhs.

The *kesha* refers to uncut hair and symbolizes acceptance of God's will by

31. Ibid., 330.

allowing the hair to grow as nature intends. Both men and women refrain from cutting their hair; women usually wear a long braid and men typically wind their hair into a topknot, which is covered by a turban. The turban itself is not one of the five Ks and while usually it is the men who wear the turban, some women wear it as well. Similar to the headscarf worn by many Muslim women, there are differences in the turban—both in color and style—that represent different political and geographical affiliations.

The *kangha* refers to the comb that is meant to keep the uncut hair in order. This is in contrast to the sages of Hinduism who often wore their hair matted. It is typically very small and almost unnoticeable. The *kirpan* was originally a full-size sword, but in modern times its size has shrunk dramatically—though not the power of the symbolism, which is a visible reminder of the fighting spirit of the Sikhs. The *kirpan* connotes both spiritual power and also physical power, the power to defend the innocent from violence. Today it is often a few-centimeter model of a sword that is affixed to the comb. The *kara* is a thin steel bangle usually worn on the right wrist. It is meant to be a daily tangible reminder that one is to do good deeds with one's hands and serve others. Finally, the *kaccha* is the special type of undergarment worn by both men and women. It is worn as a reminder to control one's desires and treat other men and women with respect.

Before leaving a discussion of the Khalsa, one more point should be noted. Traditionally, and still today, the Khalsa is often interpreted and described with very masculine imagery and language. It is the story of men, told by men, and men continue to be its exemplars in most contexts today. However, women have an equal share in the Khalsa, and they, too, participate in the initiation rites and wear the symbols proudly in their daily lives. It can be argued that their marginalization both in the history and the present-day interpretation of the Khalsa distorts its true meaning by an exclusive reliance on a hyper-masculinized version of the story. By contrast, Nikky-Guninder Kaur Singh offers an alternative interpretation in her book *The Birth of the Khalsa: A Feminist Re-Memory of Sikh Identity*.[32]

Singh notes that while the task of reinterpretation is "daunting," it is also critical because of the ways in which the "overtly 'patriarchal'" discourse of the Khalsa has reinforced and perpetuated patriarchal structures in society that continue to oppress women. She writes that by maintaining the Khalsa's identity as a "militaristic fraternity," "the guru's theological vision is neglected, and so is his compassionate and creative interior. Sikhs remember the fierce battle scenes depicted by the guru, but they miss out on how those very scenes lead to women, kitchens, sacred spaces, celebrations—to an authentic mode of life and living in our variegated world."[33] To promote such a vision, she reimagines the story of the creation of the Khalsa from a female perspective,

---

32. Nikky-Guninder Kaur Singh, *The Birth of the Khalsa: A Feminist Re-Memory of Sikh Identity* (Albany: State University of New York Press, 2005).

33. Ibid., 5.

shifting the image of the guru "from a patriarchal view to a maternal one,"[34] such that, "like a mother, the Sikh guru births his Khalsa."[35] In a similar way, she redefines the meaning of each of the five symbols of the Khalsa, describing them from a feminist point of view and infusing them with liberating and revolutionary power for women as well as men. This allows her to conclude:

> The symbols worn by the Khalsa are not weapons of war to spark violence in the public or domestic spheres. Nor are they tools that cut and divide us from the human family. Nor are they hand-me-downs from fathers and brothers. Our female understanding of the hair, the comb, the bracelet, the underwear, and the sword animates and activates each wearer's consciousness of the Infinite and knowledge of our common humanity.[36]

SIKH HOLIDAYS

There are several important holidays in the Sikh calendar, which has a complicated history. Until 2003, the calendar was based on the Hindu lunar/solar calendar, which meant that the holidays did not have a fixed date, but moved in the context of a limited number of weeks. So, for example, Hola Maholla would never show up in October but could be in February or March. This slippage caused some problems however, so in 2003, a Canadian Sikh created a new calendar, called the Nanakshashi calendar, which is now widely used in the Sikh community—even though its acceptance was not without controversy.[37]

There are two main types of celebrations: *gurpurbs*, which commemorate major events in the lives of the gurus, especially a birth or a martyrdom, and *melas*, or festivals. The dates for all *gurpurbs* are fixed, with the exception of the birth of Guru Nanak—that date fluctuates within the month of November. The dates of the *melas* continue to move according to the variances of the Hindu calendar. The main festivals are the celebration of Guru Gobind Singh's birthday, which takes place on January 5; Hola Maholla, which takes place in March; the martyrdom of Guru Arjan, June 16; Bandi Chhor Divas (Prisoner Release Day), October/November; and Guru Nanak's birthday in November.

FOUR RITES OF PASSAGE

In addition to these holidays, there are also several important rites of passage that mark growth and maturity in the life of a Sikh. The first rite that Sikhs experience is the name ceremony. Sikh children are always named in consultation with the Guru Granth Sahib. Typically what happens is that the

34. Ibid., 39.
35. Ibid., 40.
36. Ibid., 178.
37. Nesbitt, "Issues in Writing 'Introductions,'" 126.

text is opened at random and the child receives a name that begins with the first letter that appears on the left-hand page.[38] The second rite of passage is the *amrit* ceremony that many (though not all) Sikhs undergo, which initiates them into the Khalsa. This can be done at any age. This normally takes place on April 13 (the date of the original ceremony) in the local *gurdwara*. The ceremony is performed by five Sikhs who represent the first five members of the Khalsa, and they can be either men or women, though they traditionally are men. The *amrit* is prepared and stirred while hymns are sung, and as the individuals come forward, the *amrit* is sprinkled on their eyes and hair, and then it is drunk. There are prayers and singing, and then the whole community celebrates with the *langar*.

The third rite is the wedding ceremony, which is of central importance for Sikhs. Sikhism strongly encourages marriage and childbearing, and indeed, marriage is considered the foundation of Sikh society. This has had some negative ramifications for women; more will be said about women and Sikhism in general later in the chapter. Weddings have become very elaborate affairs, stretching family budgets to the breaking point. Most marriages are arranged, as a wedding is seen as a union not merely between two individuals but between two families. In a traditional Sikh wedding, a dowry is given by the bride's family, and the bride is expected to join her husband's family. The bride and groom sit in front of the Guru Granth Sahib, and the officiant, the *granthi*, explains the expectations of a married couple to them. Specific verses are read and the couple circle the holy text several times.

The last rite of passage is the death ritual. Death is not considered an enemy in Sikhism or something to be feared. Instead, it is considered part of God's ordered creation and an inevitable part of life: "mortality is imbedded in the creation of all living things."[39] Thus excessive grieving is not encouraged. Like Hindus, Sikhs also believe in reincarnation, but the hope is always that at death, the soul will be united with God. The soul is believed to be immortal but the body is not; the body is merely a temporary encasement for the soul. Cremation is the norm for Sikhism, and the traditional rite also includes hymn singing, washing the body, and sharing a meal.

WORSHIP AND THE GURDWARA

The first formal Sikh community was founded on the banks of the Ravi river, which crosses the border between modern-day Pakistan and India, and it was made up of people who lived active lives in the community—including having families—rather than monastics. They were committed to practices that still define Sikh life today.[40] Unlike other religions where the home is effectively the

---

38. N. Singh and Curcuru, "Sikhism," 122.

39. Kristina Myrvold, "Sikhism and Death," in *Death and Religion in a Changing World*, ed. Kathleen Garces-Foley (New York: Routledge, 2006), 181.

40. N. Singh and Curcuru, "Sikhism," 116.

center of one's religious life, the *gurdwara* is the heart of Sikhism—not because of any particular holiness of the structure itself, but because the *gurdwara* houses the Guru Granth Sahib. In addition, the *gurdwara* provides the place where community service (*seva*) can be done, in particular, the *langar*, the cooking and serving of a vegetarian meal for anyone who desires it. There is no one day that has been fixed as the day the community gathers, but in the diaspora, this typically occurs on Sundays.

There is no ordained priesthood in Sikhism, and the actual administration of the affairs of the Sikh community is done by lay people. There are people who are called *granthis* (keepers of the scripture), and they are the ones who tend to the scripture each day—performing the opening and closing rituals—and also the ones who read from it at Sikh services. The *granthis* also conduct the specific rites of passage in Sikhism, which can take place at the *gurdwara* or in the home. Anyone can be designated as a *granthi*, male or female; however, because of cultural custom, the vast majority of *granthis* today are men and most still come from Punjab. The primary requirement is living a life of character and virtue.

In any formal Sikh gathering, there are several key components. First is the congregation itself, the *sangat*: the company of people who are on the path and come together to give each other spiritual support and encouragement. The bulk of the service is comprised of various musicians and singers who perform *kirtan*, the singing of hymns from the Guru Granth Sahib. Often there is also a scholar who offers an interpretation of a portion of the text. The service always ends with the distribution of what is called *kara parshad*. This is a special food that is made by mixing equal amounts of flour, *ghee*, water, and raw sugar. It is received as a visible and sweet manifestation of the guru's blessing, and it is offered to everyone in the congregation as a sign of unity before God.

Finally, when the service is concluded, there is the *langar*, the free community meal that is served to everyone, all of whom eat together side by side on the floor. This, too, is a sign of the equality of all humans before God. It should be noted that while today this offering is seen primarily as an expression of generosity and service, when it was instituted it symbolized something quite different. This practice of the "free kitchen" was started by Guru Nanak, and at a time when caste distinctions strictly governed both who could eat with whom and even who could prepare one's food, it was a radical departure from Indian custom. The meal is always vegetarian, and it is served to everyone without exception. At large *gurdwaras*, it is served every day, twice a day. It is said that the *langar* at the Harmandir Sahib serves one hundred thousand people per day.

The central shrine of Sikhism is the Golden Temple complex in Amritsar, India (sometimes called the *Darbar Sahib* [divine court]). It includes the beautiful temple itself, called the Harmandir Sahib (temple of God). It sits in the middle of the holy lake of Amritsar (from which the city itself received its name), which is believed to have healing powers. Construction began under Guru Ram Das, and the foundation was laid in the late sixteenth century. It was completed in 1601 under Guru Arjan's leadership.[41]

Figure 15: The Golden Temple in Amritsar, India.

The temple is noted for having four entrances, symbolizing its openness to people of all castes and classes, and also for being built lower than the rest of the city, so that one has to go down to enter it. This is a reminder of the importance of humility and a sign that it is accessible to even the lowliest of creatures. The complex also includes the *Akal Takht* (the building where the Guru Granth is taken every evening), a walkway that surrounds the lake, a causeway that leads to the temple, and a beautiful gateway called the *Darshani Deorhi*. The Harmandir truly is the spiritual center of Sikhism worldwide, and it is a popular pilgrimage site for Sikhs and non-Sikhs alike.

The Contemporary Sikh Diaspora and Women

As noted earlier in the chapter, by far the largest Sikh community in the twenty-first century remains in India. Indeed, the term "Sikh diaspora" is a relatively recent one and some still contest its use.[42] Sikh emigration began in the nineteenth century, specifically through their service in the British army, and they settled throughout the British Empire. After the partition of India, migration began in earnest, and given the shortage of labor in the West—including Canada, the United States, and England itself—doors were opened to Sikhs in ways they had not been before.[43] Currently, there are 1.5 to

---

41. For a clear introduction to the Harmandir Sahib and worship there, see the first chapter in W. Owen Cole, *Understanding Sikhism* (Edinburgh: Dunedin Academic Press, 2004), 3–11.

42. Darshan Singh Tatla, "The Sikh Diaspora," in P. Singh and Fenech, *Oxford Handbook*, 495.

2 million Sikhs living abroad; the latest census in the United Kingdom showed almost 400,000, and in Canada the number is almost 300,000. The United States estimates a population of around 250,000.[44] Smaller but significant populations are found in the Middle East, Italy, Pakistan, Thailand, and East Africa.

Like many other religious communities who have settled in Europe and North America, the younger generation often struggles with what it means to be a Sikh outside India, especially as the religion is still so bound up with Punjabi heritage and culture. It is the challenge of balancing tradition with modernization and maintaining the symbols and practices of one's forebears in a cultural context that is often not supportive. Related to this, of course, is the increased discrimination against the Sikh community since 9/11, particularly in the United States and Europe.[45] Many people confuse Sikhs with Muslims (who are, for their part, erroneously assumed to be terrorists), and both individuals and *gurdwaras* have been attacked. In response, many Sikh communities have stepped up their outreach, working to educate and build bridges in their communities.

Nikky-Guninder Kaur Singh, mentioned previously, has written repeatedly and compellingly on the need for Sikhism to confront its patriarchal structures and return to the liberating words and practices of the gurus. So, for example, she notes while it is clear that women are allowed to serve as members of the *panj pyare*—the five Khalsa members who are chosen from the community to officiate at Sikh rites—in practice, this almost never happens.[46] In addition, many of the Sikh ceremonies that are meant to be identical for both genders are practiced very differently, with the rites for boys/men being more elaborate and celebratory than those for girls/women.[47] In addition, Sikh marriage customs, which still include the practice of arranged marriages, also reflect a sexist attitude in which "from her birth to her death, a daughter is a debit,"[48] and this is not mitigated in the Sikh diaspora. Finally, it is clear that even though sex-determination tests for fetuses are illegal in India, they are clearly practiced, with the result that female fetuses are sometimes aborted: one needs only note the current gender imbalance in the Punjab, where there are only 793 girls for every 1,000 boys.[49]

43. Ibid., 497.

44. Ibid., 499.

45. For several accounts of the latest acts of violence, see Pashaura Singh, "New Directions in Sikh Studies," in P. Singh and Fenech, *Oxford Handbook*, 625–44.

46. N. Singh, *Birth of the Khalsa*, 186.

47. N. Singh cites the name-giving ceremony as one example. Ibid., 186–87.

48. Ibid., 190.

49. Ibid., 57. See the same story in Vrinda Sharma, "Female Infanticide Affects Sex Ratio in Punjab," *The Hindu*, April 16, 2010, http://tinyurl.com/z77wptd. See also Nikky-Guninder Kaur Singh, "Female Feticide in the Punjab and Fetus Imagery in Sikhism," in *Imagining the Fetus: The Unborn in Myth, Religion and Culture*, ed. Vanessa R. Sasson and Jane Marie Law (New York: Oxford University Press, 2009).

Singh also notes how Sikh theology can benefit from a feminist perspective. For example, she describes how the symbol of the bride is at the heart of Sikh devotional life, and one of the central images in the Guru Granth Sahib. This image, she argues, can help Sikhs overcome gender dualisms by offering both men and women a means of voicing their desire for God. She writes, "This sacred volume of the Sikhs is replete with feminine symbolism and imagery. The poetry of the Gurū Granth is spoken in the bride's voice, expressing her yearning to unite with the transcendent Groom."[50] She explains how this image overcomes human/animal dualisms, helping humans experience the deep connectedness we share with all life, and observes how the text not only references human brides but female animals as well: "For instance, in a passage of superb poetic beauty, Gurū Nānak identifies himself with the females of several species to express his yearning for union. He wishes he were a she-deer (*harṇi*) living the jungles, or a koel (*kokil*) singing in the mango grove, or a fish (*machuli*) dwelling in the waters, or a she-serpent (*nāgin*) within the earth, in each case enjoying the proximity of the beloved."[51]

Finally, she also emphasizes how this image overcomes mind/body dualisms, as the descriptions of the young bride's physical adornments—heavy necklaces, makeup, plaited hair, elaborate dress—mirror her inner readiness: "Her bodily adornment represents her mental purification. Her cosmetics not only enhance her physical appearance, they also contribute to her intellectual strength. For example, the mascara (*anjani*) that she uses to darken and beautify her eyes is to be interpreted as *jnāṇa* (knowledge)."[52] In this way, Singh works to recapture the essential liberatory core at the heart of Guru Nanak's teaching, which emphasizes the dignity of all people—men and women—and inspires each person to rise to union with God.

This famous statement by the tenth guru sums up well Sikhism as a whole:

Hindus and Muslims are one.
The same Reality is the Creator and Preserver of all;
Know no distinctions between them.
The monastery and the mosque are the same;
So are the Hindu worship and the Muslim prayer.
Humans are all one![53]

50. Nikky-Guninder Kaur Singh, "The Sikh Bridal Symbol: An Epiphany of Interconnections," *Journal of Feminist Studies in Religion* 8, no. 2 (Fall 1992): 44.
51. Ibid., 45.
52. Ibid., 46.
53. N. Singh, *Name of My Beloved*, 8.

3

A Brief Introduction to Confucianism

Confucianism in the Chinese Context

In many world religions textbooks, Confucianism and Daoism are lumped together under the larger category of Chinese religions, even though they are quite different—some might even say polar opposites. What is the justification for that? Generally speaking, there are three primary reasons for this consistent pairing: the first is geography, the second is Chinese history and a shared language, and the third is the complementary nature of the religions themselves. In spite of these commonalities, they are each given their own chapter in this text, primarily to better help Western readers, who are often unfamiliar with both religions, get a clearer sense of each on its own terms. At the same time, it should be noted that there is some overlap in these two chapters given the religions' shared history and culture. Therefore, in this chapter in particular, some introductory groundwork is laid regarding salient points in Chinese history in order to gain a better understanding of how both of these religions developed together and how deeply they shaped—and were shaped by—the Chinese context in which they came to fruition.

To that end, for those who are not familiar with the spelling and pronunciation of transliterated Chinese words, a few sentences of introduction are necessary. There are two different spelling systems that typically have been used in the West when converting Chinese words into English: Wade-Giles and *pinyin*. Wade-Giles is the older form, named for its two founders. It was the most common system up through most of the twentieth century, but it has subsequently been replaced by the *pinyin* system, which was developed by the Chinese government in the 1950s and serves as the new international standard. Wade-Giles can still be found in older texts, however, and this can create some confusion. For example, one of the primary Confucian thinkers is named Xunzi. However, in the Wade-Giles system, his name is spelled Hsün Tzu. One would be excused for not initially realizing they are the same person. Thus when reading a text about either Confucianism or Daoism, it is important to note which spelling system is being used—and hope it is consistent throughout. *Pinyin* spelling is used in both this chapter and the following chapter on Daoism.

Finally, let me say a few words about pronunciation. Transliterated Chinese follows very different pronunciation conventions from English, which makes many of the names and words sound much different than they look. It is both respectful and helpful to have at least a general sense of how one might pronounce Chinese words. To that end, then, what follows is a quick guide to a few of the more difficult examples. (Note these are only approximations, as the Chinese pronunciation of most vowels also differs from English as well.) The letter *x* is pronounced *sh* and *z* is pronounced *ts*—so the name *Xunzi* is pronounced *Shuntsi*. The letter combination *zh* is pronounced *j*—so the *Zhou* dynasty is pronounced *Joh*. The letter *q* is pronounced *ch*—so the word *Qi* is pronounced *Chi*.[1]

RELIGIOUS DIVERSITY AND THE CHINESE CONTEXT

One other point of introduction is needed before beginning an examination of Confucianism proper. It is important to be reminded of how dissimilar a Chinese context is from an American context, particularly when it comes to religion. Many writers have noted how different the traditional Asian religious dynamic is from the traditional Western religious milieu. Even though this is a broad generalization, it remains accurate to say that the high level of pluralism, inclusivity, and "multiple-religious belonging" that occurs quite naturally in various Asian countries has a long history and is quite well established. Certainly, this has been true for millennia in China. Judith Berling notes that a "Chinese cultural practice of religious crossover is the antithesis of historical Christian patterns of exclusivity. It is grounded in a history of religious interaction very different from that which characterized Christianity in Europe and North America."[2] Religion always has been important in Chinese history, and it always has had a major role in shaping the destinies of both individuals and dynasties. Indeed, religion has even had a hand in shaping Chinese geography, as the borders of the country we call China are still contested today; the current situation of Tibet is only the most well-publicized example.

Although many different religions have been significant in Chinese history and culture, certainly the most important have been are traditionally called the three teachings: Daoism, Confucianism, and Buddhism. A full examination of Chinese Buddhism is outside the scope of this chapter; therefore, only a brief word is offered here. Buddhism came into China in the very early centuries

---

1. There are many internet sources where more information can be found. For a source that includes audio examples, see "Cal Poly Pomona Asian Name Pronunciation Guide: Mandarin Names," California State Polytechnic University, Pomona, last updated June 22, 2005, http://tinyurl.com/h8kv3q2. See also David K. Jordan, "Guide to Pronouncing Mandarin in Romanized Transcription (Beginners' Page)," University of California San Diego Division of Social Sciences, last updated June 21, 2015, http://tinyurl.com/ojj7pjo.

2. Judith A. Berling, *A Pilgrim in Chinese Culture: Negotiating Religious Diversity* (Maryknoll, NY: Orbis Books, 1997), 42.

CE, sometime during the Han dynasty. The first Buddhists came on the Silk Road, coming up from India through Central Asia, and were probably simple traders and merchants who left no records. The official recorded transmission of Buddhism happened through the work of Buddhist monks, most of whom were affiliated with what are traditionally called the Mahayana schools. These schools were the ones that grew and flourished in China over time.

During this period, and in the centuries to follow, much effort was invested in translation of Buddhist texts. In the process of translating documents from Sanskrit into Chinese, which are very different languages, Daoist vocabulary often was used for Buddhist philosophical terms, which resulted in close communication—but not necessarily understanding—between the two traditions, including mutual borrowing back and forth, both ritual and conceptual.[3] (One example of this is the Daoist concept of *wu-wei* [non-action] being used to translate the Buddhist concept of nirvana.[4]) This dynamic was mitigated with the coming of Kumarajiva (344–409/413), widely considered to be the greatest translator in Chinese Buddhist history. His superior translations facilitated an understanding of Buddhism on its own terms, rather than in the terminology of Daoism. And while the relationship between the two traditions ebbed and flowed over time as Buddhism gained influence in China, the lines between the two religions became more firmly established.

CONFUCIANISM AND CHINESE HISTORY

Brief Chronology of Chinese History	
Shang (Yin) Dynasty	1600–1050 BCE
Zhou Dynasty	1046–256 BCE
Confucius	551–479 BCE
Mencius	371–289 BCE
Xunzi	298–238 BCE
Qin Dynasty	221–206 BCE
Han Dynasty	206 BCE–220 CE
Tang Dynasty	618–906 CE
Song Dynasty	960–1279 CE
[Neo-Confucianism originated during the Tang/Song dynasties]	
Yuan Dynasty (Mongol rule)	1279–1368 CE
Ming Dynasty	1368–1644 CE
Qing Dynasty (Manchu)	1644–1912 CE
Republic of China	1912–1949 CE
People's Republic of China	1949–present

3. Ibid., 50–56.
4. Mario Poceski, *Introducing Chinese Religions* (New York: Routledge, 2009), 121.

As one of the earliest documented human civilizations, China has a long, rich history that includes many technological innovations that have enriched cultures all around the world, including what commonly are referred to as the four great inventions: paper, gunpowder, the compass, and both wood-block and movable-type printing. In addition, China also developed silk, tea, and porcelain. China's contributions to human economic and political development are also substantial. In the context of this chapter, however, I want to only briefly mention several periods that are particularly noteworthy for their religious significance, especially as it relates to the development of Confucianism.

Confucianism is typically understood to have gone through several major periods of expression in China. The first is considered to be the "classical age" of Confucianism (fifth century–third century BCE), which began with Confucius himself and includes the life and work of the next two most important scholars: Mencius and Xunzi. The next most important period for Confucianism is the period of the Han dynasty (206 BCE–220 CE), which was the first ruling dynasty to make Confucianism the official state philosophy. The third major period came during the Song dynasty, and the revival of Confucianism that occurred at this time is known as Neo-Confucianism. (Some scholars would argue that the time of the Qing dynasty should be viewed as its own period of Confucian history, but others see this instead as the culmination of Neo-Confucianism.) Regardless, the final period is what is called New Confucianism, which began in the late nineteenth century and is still ongoing today.[5]

SHANG DYNASTY

Chinese history is typically divided into periods called dynasties. This was true up until the formation of the Republic of China in 1912, which formally ended Chinese imperial rule. (When Mao Zedong took over in 1949, he inaugurated the People's Republic of China.) While traditional sources list the legendary Xia dynasty as the first Chinese dynasty, the first recorded dynasty in China is the Shang (or Yin) dynasty, which was in power from around 1600 BCE to around 1100 BCE. One important practice of this period that has been discovered from the textual and archeological evidence is the divination system of oracle bones, which were used to communicate with the different spirits who were believed to be active in the lives of the community. These bones were first discovered late in the nineteenth century, and they comprise the first written records of Chinese religious practice and belief.[6]

---

5. Scholars differ in how they divide Confucian history. Leonard Swidler describes a five-period model in "Confucianism for Modern Persons in Dialogue with Christianity and Modernity," *Journal of Ecumenical Studies* 40, no. 1–2 (Winter–Spring 2003): 14. John Berthrong describes a four-period model in "Confucian Formulas for Peace: Harmony," *Society* 51, no. 6 (2014): 645–46. See also John Berthrong and Evelyn Nagai Berthrong, *Confucianism: A Short Introduction* (Oxford: Oneworld, 2014), 11–20.

6. Poceski, *Introducing Chinese Religions*, 13.

Typically, oracle bones were made from either turtle shells or the shoulder blades of oxen, and they record both the questions that were posed to various spirits and also the answers that were received through the process of heating the bones and then reading the cracks that were produced. Most of the bones discovered were used in rituals performed by the Shang dynasty kings, and thus the information they contain relates primarily to the practices of royalty rather than those of the average citizen. The kings were concerned with gaining the approval of these spirits for particular actions they were hoping to take, looking for insight into their own destinies, and/or asking for agricultural or meteorological advice. The questions were also often directed at ancestors, which is evidence that both ancestor veneration and filial piety—still important parts of many Asian cultures today—have an exceptionally long history in Chinese society.[7]

ZHOU DYNASTY

The transition from the Shang dynasty to the Zhou dynasty was marked by both continuity and change. For example, the role of ancestors and the reciprocal relationship between dead and living relatives continued unabated. At the same time, however, the important concept of Heaven came to the fore. In the Shang dynasty, there were a multitude of gods, organized in a hierarchy with *Di* or *Shangdi* at the pinnacle; his power was superior to all other gods, particularly his power over the natural elements.[8] In the Zhou dynasty, *Shangdi* was replaced by *Tian* (heaven, sky). Additionally, Heaven was accorded a moral character—that is, it was seen as a non-personified force (for the most part) for good. This shift had significant ramifications for both an understanding of humanity and human behavior and also for an understanding of humanity's relationship to the divine realm. Not only did human beings begin to ascribe to the gods a desire for human moral behavior rather than simply ritual offerings, they also began to emphasize their own moral capacities, ascribing to themselves the potential for radical spiritual transformation into sages or immortals.

A related development here concerns the concept of a "mandate from Heaven." As Heaven became imbued with a moral character, a certain amount of agency was also ascribed to Heaven, with the result that one could speak of receiving and/or doing the will of Heaven. The early Zhou kings adopted this idea and made the claim that they had received a mandate from Heaven to rule—that is, they claimed moral authority directly from Heaven. The result was that "their conquest was thus not simply a change of regime brought about by the force of arms; rather, it was the realization of a divine plan."[9] In a related move, then, each Zhou king conferred upon himself the title "Son of Heaven."

7. Ibid., 19.
8. Ibid., 17.
9. Ibid., 29.

This was to emphasize his role as a mediator between the will of Heaven and the sphere of human engagement. This did not mean to suggest that the king himself was divine, only that he was both a legitimate ruler and also that he could discern the wishes of Heaven. However, this was no permanent designation; natural calamities could be interpreted as signs that Heaven's favor had been removed from a specific king due to his lack of virtue. In this case, another ruler would be sought. The term "Son of Heaven" continued to be used down through the centuries, up until the modern period.

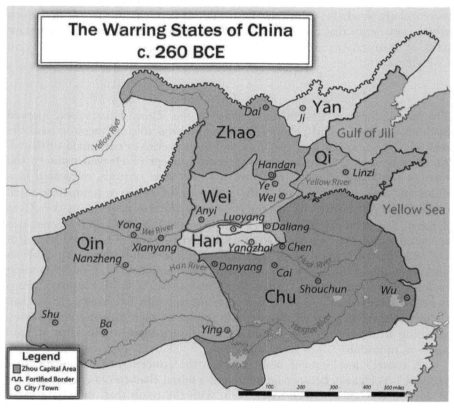

Figure 16: A Map of China during the Warring States Period, 475–221 BCE. This period came to an end when the state of Qin conquered them all.

It was under the Zhou dynasty that both Confucianism and Daoism had their formal inception. Most of the important early figures for both traditions lived during this period: Confucius (551–479 BCE) lived during what is called the Spring and Autumn Period (771–476 BCE) of the Zhou dynasty. Mencius (fourth century BCE) and Xunzi (third century BCE) lived during the Warring States Period (475–221 BCE). In addition, the legendary life of Laozi is dated to this time, as are the two primary Daoist texts: the *Daode jing* (fourth century BCE), and the *Zhuangzi* (third century BCE). Also important for both Confucianism and Daoism was the shift that occurred with the dynastic transition from the system of oracle bone divination to the use of the *Yijing* or *Book of Changes* (perhaps best recognized by its Wade-Giles spelling, the *I-Ching*). Unlike the oracle bones, which were used to provide more direct yes/no answers to specific questions, the *Yijing* was used in a more general, one might even say philosophical, way—that is, to divine the will of Heaven, understood here as an abstract, non-personified representation of the forces of nature. The idea was to gain insight into the natural flow and rhythm of the cosmos to help determine the best course of action in any given situation.

The *Yijing* rests on the dynamic of the interplay between the two cosmic forces of yin and yang. Originally, they simply referred to complementary natural phenomena, related specifically to the earth's rotation around the sun. So, for example, yang was the sunny side of a hill and yin was the shady side. One was not better than the other; they were different but harmonious complements. In time, yin and yang took on additional, gendered characteristics: yin came to represent the feminine, which was dark, cool, passive, and yielding, and yang came to represent the masculine, which was bright, hot, aggressive, and hard. Together, they stood for the dynamic interplay of heaven and earth, and the fluid balance of the fabric of nature.

In terms of their use in the *Yijing*, both yin and yang are represented by written lines: yang is depicted by a solid line, while yin is depicted by a broken line. These lines are combined in a variety of patterns—first into four symbols, then into eight trigrams, each of which is linked to some natural phenomenon, like fire, wind, or mountain. Finally, these trigrams are combined into sixty-four hexagrams. It is these symbols that the book "reads" in order to provide wisdom and guidance. The *Yijing* was a foundational text for both Confucianism and Taoism, and while the method of reading and interpreting it changed over time, its influence remained strong up through the modern period of China. In addition, the text came over into the West through the Jesuit missionaries, and Gottfried Leibnitz wrote a commentary on it in the early eighteenth century. It enjoyed a period of popularity in the 1960s and 70s in the United States, but its use has since waned.

HAN DYNASTY

The Qin dynasty was the first to unify China as a country, but that unification came at a cost: it was a short-lived empire. During that time, Confucianism was banned and Confucian books were burned—some lost forever. The dynasty ended in squabbling and revolt. However, in the subsequent Han dynasty, Confucianism thrived. It was during this time that Confucianism became the official teaching of the state, in large part due to the new Imperial Academy

Figure 17: A yin/yang symbol surrounded by the Yijing trigrams.

where students studied Confucian classics in order to pass examinations that would lead to government appointments.

Daniel Gardner states that the importance of these steps "can hardly be overestimated. . . . As a consequence of the ideological dominance of Confucianism in government, education in imperial China would center on mastery of Confucian writings."[10] He goes on to note the result: "Virtually all literate Chinese, particularly during the millennium leading up to the end of imperial China in 1912, were Confucian-schooled and Confucian-socialized. Thus the lives and work of almost all educated Chinese, not just officials but poets, essayists, novelists, artists, calligraphers, historians, scholars, teachers and the small percentage of literate women were shaped, to one degree or another,

10. Daniel K. Gardner, *Confucianism: A Very Short Introduction* (Oxford: Oxford University Press, 2014), 7.

by the beliefs and ideals embodied in Confucians texts."[11] It was during this time, too, under influential Confucian teachers such as Dong Zhongshu, that the state was brought into a larger cosmological picture that synchronized human society and Heaven, with the emperor as the Son of Heaven and the key contact point between the two realms, the one with the most responsibility to secure their harmonious relationship.

Yet interestingly enough, Confucianism's ascendance did not equate to either the marginalization or suppression of other schools of thought. Rather, the Han dynasty was a time of both syncretism and pluralism, as many diverse schools of thought engaged one another and exerted influence in a wide variety of public spheres. "There was rich cross-fertilization of diverse political philosophies, systems of ethics, and cosmological theories, with leading thinkers not being shy about incorporating into their theoretical models, concepts, and ideas derived from other traditions."[12]

Perhaps as a result of this cross-fertilization, and, in a way, corresponding to it, this was also a period in which distinctions were made between the religious traditions, and there were efforts to categorize and distinguish them. Judith Berling observes that "in an attempt to impose some order in the Chinese religious world, the labels 'Confucian,' 'Buddhist,' and 'Taoist' were adopted by Han dynasty (206 BCE–202 CE) historians as classifications for writings, biographies, and temples or shrines."[13] The categories were text based, and the divisions were determined by which books were given authoritative status by different groups. However, Berling also notes that "the borders between groups were by no means absolute, and—most significantly—their devotees, patrons, and even occasionally their religious professionals overlapped and crossed boundaries."[14] Burton Watson argues something similar when he writes, "One should therefore think of Confucianism and Taoism in Han times not as rival systems demanding a choice for one side or the other, but rather as two complementary doctrines, an ethical and political system for the conduct of public and family life, and a mystical philosophy for the spiritual nourishment of the individual, with the metaphysical teachings of the *Book of Changes* acting as a bridge between the two."[15]

Speaking of texts, Confucianism is and always has been a text-based religion. Initially there were six classic Confucian texts, all of which originated before Confucius's own lifetime. However, one of those books, the *Book of Music*, was completely lost in what was called the "burning of the books" during the Qin dynasty, in 213 BCE. From then on, the six classics became five, described briefly here. Typically, the first book mentioned in this list is the

---

11. Ibid.

12. Poceski, *Introducing Chinese Religions*, 55.

13. Berling, *Pilgrim in Chinese Culture*, 43.

14. Ibid., 44.

15. Chuang Tzu, *Chuang Tzu: Basic Writings*, trans. Burton Watson (New York: Columbia University Press, 1996), 10–11.

Yijing (described above), the divination manual that dates back to the Zhou dynasty. Second is the *Book of Documents/Book of History* (*Shang Shu*), which is basically a historical record of stories and speeches by different kings from both the pre-Zhou and Zhou dynasties. Third is the *Book of Rites/Rituals* (*Li Ji*), a text that describes proper etiquette and traditional rituals from the Warring States and Han periods. Fourth is the *Book of Odes/Book of Songs* (*Shijing*), a book of Chinese poetry that dates back to the early Zhou dynasty. The final book is the *Spring and Autumn Annals* (*Chun Qiu*), which contains documents from the state of Lu up to the time of Confucius himself. Tradition holds that all five of these texts were compiled and edited by Confucius himself, but textual scholarship has shown that their compilation took place over the course of many centuries—including periods both well before and after Confucius's life span.

Neo-Confucianism

The Sui and the Tang dynasties came between the Han and the Song, and during that time, while Confucianism remained a viable component of Chinese society—particularly governmental life—Buddhism dominated the religious scene in China. There were no significant developments of note in Confucianism until the revival that began in the early ninth century. This is the reform movement that took place primarily during the Song dynasty (960–1279), which led to the development of what is called Neo-Confucianism by the great thinker Zhu Xi (1130–1200) and others. It is this form of Confucianism that was solidified as orthodox imperial teaching and endured until the early twentieth century.

Much time elapsed between the heyday of the classical Confucianism of the Han dynasty, which ended in the third century CE, and the rise of Neo-Confucianism in the tenth century. This period is typically classified as a period of steady decline and a loss of influence, particularly as both Daoism and Buddhism were on the rise. However, this is somewhat of a false generalization. Better is the description of the harmonization of the three traditions, particularly during the Tang dynasty (618–907 CE): "Confucianism for the external (world) . . . Buddhism and Daoism for the inner (world)."[16]

Nonetheless, what is clear is that beginning even in the ninth century, influential Confucian voices had begun to clamor for a return to a more "authentic" form of Confucianism. While this movement has been dubbed Neo-Confucianism in the West, in China itself it was called *Daoxue* (Study of the Way) or *Lixue* (Study of Principle).[17] The main authors of Neo-Confucianism shared a passion for the repristination of Confucianism and a critical attitude toward many central Buddhist practices and doctrines, like the doctrine of emptiness, for example. At the same time, an important aspect of their work was an expansion of traditional topics of Confucian thought

16. Poceski, *Introducing Chinese Religions*, 191.
17. Ibid., 193.

into more metaphysical topics and an increasing emphasis on the inner life by adapting forms of Buddhist meditation. They were not afraid to borrow from Daoism in this endeavor, either. They did this, however, while maintaining traditional Confucian emphases on personal ethics and proper societal relationships. "The end result was a substantial broadening of the field of Confucian learning and the growth of new trends within it."[18]

Many voices were involved in the Neo-Confucian movement, but one in particular stands out: Zhu Xi (1130–1200). Widely regarded as the greatest and most influential Neo-Confucian scholar, he, more than anyone else, was responsible for synthesizing all of the various threads of the different Confucian thinkers of the previous several centuries into one cohesive school of thought that endured up until the Republic of China. As a part of his doctrinal reform, Zhu Xi also reformed the Confucian canon, replacing the Five Classics with what became known as the Four Books: *The Analects*, the *Book of Mengzi*, the *Great Learning*, and the *Doctrine of the Mean*. These four books became extremely important in the ensuing centuries and served as the primary source material for studying Confucianism throughout China. All of this work culminated in the integration of Confucianism in general—and the Five Classics in particular (replaced by the Four Books in the fourteenth century)—into the official civil service examinations. As noted above, the development of state exams began in the Han dynasty and was extended during the Sui dynasty in the late sixth/early seventh centuries. However, it was in the late Tang dynasty (618–907) where this practice was codified, and Confucianism held this privileged status until state examinations were abolished in 1905.

The other place Neo-Confucianism demonstrated its influence was in Korea; Korea is second only to China in terms of the role Confucianism played in the historical and cultural development of the country. Confucianism had been a part of the educational system of the Korean elite since the third century CE, but it was only with the beginning of the Joseon/Yi dynasty, under the influence of Neo-Confucian scholars, that Confucianism replaced Buddhism as the de facto state religion in Korea. However, its influence lasted only as long as the dynasty itself, and with the annexing of Korea by Japan in 1910, Confucianism's influence also declined.

CONFUCIANISM THE RELIGION

The name Confucius is a Western coinage—a Latinized version of his popular moniker *Kongzi* or *Kong fuzi* (Master Kong). Not surprisingly, then, the name Confucianism is also a Western construction. It was coined by the Jesuits who came in contact with it when they came to China in the sixteenth century. In China itself, this "school of the scholars" was known as *rujia*, *rujiao*, or *ruxue*, where *ru* refers to the scholars themselves—those we now call Confucians.[19]

---

18. Ibid., 194.

Naturally, they were considered the educated elite of Chinese society, and they were almost all employed by the government. Thus as was noted earlier, Confucianism played a key role in Chinese imperial society for centuries, helping shape the values of the government by contributing to the overarching political philosophy and offering models for structuring society.

This emphasis on political and social life perhaps begs the question of whether or not Confucianism should be characterized as a religion or as a philosophical or, even more, an ethical system.[20] Certainly there is no denying that a focus on ethics and the moral life is one of the hallmarks of Confucianism. However, it is also clear that the whole category of "moral behavior" is much broader and all-encompassing in Confucian thought than typically is seen in the West. Yet the question of proper categorization still comes up repeatedly, and it is discussed in practically every Western introduction to Confucianism. The answer, of course, depends a great deal on how religion is defined. This leads to the consequent realization that Western definitions of religion are based almost exclusively on the model of Christianity, into which many Asian religious traditions do not neatly fit.

A single personified deity with specific characteristics and attributes, a defined afterlife, an official religious hierarchy—Confucianism lacks all of these. However, Confucianism has other characteristics that would commend its religious classification: "recurrent expressions of belief in Heaven, often accompanied by efforts to divine its will and act accordingly"; "tacit acknowledgement of a supernatural realm, populated with various gods and spirits, along with a pervasive emphasis on ritual"; and "the quest for sagehood."[21] All this pushes Western scholars of religion to rethink their presuppositions about what counts as a religion and the different ways religions function in the lives of individuals and societies.[22]

WOMEN AND CONFUCIANISM

A word should be said here about the role of women in Confucius's own thought and in later Confucianism as well. Historically, the subjugation of women in Confucianism is undeniable. Women were not accorded the same status and dignity as men, and this was true both in Confucius's own thought and also in Chinese society as a whole. Gardner writes, "Indeed, nowhere in the *Analects* or other canonical texts is there the suggestion that the Confucian program for self-cultivation and moral perfection was applicable to women. The teachings of Confucius—and those of most of his later followers—were

---

19. Xinzhong Yao, *An Introduction to Confucianism* (Cambridge: Cambridge University Press, 2000), 17.

20. For a more detailed examination of this question and an explication of some differing opinions, see ibid., 39–46.

21. Poceski, *Introducing Chinese Religions*, 36.

22. Yao, *Introduction to Confucianism*, 183.

seemingly intended for men."[23] However, as is true in all cases, religions both influence and are influenced by the cultures in which they develop, and in this situation, Confucianism originated and grew in a deeply patriarchal context.

Here is one description of the pre-Confucian expectations of a woman, emphasizing the "three obediences" and the "four virtues":

> A woman is to obey or follow her father when young, her husband when she marries, and her son when she is old and her husband is dead. The four virtues include her obligations, her appearance, her behavior, and her speech. She must perform well her household and ritual duties; she must keep herself neat and clean, and always dress simply and not seductively; she must be gentle, kind, and compliant; and she must be soft-spoken and not quarrelsome. She must not gossip.[24]

However, Confucius not only inherited this system, he adhered to it, which meant that he was, at the very least, an "accomplice to the continued cultural minimization of women."[25] Throughout the evolution of Confucianism, there certainly were differences in how Confucian ideas were articulated by subsequent teachers. Nonetheless, there was consistency in the teaching of the subordination of women and the emphasis of obligation over freedom, particularly in relationship to family: for women, marriage and children were a duty, not a choice. Indeed, it was only through marriage and the bearing of children, particularly sons, that a woman had any chance of influence and power—as a mother, mother-in-law, or wife. With very few exceptions, a woman's authority was limited to the context of her family. In light of this long history, the role of women in Confucianism and the relationship between Confucian ideals and feminist thought is an important area of current scholarship.[26]

---

23. Gardner, *Confucianism*, 105.

24. Terry Woo, "Confucianism and Feminism," in *Feminism and World Religions*, ed. Arvind Sharma and Katherine K. Young (Albany: State University of New York Press, 1999), 141.

25. Ibid., 117.

26. See for example the following sources: Xiongya Gao, "Women Existing for Men: Confucianism and Social Injustice against Women in China," *Race, Gender & Class* 10, no. 3 (2003): 114–25; Dorothy Ko, JaHyun Kim Haboush, and Joan R. Piggott, eds., *Women and Confucian Cultures in Premodern China, Korea, and Japan* (Berkeley: University of California Press, 2003); Chenyang Li, ed., *The Sage and the Second Sex: Confucianism, Ethics, and Gender* (Chicago: Open Court, 2000); Susan Mann and Yu-yin Cheng, eds., *Under Confucian Eyes: Writings on Gender in Chinese History* (Berkeley: University of California Press, 2001); Vivian-Lee Nyitray, "The Real Trouble with Confucianism," in *Love, Sex and Gender in the World Religions*, ed. Joseph Runzo and Nancy M. Martin (Oxford: Oneworld, 2000); Vivian-Lee Nyitray, "Treacherous Terrain: Mapping Feminine Spirituality in Confucian Worlds," in *Confucian Spirituality*, ed. Tu Weiming and Mary Evelyn Tucker, vol. 2 (New York: Crossroad, 2004); Lisa Raphals, "A Woman Who Understood the Rites," in *Confucius and the Analects: New Essays*, ed. Bryan W. Van Norden (New York: Oxford University Press, 2002); Barbara Reed, "Women and

Confucius and the Origins of Confucianism

Figure 18: Confucius.

Confucius was born in 551 BCE, in the state of Lu, which is located in the present-day Chinese province of Shandong (Northeast China). His given name is Kong Qiu or Kong Zhongni, and from the sparse information available about his early years, it is believed that he was born into an upper-middle-class family that had experienced a decline in fortunes. It is said that his father died when he was only three years old, leaving his mother to raise him by herself with few resources. Confucius was said to have been an unusually intelligent child with a strong desire to learn. Upon adulthood, he became a member of the "scholar-official" class of society, and he held a series of relatively low-level governmental bureaucratic positions.

The period of time in which he lived was called the Spring and Autumn Period of the Zhou dynasty. This was a particularly turbulent time in Chinese history, when the Zhou feudal system was collapsing, causing disruption in both the political and economic balance. The result was that some feudal states began to challenge each other for supremacy, while others simply fought to survive. Confucius stepped into this chaos and proposed a means of restoring order: he wanted to call the rulers back to moral conduct and proper behavior in all actions—propriety in daily life—as modeled by the ancients. In a nutshell, Confucius's purpose was "to reinstate the timeless Way (Dao) that was revealed

Chinese Religion in Contemporary Taiwan," in *Today's Woman in World Religions*, ed. Arvind Sharma (Albany: State University of New York Press, 1994).

and followed by the ancient sages, which echoed the norms and designs of Heaven and brought perfect harmony between Heaven and humanity."[27]

During his lifetime, Confucius was, for the most part, unsuccessful in his attempts. It is said that for thirteen years he traveled all around China looking for the right ruler who could implement his philosophy—and under whom he could serve as a high-ranking counselor—but never found him. He therefore resigned himself to returning to Lu and teaching his philosophy to what turned out to be an ever-growing band of followers. While he had little success in influencing government policy, he turned out to be an excellent educator, and he is the first individual in recorded history to have made teaching his primary vocation.[28] His emphasis on education and learning is perhaps unmatched in any other religious tradition. He died in Lu in 479 BCE, but his teachings lived on and became an indispensable part of Chinese culture, education, and worldview.

PRIMARY CONFUCIAN TEACHINGS

Confucius's most famous work is titled *The Analects*, although he did not write it himself. Instead, it consists of lectures and teachings that were compiled by his students. After many generations of editing, it attained the form it has today in the second century BCE, three centuries after Confucius's death.[29] In Confucian studies, it continues to be one of the main sources of information about Confucius's thought, even though it is sometimes difficult to distinguish between his own teachings and the views of his disciples who were transcribing his thoughts. In addition, this text also contains much of the biographical information about Confucius we have. For example, book 10 is filled with descriptions of Confucius, such as: "At court, when speaking with Counsellors of lower rank he was affable; when speaking with Counsellors of upper rank, he was frank though respectful. In the presence of his lord, his bearing, though respectful, was composed."[30] Other, more menial details are also given: "Even when there was plenty of meat, he avoided eating more meat than rice."[31] And, "He did not converse at meals; nor did he talk in bed."[32]

The Analects is composed of twenty books, which contain around five hundred verses. Many people at first find *The Analects* hard to read, as it doesn't seem to have a logical structure or flow. Nonetheless, throughout the text, there are two overriding concerns that thread together the different parts: "What makes for a good man?" (Man is used intentionally here, and throughout the rest of the chapter, because Confucius and his followers were,

27. Poceski, *Introducing Chinese Religions*, 41.
28. Ibid., 41.
29. Gardner, *Confucianism*, 6.
30. Confucius, *The Analects*, trans. D. C. Lau (London: Penguin Books, 1979), 10:2, 101.
31. Ibid., 10:8, 103.
32. Ibid., 10:10, 103.

indeed, primarily concerned with men and not women) and "What makes for good government?"[33] These two questions center the text and provide a helpful interpretive key for the reader. Quotes from *The Analects* will be used to illustrate various aspects of Confucius's thought in the following pages.

Before moving to a discussion of specific Confucian ideas, it should be noted that it is not always easy to distinguish where Chinese culture ends and Confucianism begins. One such example is the notion of filial piety. There is no question that this value is of central importance for Confucius and plays a key role in his ethical understanding of humanity, but it is also true that this concept was important in Chinese culture long before Confucius was even born.[34] It also should be noted that Confucianism was primarily directed toward the educated elite—the majority of Chinese were poor and illiterate and had no access to Confucian teachings or texts. So, while they perhaps technically should not be called Confucian, if that means explicitly and intentionally reading and adhering to Confucian doctrines, in light of the fact that Confucian ideas and values so permeated Chinese culture, all Chinese—regardless of economic or social class—certainly were influenced by Confucianism, whether they knew or chose it, or not.

THIS-WORLDLY LIFE

One of the most well-known characteristics of Confucianism—and one of its defining beliefs—is an emphasis on human life in the here-and-now, and on proper human behavior in a variety of relational contexts. This means that ethics are of critical importance rather than, for example, eschatological speculation, and a premium is placed on education and study to further one's moral character and the good of society as a whole. It's not that Confucius didn't believe in spirits or the supernatural, or that he was unconcerned about Heaven—more about that shortly—rather, it was simply that he didn't value speculation on these things and wasn't eager to ponder them. His disposition on the afterlife, including either rewards after death or even one's existence after death, can accurately be defined as agnostic.[35]

For Confucius, then, what this meant was that one's behavior in this life was not a preparation for an afterlife, nor was it the means to an end—some kind of heavenly reward. Instead, this life is the point—one does not live a moral life for any other purpose save that of its own cultivation; the life itself is its own reward. An oft-quoted remark from *The Analects* reads, "I have yet to meet the man who is as fond of virtue as he is of beauty in women" (sometimes translated as, "I have never seen one who loves virtue as one loves sex").[36] By this, Confucius was pointing to the idea that it was not enough to merely

33. Gardner, *Confucianism*, 15.

34. Ibid., 97.

35. Confucius, *The Analects*, 12, 112–17.

36. Ibid., 15:13, 134.

know—or even do—the right thing; the point was to take joy in it: "The Master said, 'To be fond of something is better than merely to know it, and to find joy in it is better than merely to be fond of it.'"[37] In other words, "The ideal person in Confucianism is not merely the one who does the right thing but the one who also loves doing it, finds joy in doing it, and becomes effortless in doing it."[38] Thus Confucius chose to focus his teaching on the present and how human beings should live in order to have a peaceful, happy life and a peaceful, well-ordered society. It is said that "he developed his ethics around two central theses; that goodness can be taught and learned, and that society can only be in harmony and at peace under the guidance of wisdom."[39]

There are two important sets of principles that shape Confucian thinking. This first is the Three Guiding Principles (*san gang*), which are to govern social interactions: the obedience of a subject to a ruler, the obedience of a son to his father, and the obedience of a wife to her husband.[40] Intrinsically related to this code of conduct are what are called the Five Regulations (*wu chang*), which are also considered to be the cardinal Confucian virtues meant to govern all human activities in all spheres of life. These are as follows: humanity/humanness or benevolence (*ren*—Wade-Giles spelling: *jen*), ritual etiquette (*li*), righteousness (*yi*), wisdom (*zhi*), and faithfulness (*xin*).

Of these five, two are typically viewed as most important—*li* and *ren*—and about them a bit more needs to be said. As indicated previously, *li* is one of the two basic principles of Confucianism, and it points to the proper ritual actions performed in the proper manner—ritual etiquette, if you will. Originally it signified the specific ritual offerings that were made to gods and ancestors, but later it was expanded to encompass all human ceremonial behavior. What was particularly interesting about this expansion was the way that it links explicitly religious activities with ethical social conduct: "That, in a sense, implied the introduction of a sacramental dimension of all aspects of human life."[41] *Li* came to govern an elaborate, overarching social order in which everyone had his or her place and knew what principles of conduct governed interactions with both those above and below them in status.

Ren can be translated in a variety of ways, including "benevolence" or "humanity." This word points not so much to behavior as it does to attitude; it indicates a disposition of affection and care for others, and a concern for their well-being. Book 12 of *The Analects* is all about benevolence, and there one finds many different definitions and examples of what benevolence looks like in concrete, real-life situations. The core of them all, however, can be found in one simple statement: "Fan Ch'ih asked about benevolence. The Master said, 'Love

37. Ibid., 6:20, 84.
38. Yong Huang, "Confucianism," in Sullivan, *Religions of the World*, 151.
39. Yao, *Introduction to Confucianism*, 26.
40. Ibid., 34.
41. Poceski, *Introducing Chinese Religions*, 44.

your fellow men.'"[42] For Confucius, disposition matters as much as action. The goal here is to move one away from selfishness and self-preservation and instead seek the general flourishing of society as a whole, regardless of one's personal good or ill fortune. These two virtues work together, reinforcing each other as they mutually form an individual both internally and externally, both in attitude and behavior.

The fundamental loci for this personal growth and development can be found in five core relationships that stand at the heart of a well-functioning Confucian society. They represent the patriarchal mentality of the time, as well as an unquestioning acceptance of normative social hierarchies. The first and most important relationship is that of a father and his son; the other four relationships are built on and modeled after that one. The centrality of this relationship, and the general responsibility children have to honor their elders, continues to be of central importance in contemporary Chinese society. The subsequent four relationships are as follows: ruler and subject, husband and wife, elder and younger brother, and the relationship between two friends of equal status. It should be noted that even though there is a clear imbalance of power in most of these relationships, Confucius expected that the person "on top" would act fairly and justly, such that rulers would not be oppressive, nor husbands abusive. One can well imagine that this principle often was more effective in theory than in practice.

HARMONY

The concept of harmony is also important in Confucian thinking, and it emphasizes the necessity of all things working together in a complementary way for the smooth functioning of the cosmos. This principle operates at a micro level, at all levels of human society, from the family to the empire, and it also operates at a macro level, governing the relationship between Heaven, earth, and humanity. These three "powers"—Heaven, earth, and humans—"work together in an organic cosmos so that 'Heaven, Earth and humans are the origin of all things. Heaven generates them, Earth nourishes them and humans perfect them.'"[43] Another key term for understanding this principle is one more typically associated with Daoism: the Way (*dao*). In Confucianism, the Way is a universal principle that originates from Heaven and reveals itself in human society. Consequently, humans have the responsibility for maintaining it: "the Way is not distinct from human beings and cannot be separated from human life, since it exists in daily life, in ordinary behavior and in mundane matters. It is up to humans to enlarge or belittle it, to manifest or obscure it."[44]

---

42. Confucius, *The Analects*, 12:22.
43. Yao, *Introduction to Confucianism*, 139.
44. Ibid., 140.

HEAVEN

The role of Heaven can hardly be overestimated in Confucian thought, even though a clear definition is difficult to find. Heaven has a variety of meanings and descriptions, depending on which text and which Confucian thinker one reads. Yet, one thing is clear: whatever Heaven means in Confucian thought, it does not have the same meaning found in Christianity. Christians, of course, have a very specific definition of heaven: in essence, it is the place of reward where one goes after death. In Confucianism, however, Heaven is not a destination or a reward. Instead, Heaven is a disembodied power, the source of the laws of the universe as well as the source of all moral conduct and right relationships. However, this power should not in any way be equated to the concept of God in Christianity. Confucius himself did not describe any kind of single creator deity in *The Analects*—and in fact, this belief is absent from practically all Chinese religious traditions. Thus whatever Heaven means in Confucianism, it does not equate to a Christian conception of either heaven or God.[45] Instead, it is better equated to the sense of orderly repetition characteristic of cosmic realms, including not only the cyclical movement of the planets but also the cycle of the seasons, the ebb and flow of the tides, and so on.[46]

Xinzhong Yao offers three constellations of meaning of Heaven that are regularly employed in different contexts:

> In its metaphysical and physical connotation, Heaven, often in conjunction with, and/or in opposition to, the Earth, refers to the universe, the cosmos, the material world, or simply, Nature. Applied in the spiritual realm, it signifies an anthropomorphic Lord or a Supreme Being who presides in Heaven, and rules over or governs directly the spiritual and material worlds. In a moral context, it is understood to be the source of ethical principles and the supreme sanction of human behavior.[47]

In all cases, what is clear is that Heaven has active agency and plays a dynamic role in the moral life of human beings. Indeed, there is a deep complementarity and significant interplay between Heaven and humanity: the way of one is supported and fulfilled in the way of the other. While early Chinese history talks about the necessity of rulers obeying the decree of Heaven, by Confucius's

45. David Gardner makes an interesting point here, noting one possible ramification of this difference. He suggests that one reason why ancestor veneration was so important in China is that, in the absence of a creator deity, the ancestors are the ones who created life, and therefore they are the ones who deserve an individual's highest praise and gratitude. Gardner, *Confucianism*, 101.

46. I am indebted to Richard Payne, personal correspondence with the author, July 11, 2015, for this conception.

47. Yao, *Introduction to Confucianism*, 142.

time it was believed that every individual had a mandate from Heaven and was required to obey the demands of that mandate.

Here are some descriptions of Heaven from *The Analects*: "Heaven is the author of the virtue that is in me";[48] "If I am understood at all, it is, perhaps, by Heaven";[49] "If Heaven does not intend this culture to be destroyed, then what can the men of K'uang do to me?",[50] and finally, "The Empire has long been without the Way. Heaven is about to use your Master as the wooden tongue for a bell."[51] It can be said, therefore, that Confucius taught an understanding of Heaven whereby it is possessed of consciousness and agency and does seem invested in the affairs of human society—for this reason, Heaven can and does offer ethical guidance.

HUMANITY

The importance of this harmonization for peace and prosperity is one reason for Confucianism's emphasis on one's own moral behavior in this life and the ability of humanity to practice and perfect that behavior. Naturally, this activity takes place firmly within the context of human society—retreat and isolation have no place in the cultivation of one's true humanity. It is believed that it is possible to both know what good behavior is and how to cultivate it. Thus for each individual, the goal is to become a *junzi*—a term with a long history. Literally, it means "ruler's son," and so etymologically it refers to a member of the nobility. For Confucius, however, it meant a person of *moral* nobility, a morally superior person—an ideal man. This was, in fact, a radical redefinition, which opened to anyone who worked hard enough what was previously an exclusive, closed category: "Here Confucius lays down a novel challenge to his contemporaries: through effort, any one of you can *become* a noble person."[52] The contrast to a *junzi* is a *xiaoren* (small man) where, again, that term refers to a *morally* small man. This is a man who is vulgar, small minded, selfish, and uncultivated. The small man is often contrasted with the gentleman or noble man. For example, in *The Analects*, Confucius writes, "The gentleman is easy of mind, while the small man is always full of anxiety."[53]

Related here, too, is the concept of the sage, which is also a complex term with a variety of meanings. The basic meaning is a man who has perfected his character in this life, someone who has "manifested the greatest virtue which corresponds to Heaven and [has] been given the blessing of Heaven."[54] He is perfect in every sense of the word that matters, and for this reason, he is

48. Confucius, *The Analects*, 7:23.
49. Ibid., 14:35.
50. Ibid., 9:5.
51. Ibid., 3:24.
52. Gardner, *Confucianism*, 18.
53. Confucius, *The Analects*, 7:37, 91.
54. Yao, *Introduction to Confucianism*, 159.

also considered an immortal, but again, not in the way Christians typically understand that word. Immortality does not point to a single individual living forever but rather the lasting impact of a man's virtue. In this understanding of immortal, a sage "has brought the greatest benefits to the world, established an immortal influence and bequeathed an admirable model to all people of all generations."[55] A sage is one who is so virtuous that he can actually help others in the cultivation of their own virtue and in this way actually participates or shares in the virtuous nature of Heaven.

As has been noted above, foundational for a Confucian understanding of humanity is the family: the family is the bedrock on which all other human relationships are built and the model for proper interaction in all other social contexts. If the family is strong, the society and the government will also be strong; if sons know how to treat their fathers, subjects will know how to treat their rulers; if children love their elders, society as a whole will be humane and compassionate. Confucius writes, "Being good as a son and obedient as a young man is, perhaps, the root of a man's character."[56] What all this means is that in a Confucian worldview, "[the] concern is not about life in the other world, but about the life fulfilled in this world, not about the possibility of salvation from without but about the process of self-transformation or self-transcendence through moral cultivation and social engagement. The question 'how to become good' in the Confucian tradition becomes as resourceful and profound as the question 'how to be saved' in many other religious traditions."[57]

RITUAL

The last aspect of Confucian practice and belief noted here concerns ritual (*li*) and the proper rites and ceremonies that are necessary in order to maintain cosmic and social harmony. This is one specific place where Confucianism was particularly influential in both Korean and Chinese state governance. There are a wide variety of rituals and different levels of performance: some rituals are performed only by rulers; others are performed in the privacy of one's own home. When understood in a religious context, *li* is believed to be a way in which humans can communicate with spiritual powers and various deities and also provides the means by which they can express their thanks to ancestors and ask for continued guidance and benevolence. There are three primary functions of rituals in what Christians might call a worship context: prayer to the spirits and/or gods for benevolent action and favor, thanksgiving to them for good fortune and blessing, and reporting important political events.[58] In addition, *li* also has a purely sociological function when seen in the context of

---

55. Ibid., 159.
56. Confucius, *The Analects*, 1:2, 59.
57. Yao, *Introduction to Confucianism*, 157.
58. Huang, "Confucianism," 149.

human society and that is to reinforce proper conduct, establish harmony, and strengthen traditional relational hierarchies.

In almost all cases, sacrifice is a key component of ritual performance in Confucianism. From the early Zhou period, different categories of sacrifice were recorded, from elaborate sacrifices of jade and silk down to ordinary sacrifices of vegetables and small animals.[59] However, in all sacrifices what is critical is one's attitude and disposition. It is not simply the fact of the offering—or its size—that matters, nor is the point of the offering simply to gain some reward. Instead, in Confucianism, sacrifice is a central means of cultivating virtue and morality, a way of facilitating social harmony and harmony between Heaven and earth. Xinzhong Yao writes, "Confucianism appreciates that sacrifice may bring about good fortune, such as material gain, physical longevity and spiritual protection, but it constantly emphasizes that personal gain is not the primary purpose. The important thing is to have a sincere attitude, a reverential heart and a virtuous motive. . . . Those who are engaged in ritual should experience a spiritual and moral reunion with the spirits."[60] This is consistent with Confucius's belief that what was of paramount importance to the ancestors and the spirits was a person's inner disposition and moral perfection—not the quality or quantity of the sacrifice itself. Thus the very practice of sacrifice was not exclusively for the sake of the relationship between humanity and Heaven/spirits/ancestors, but equally for the sake of cultivation of one's own virtue.

IMPORTANT CONFUCIAN TEACHERS

There were many other important Confucian teachers who followed in the path of their master. Of these, two are worth particular note: Mencius (371–289 BCE) and Xunzi, also spelled Hsün-tzu (298–238 BCE). These two Confucian teachers were active during the Warring States Period (475–221 BCE) and are often mentioned together because they represent two different strains of Confucian thought regarding human nature. One of the interesting dynamics apparent in their writing is that while they shared similar convictions about human behavior and human society, they disagreed on one fundamental point of anthropology. To the question, "What is the core disposition of human nature?" Mencius said that human beings are fundamentally good, while Xunzi said that human beings are fundamentally evil. This has led to Mencius being named as the representative of the idealistic strain of Confucianism and Xunzi the representative of the rationalistic strain.[61] Note here that good and evil are not metaphysical categories—they are simply ethical categories to describe human behavior and disposition.

59. Yao, *Introduction to Confucianism*, 193.

60. Ibid., 194.

61. Poceski, *Introducing Chinese Religions*, 50.

Figure 19: Mencius.

In his writings, Mencius emphasized the "four inborn virtues" of benevolence, righteousness, ritual, and wisdom,[62] which he believed were present in all human beings from birth and simply needed cultivation to develop. Thus for Mencius, evil typically results from a lack of cultivation and nurturing of our inborn virtue: "evil is none other than underdevelopment, deprivation, degradation and non-completion of our original good nature. Whatever erosion or corruption one may suffer, one's original goodness cannot be totally eradicated. Learning and education would be sufficient to help one seek the

62. Ibid., 52.

lost heart, and by natural growth and conscious cultivation its original goodness could be restored."[63]

In the collection of his teachings, also titled *Mencius*, we see this most clearly in the concept of "heart" and his insistence that all men are born with this inherent sense of compassion and goodness. The classic example from his writing is the story of the boy in the well:

> My reason for saying that no man is devoid of a heart sensitive to the suffering of others is this. Suppose a man were, all of a sudden, to see a young child on the verge of falling into a well. He would certainly be moved to compassion, not because he wanted to get in the good graces of the parents, nor because he wished to win the praise of his fellow villagers or friends, nor yet because he disliked the cry of the child. From this it can be seen that whoever is devoid of the heart of compassion is not human.[64]

Another important example that makes the same point is his story about Ox Mountain. Mencius compares the man who has let go of his "true heart" to the mountain that is bald, clear-cut of all its trees. While people may begin to think that baldness is the true nature of the mountain, it is not. In the same way, a man without a heart is not the natural state of things, but it can happen without proper nourishment and tending.[65] People may be so conditioned to act without virtue that it is easy to conclude they must have been born that way, but this is not the case. Everyone is born with natural compassion and goodness, but without development, these virtues can be lost.

Not surprisingly, then, Mencius spoke out against war and instead believed that good governmental leaders could influence people by their own morality, which naturally would lead people to respect and honor them and also try to emulate them in their own lives. He believed this positive example was more effective than threats or punishments.

By contrast, Xunzi argued that humans' basic disposition was toward evil and the overriding human impulse was to seek one's own selfish good through unethical and deceitful means. Xunzi did not believe humans were born with virtues but rather that those virtues had to be taught and learned—this was the main purpose of a Confucian education. Without this education, humans would simply follow their own selfish needs and desires, and both individuals and society as a whole would suffer. This is why sages were necessary, why propriety was necessary: "virtues are not innate, but are the result of the activities of the sages. As a potter shapes the clay to create the vessel, or as an artisan carves a vessel out of a piece of wood, ancient sages created propriety and righteousness by accumulating their thoughts and ideas, and established

---

63. Yao, *Introduction to Confucianism*, 161.
64. Mencius, *Mencius*, trans. D. C. Lau (London: Penguin Books, 2003), 2:A:6.
65. Ibid., 6:A:8.

goodness mastering what had been gained in learning and practice."[66] This belief in education as a means of training virtue and building a harmonious society was something both thinkers shared, in spite of their differing anthropological views.

Figure 20: Xunzi.

NEW CONFUCIANISM

Finally, a brief word should be said about so-called New Confucianism, a movement (distinct from Neo-Confucianism) that seeks to reinterpret

66. Yao, *Introduction to Confucianism*, 163.

Confucianism in a more modern, Western context and bring Confucian ideals to bear on contemporary social issues, such as human rights, democracy, and even feminism. The early twentieth century and the changes that it inaugurated precipitated a crisis moment for Confucianism as serious questions were asked about its ability to adapt and survive. Some even suggested it should be abandoned altogether, seeing fundamental contradictions between a Confucian view of life and humanity and the values espoused by Enlightenment modernity.[67] Lin Hang notes that "for the vast majority of East Asians, modernity had come to mean overcoming Confucianism."[68]

Nonetheless, many other scholars were not content with that conclusion and sought another way, and so-called New Confucianism was the result. One definition reads as follows: "New Confucianism . . . aims at culling the deep, lasting values from the 2,500 year Confucian tradition and bringing them into dialogue with Christianity and Modernity, especially Western philosophical and scientific thought and democracy."[69] This form of Confucianism originated in China in the early 1900s when Confucianism lost its official status and scholars began interpreting it with fresh eyes in light of new contextual realities. They were responding to the dramatic social and economic changes that were taking place in China as more aspects of Western culture seeped into Chinese life. This movement, which only later came to be known as New Confucianism, went through a series of evolutions, leading to the contemporary New Confucian scholars, who seek to mold Confucianism into a dynamic, constructive dialogue partner with the West as a tradition with a distinct perspective to offer in global religious dialogues.[70]

This new Confucian movement was not limited to China, and it has been influential in the United States as well. One of the main schools of contemporary Confucianism is called Boston Confucianism, and its leading proponents are Robert Neville and John Berthrong—both of Boston University—and Tu Weiming of Harvard University. These scholars are working specifically to mine the riches of Confucianism as a resource for furthering interreligious dialogue, promoting transnational justice and peace work among different nations and religions, and offering constructive guidelines for ethical human behavior—including environmentalism.[71] They are convinced that not only is Confucianism not outdated and obsolete, but in

---

67. For example, some argue that the rigid hierarchy of Confucianism—including its patriarchal norms—makes it fundamentally incompatible with a democratic society. See Zehau Liu and Quan Ge, "On the 'Human' in Confucianism," *Journal of Ecumenical Studies* 26, no. 2 (Spring 1989): 313–35. John Berthrong also notes the diversity of opinion around the possible relevance of Confucianism in a modern context. See Berthrong, "Confucian Formulas for Peace," 652–53.

68. Lin Hang, "Traditional Confucianism and Its Contemporary Relevance," *Asian Philosophy* 21, no. 4 (November 2011): 438.

69. Swidler, "Confucianism for Modern Persons," 12.

70. Ibid., 13.

71. Mary Evelyn Tucker and John Berthrong, eds., *Confucianism and Ecology* (Cambridge, MA: Center for the Study of World Religions, 1998).

fact, it has a unique perspective on human society that is desperately needed in today's multicultural, international context.

CONCLUSION

Thus in the early years of the twenty-first century, Confucianism is having a moment again. A growing number of Confucian scholars on both sides of the Pacific are committed to dialogue, openness, and the need for shared ethical commitments. These scholars believe that Confucianism has much to offer the global community, not least in its "concern about moral responsibilities of an individual and the humanistic recognizing of human life."[72]

Julia Ching offers this assessment. If by Confucianism, one points to

> a dynamic discovery of the worth of the human person, of the possibilities of moral greatness and even sagehood, of one's fundamental relationship to others in a society based on ethical values, of an interpretation of reality and a metaphysics of the self that remain open to the transcendent—all this, of course, the basis for a true sense of human dignity, freedom, and equality—then Confucianism is very relevant, and can remain so, both for China and for the world.[73]

72. Hang, "Traditional Confucianism," 441.
73. Swidler, "Confucianism for Modern Persons," 25.

4

A Brief Introduction to Daoism

INTRODUCTION

As in the previous chapter,[1] before a discussion of Daoism in particular, a few words of introduction and orientation are in order. First, the reminder that opened that chapter is also relevant here: the Chinese context is different from a Western context in many ways, and more specifically, those differences often complicate an understanding of traditional Chinese religions for those coming out of a Western European Christian background. So, for example, for someone used to the relative precision of Christian creedal statements, sacraments, and sacred texts, the amount of ambiguity around both Daoist doctrine and practices and the fluidity of insider/outsider boundaries can frustrate even the most dedicated and eager learner.

In his introduction to Daoism, James Miller writes, "Day by day, Daoism is truly becoming a world religion, but as it does so, it seems to resist being pinned down in neat categories. Not many people know what Daoism is, and when people do have an understanding of it, often it is quite different from someone else's."[2] A mental shift of sorts is required, then, in order to prevent an attitude that simply concludes, "If you can't provide clear answers to my questions, I'm giving up."

A second point to note when studying Daoism is a distinction that existed in Western Daoist scholarship for many decades, which one still sees in certain secondary texts on Daoism: the split between "philosophical Daoism" and "religious Daoism." This attempt to separate the more theoretical and metaphysical aspects of a religion from the lived experience involving rituals and physical practices is not unique to Daoism. In the nineteenth and early twentieth centuries—and before—many Western scholars sought to make sense of the different religious/spiritual practices they encountered in Asia by using

---

1. As in the chapter on Confucianism, this chapter will follow *pinyin* spelling conventions for the transliteration of Chinese words. Here is a brief list of some of the most common Daoist words (in the order of the *pinyin* spelling, the Wade-Giles spelling, and the English translation): (1) Dao; Tao; Way, path; (2) de; te; virtue, moral force, power; (3) jing; ching; classic, scripture; (4) Tian; T'ien; Heaven, nature; and (5) ziran; tzu-jan; spontaneity, naturalness.

2. James Miller, *Daoism: A Short Introduction* (Oxford: Oneworld, 2003), ix.

the template of Christianity. This involved privileging texts and concepts that appeared more universal, more theoretical, and less bound to a specific historical and geographical context. The specific rites and practices of different communities often were dismissed as less sophisticated, superstitious customs of the "common people" and therefore not worthy of serious study or consideration.

In the case of Daoism in particular, Louis Komjathy calls this the "Victorian" or "Leggean" view of Daoism after James Legge (1815–97), a Protestant missionary who promulgated this "bifurcated" view of Daoism.[3] In this interpretation, the textual tradition represented by the *Daodejing* and the *Zhuangzi* is considered to be the "pure" form of the tradition (philosophical Daoism), and the religious aspects of Daoism (specific cosmological ideas, breathing practices, sacrificial rites, etc.) are considered "degenerate and superstitious" accretions of the former. Komjathy is clear: "Such a bifurcated interpretation of Daoism is flawed and inaccurate."[4] Therefore, in order to avoid perpetuating such bifucation, in what follows, Daoism is explored as an organic whole, integrating aspects of Daoist mysticism, theory, worldview, and concrete religious experiences.

Finally, I noted previously the close synergy that has existed and continues to exist in China between Confucianism, Daoism, and Buddhism, making sharp distinctions difficult, particularly in popular religious devotional practices. While Westerners often pejoratively name this boundary crossing *syncretism*, another way to think about it is as "flexible attitudes toward religious categorization, affiliation and identity formation."[5] This language of flexibility is helpful in that it foregrounds the fact that, in general in the Chinese context, this synergy is and has been seen positively, not negatively. Indeed, it is a fundamental characteristic of a quintessentially Chinese religious orientation.

Brief Chronology of Chinese History	
Shang (Yin) Dynasty	1600–1050 BCE
Zhou Dynasty	1046–256 BCE
Laozi	Sixth Century BCE (mythic-historical)
Warring States Period	475–221 BCE

3. Louis Komjathy, *The Daoist Tradition: An Introduction* (London: Bloomsbury, 2013), 4.

4. Ibid., 5.

5. Poceski, *Introducing Chinese Religions*, 164. The whole concept of syncretism deserves more discussion than is possible here. In particular, the Western characterization of it—as something entirely negative and something from which Christianity is free—needs to be reconsidered. In this vein, what Poceski says is helpful: "Syncretism is a basic component of interreligious interaction and to some degree it is found in all religions, notwithstanding the ahistorical claims of individual religious traditions that they are pure and unique, representing god-given dispensations free from external accretions or influences." Ibid., 166.

Zhuang Zhou	370–29 BCE
Qin Dynasty	221–206 BCE
Han Dynasty	206 BCE–220 CE
Beginnings of Organized Daoism	Second Century CE
Celestial Masters	Second Century CE
Taiping Dao	Second Century CE
Lingbao Dao	Fourth Century CE
Daoist Monasticism	Fifth Century CE
Tang Dynasty	618–907 CE
Song Dynasty	960–1279 CE
Quanzhen Dao	Twelfth Century CE
Yuan Dynasty (Mongol rule)	1279–1368 CE
Ming Dynasty	1368–1644 CE
Qing Dynasty (Manchu)	1644–1912 CE
Republic of China	1912–1949 CE
People's Republic of China	1949 CE–present

DAOIST HISTORY IN CHINA

While Daoism has moved far beyond its Chinese origins, and while it also has an important history in Korea and other East Asian countries, its roots in China have been formative in shaping the contours of contemporary Daoism. According to Komjathy's revisionist interpretive framework, Daoism may be divided into four periods, which correspond to historical political developments in China. The first period, Classical Daoism, comprises the time from the fifth century BCE up until the second century BCE. The second period, Early Organized Daoism, took place from the first/second century CE up until the seventh century. The third period, Later Organized Daoism, spanned the time between the seventh century and the beginning of the twentieth century, which saw the end of the Qing dynasty. Finally, Modern Daoism reflects the development of Daoism in the modern period of China, from 1911 up to the present, which includes its ongoing globalization.[6]

Classical Daoism constitutes the beginning of the Daoist tradition and is best known for the compilation and promulgation of the earliest sacred texts—in particular, the *Daodejing* (also spelled *Tao Te Ching*) and the *Zhuangzi* (also spelled *Chuang Tzu*)—more about both of these texts below. During this time, a variety of Daoist lineages developed, often loosely organized around a sage or master, but also at this time many individuals practiced a more solitary form of renunciation and self-discipline.

Early Organized Daoism began in the first/second century CE and marks the time when Daoism developed into a (loosely) structured community. A

---

6. The names for these periods are taken from Komjathy, *Daoist Tradition*, 11–15. For a different organizational structure, see J. Miller, *Daoism*.

variety of important Daoist movements began during this time, of which the Celestial Masters is the most influential. Two other important events for the development of Daoism happened during this time. First, Buddhism was brought into China by missionaries from Central Asia and India. Over time, many Buddhist ideas were incorporated into Daoism (the reverse also occurred), notwithstanding the fact that there were serious rivalries between representatives from each tradition, especially when they were seeking political favor. Second, it was toward the end of this period, during the rise of the Tang dynasty, when Daoism became the official religion of the imperial court, which enabled it to thrive. During this time, many of the characteristic Daoist rituals and texts were solidified and Daoist monasticism was established. Finally, during this period, Daoism was introduced into Korea.

The beginning of the Tang dynasty in the early seventh century CE marked the beginning of the third period of Daoism, Later Organized Daoism. It was during this long period, which extended up until the end of dynastic China in 1911, that Daoism solidified its place in China with the growth of monasticism, institutionalization, and a standardization of ritual practices. In this period, the most important movement was *Quanzhen dao* (the Way of Complete Perfection). Daoist alchemy also became widely popular during this time. Another trend that continued, particularly during the early part of this period, was further overlap and sharing between Buddhism, Daoism, and popular Chinese religious practice, such that in many cases distinguishing between them became difficult. In addition, Komjathy notes that during the late imperial period, many new deities were incorporated into the Daoist pantheon. These include *Doumu* (the Dipper Mother), *Wenchang* (the God of Literature), *Zhenwu* (the Perfect Warrior), and *Tianfei* (the Celestial Consort).[7] This period ended with the encroachment of the West into China in the nineteenth century.

James Miller judges the final period of Daoism as "a near-total catastrophe . . . particularly during the period of the Great Proletarian Cultural Revolution (1966–76)."[8] This was a period of general religious persecution, and during this time most Daoist temples—along with Buddhist temples and others—were destroyed, monasteries were closed, monks were put to work, and public rites and rituals were prohibited. During this time, "the overt functioning of the religion to all intents and purposes ceased to exist in mainland China."[9]

In the past few decades, however, there has been a relaxing of restrictions against religions and more support for Buddhism and Daoism in particular, including a substantial rebuilding project of Buddhist and Daoist temples. Since the 1980s, more specifically with the death of Mao Zedong in 1976 and the leadership of Deng Xiaoping, Daoism has once again become a public religion

---

7. Komjathy, *Daoist Tradition*, 33.
8. J. Miller, *Daoism*, 3.
9. Ibid.

in China, and new Daoist leaders have begun to be trained there. Nonetheless, the loss of a whole generation of leaders and lay practitioners is not easily overcome or forgotten.

One other point must be mentioned in relation to Modern Daoism. The other side of this religious persecution was the accelerated development of Daoism in the West. Komjathy observes, "the Chinese Communist revolution had the unintended consequence of disseminating Chinese religious culture throughout the world and helping to make Daoism a 'world religion.'"[10] As more and more Chinese immigrants left China for the United States, Europe, and other places, Daoism also spread, and unsurprisingly, it adapted to the new contexts in which it found itself. Thus the future of Daoism no longer seems so dire, even if Daoist identity is in flux. This fluidity will be evident in what follows.

DAOISM AND POPULAR CHINESE RELIGION

Before leaving the Chinese context, it is necessary to elaborate on what is typically called Chinese "popular religion." It is a broad category, but for the sake of the discussion here, the following definition will suffice: "often local manifestations of popular piety [that] have over the centuries constituted a vibrant, widely diffused, and immensely significant part of Chinese religious life."[11] There are two specific reasons why it is particularly appropriate to include a brief discussion of Chinese popular religion in a chapter on Daoism. First is the fact that popular religion both influences and is related to various Daoist practices in China; this is true today and has been true for millennia. Second, Daoism itself sometimes has been characterized as an "elevated expression of popular religion," and even scholars have trouble distinguishing where one ends and the other begins.[12] Thus a brief introduction to Chinese popular religion is both helpful and warranted here.

The category "popular religion" is, of course, a scholarly convention, used as a means of categorizing and discussing a wide variety of practices and customs that don't neatly fit into any one of the traditional three teachings (Confucianism, Daoism, and Buddhism). However, even though the roots of these practices might not be in one of these traditions, their presence is still felt strongly in all three of them and is visible in a very public way in many Chinese temples, festivals, and local villages. What this means is that "popular religion constitutes a rich substratum of religiosity that is shared by most Chinese people and reflects prevalent norms, values and worldviews."[13] As a means of introducing this category of religious practices and beliefs, I will briefly mention three aspects of popular religion that have a significant presence

10. Komjathy, *Daoist Tradition*, 35.
11. Poceski, *Introducing Chinese Religions*, 163.
12. Ibid., 62.
13. Ibid., 165.

in a contemporary Chinese religious context: the presence of various deities in local temples, the veneration of local gods, and the practice of divination.

THE SYNCRETIC NATURE OF CHINESE TEMPLES

Figure 21: Main Hall, Wong Tai Sin Temple, Hong Kong (author's picture).

A natural question that a Christian might first ask when visiting a Chinese temple is "What kind of temple is it—is it a Daoist temple or a Confucian temple?" Very often, the answer is "yes"—any given temple might include not only Daoist and Confucian altars but altars to other popular deities as well. Let me offer a few examples from Hong Kong. One of the largest and most popular Chinese temples in Hong Kong is the Wong Tai Sin Temple. It was originally founded in 1921 by Daoist priests as a place to worship the Daoist god Master Wong Tai Sin. While the temple is Daoist in origin, it is currently home to Confucianism, Daoism, and Buddhism, and there are various buildings in the complex with altars dedicated to different figures in all three religions. So, on one side of the main temple are altars to the God of Medicine, the Daoist priest called Master Sun, and the Daoist Martial God of Fortune, Master Zhao. The Yue Heung Shrine is a Buddhist shrine, and Confucian Hall is dedicated to Confucius and a group of his followers. There is also a memorial hall commemorating deceased Taoist priests.

Figure 22: Yue Heung Shrine, Wong Tai Sin Temple, Hong Kong (author's picture).

By contrast, another popular temple, the Tin Hau Temple, has little to do with any of the "three traditions," and is focused primarily on local deities: the main altar is for Tin Hau (also known as Mazu), the patron goddess of sea travelers, and there are side altars dedicated to local earth gods as well. This goddess is particularly important in the pantheon of popular Chinese religions, and temples to her are found all over the southeast China provinces and even in other southeastern Asian countries. Another popular local temple, the Tam Kung temple, is also dedicated to a god of the sea; Tam Kung was said to be a young boy who had healing powers and could also control the weather. The temple contains not only a main altar to him but side altars to various other gods and goddesses, including the God of War, the God of Medicine, and the Goddess of Mercy.

DIVINATION

Divination has a long history in Chinese culture. Today, one often finds individuals practicing divination at local temples, where they can use a variety of methods to get advice about an impending decision or foretell the future. One popular means of divination is the use of oracle sticks (pictured below). This practice is called *Kau Cim/Chim* and is very popular at Wong Tai Sin Temple. There, one first procures a container of sticks from a stall located in

Figure 23: Main altar, Tin Hau Temple, Hong Kong (author's picture).

the temple. The container is brought to a location in front of the altar, and then, after making an offering, the container is shaken—either while kneeling or standing—until one stick comes out. Each stick has a single number, which corresponds to a specific oracle. Interpretation can be done by the petitioners, by a temple priest, or by one of the many fortune tellers in stalls outside the temple.

WHO IS A DAOIST?

A key question that comes early in the study of Daoism is the question of identity: Who, exactly, is a Daoist? Unlike Western religions, there is no universal ritual practice that identifies a Daoist, nor any single shared confession or creed. Instead, there are many different ways to define both individual Daoists and the Daoist religion itself. As already has been mentioned, one way of defining Daoism is to link it specifically to its origins in China and emphasize the "Chinese-ness" of Daoism. This kind of definition can be found in many earlier books on Daoism, but today this is seen as more problematic given the fact that such an identification ignores the complex diversity of Chinese history, the ethnic heterogeneity in China, and the varied geographical components

Figure 24: Divination sticks used at Wong Tai Sin Temple, Hong Kong (author's photo).

involved in the development of a Chinese national identity—to say nothing of the contemporary globalization of Daoism. At the same time, the Chinese character of Daoism is undeniable, particularly given that the most important Daoist texts are all written in Chinese, and relatively few of them have been translated. This requires that any serious scholar of Daoism also become a serious scholar of Chinese language and culture.

Another way to think about Daoist identity is to link it to specific priestly (and lay) ordination lineages. While few Daoist communities have ever ordained all members, many still ordain priests, and as part of their ordination, they receive information that allows them special access to the pantheon of deities and spiritual powers in order to make petitions on behalf of individuals. However, the main weakness here is not only the vast number of Daoists who are not ordained and who do not take advantage of the services of Daoist priests, but also the number of Daoist monks who may or may not be ordained but who spend at least some time in monasteries focusing on alchemical practices that cultivate and refine the body.

Perhaps the most general, overarching definition of Daoist identity describes Daoism as "a universal mystical path that exists and functions independently of any particular lineage transmission or cultural context."[14] This is the definition that resonates most in a contemporary Western context, and it also reflects a historical connection with the two seminal Daoist texts, the *Daodejing* and the *Zhuangzi*. This is certainly the most inclusive and most expansive definition, and for that reason, many welcome it, at least in the West. Less certain is how well such a definition is received by Daoists themselves, however.[15]

For this reason, two cautions much be flagged here. First is the danger of perpetuating the attitude prevalent in many Western missionaries who came to Eastern countries and tried to learn about the religions they discovered there. Being "people of the book" themselves, they privileged sacred texts and the philosophical concepts that went along with them; James Miller notes that, in general, the Western academic system is biased "towards engaging reality through words and ideas,"[16] with the result that important rituals are dismissed as local superstitions. Therefore, one must be careful to not assume Daoism is simply, at its core, a universal philosophy that transcends any specific cultural connections or historical practices.

The second caution is related, and that is the assumption that Daoism is only about an attitude toward life, a set of ideas that one can learn and apply according to one's own situation and proclivities. This carries with it two negative ramifications. First is how this feeds into a colonial mentality, which appropriates from Daoism that which suits a specific construction of an idiosyncratic Western spirituality. Second, this assumption denies the central role the body plays in Daoism and the holistic views Daoism propounds regarding the human person. The Dao is not experienced only or purely as a mental reality but rather in and through one's body, again in a very holistic way. Daoism always has included physical practices as an important part of its self-understanding, and this conviction must be acknowledged and respected.

---

14. J. Miller, *Daoism*, 29–30.

15. For example, Louis Komjathy defines Daoism as "Indigenous Chinese religious tradition. Now a global religious tradition characterized by cultural, ethnic, and linguistic diversity, which recognizes Chinese Daoism as source-tradition." Komjathy, *Daoist Tradition*, 318.

16. J. Miller, *Daoism*, 31.

CENTRAL DAOIST CATEGORIES

THE DAO

The opening words of *Daodejing* have become the classic definition of the Dao:

> The tao that can be told is not the eternal Tao;
> The name that can be named is not the eternal Name.
> The unnamable is the eternally real;
> Naming is the origin of all particular things.[17]

James Miller argues that "the question of the Way (in Chinese 'Dao') is the single most important question that shaped Chinese religious civilization."[18] Therefore, the starting point of Daoism can be nothing else but the Dao itself. For Miller, this question is significant because it distinguishes the Chinese context from a classical Greek context on the one hand—where the fundamental questions were philosophical ones: What is truth? What is goodness?—and a Semitic context on the other—where the fundamental questions related to a belief in a monotheistic god: "How do I obey God's will?"[19] The Chinese context was different and reflected the concern for stability and guidance in the time of upheaval and instability that characterized the Warring States Period in particular.

The Dao in its most basic meaning refers to "way" or "path," but in a religious context, it means much more. The Dao is the focal point of all Daoist thinking and, indeed, the focal point of all life. It is simultaneously everything and nothing, both "the creative source of life in all of its richness and variety that antecedes the formation of heaven and earth," and also "void, ineffable, and mysterious." It has no name and no form, and yet "it is manifest everywhere and permeates everything." It is "an impersonal natural principle, operating constantly and spontaneously, irrespective of purposeful human action and impervious to pious supplication."[20]

Specifically for a Christian audience, one point of clarification is warranted here as it is important to state explicitly that the Dao is not God—it is neither a personified force nor is it relational. Thus the Daoist universe is not theistic in the way the Christian universe is conceived. Instead, the universe is said to be composed of three primary components: heaven (here understood as spiritual powers and deities), earth, and humanity. As force and matrix, the Dao governs and encompasses all three aspects of life. Daoism operates out of the basic idea that there is a harmonious relationship between these three components, which humans must participate in and understand. This relationship is, at its heart,

---

17. Laozi, *Tao Te Ching*, trans. Stephen Mitchell (New York: HarperCollins, 1988).
18. J. Miller, *Daoism*, 37.
19. Ibid.
20. Poceski, *Introducing Chinese Religions*, 65.

dynamic—always flowing, never standing still. Thus the Daoist universe is in a constant process of going out and returning, ebbing and flowing. James Miller writes, "The universe is dynamic and alive, but it dances to a clearly discernible pulse, a binary pulse or cosmic heartbeat according to which everything around us is undergoing a process of expansion and contraction. Nothing in the world stays the same."[21]

YIN/YANG

This relates to another fundamental component of a traditional Chinese worldview, yin and yang. This was defined in the previous chapter on Confucianism, but it is also important to discuss it here, as it plays a key role in shaping a proper understanding of the Daoist universe.

Figure 25: Yin/Yang Symbol.

Most people recognize the yin/yang symbol, as it has been used in a wide variety of contexts to illustrate the principle of harmony. Originally yin referred to the shady side of a hill and yang referred to the sunny side. Obviously these categories aren't static; as the sun moves, the sunny side will slowly become shady and vice versa. So, when you look at the yin/yang symbol, starting at the bottom of the circle, where yang (the white segment) is at its weakest, you move clockwise as yang gains power, until it is at its full strength at the top. Then it recedes as yin (the black segment) comes into ascendance, until it

21. J. Miller, *Daoism*, 34.

reaches its full strength at the bottom, where yang is at its weakest. The whole cycle continuously repeats.

One of the main points of this symbol is that yin and yang are not antagonist opposites but complementary principles: there is no yang without yin, no light without dark, no warmth without cold, no happiness without sadness. This is also the meaning of the opposing color dot in each droplet. Even at its strongest, yin is present in yang and vice versa. They go together, and the harmony of the universe depends on the presence of both.

Stepping back for a minute into the broader landscape of Chinese religion, one of the reasons why Daoism is often seen as so compatible with Confucianism is that, in a simplistic way, Daoism is the yin to Confucianism's yang. That is, where Confucianism focuses on society, on the proper hierarchical relationships between individuals, on structure and order, and on civilization and moral action, Daoism focuses on nature, on the spontaneous, on the individual, on internal cultivation, and on freedom. Where for Confucianism, the perfect world is a flawlessly ordered society, for Daoism, the perfect world is the natural world, naturally changing, with all elements in harmony. Thus where in Confucianism the way of order and peace is through structured social and familial relationships, proper ritual, and civic virtue, in Daoism, to follow the way is "to harmonize oneself with the natural flow of water which, though soft, overcomes all obstacles in its path."[22] It is possible to see these as complementary ideas and practices, although they have not always functioned that way in Chinese society.

The importance of harmony and flow relates directly to another key concept in Daoism: *wuwei* (non-action). This does not point to passivity, but rather nonresistance, effortless activity, and noninterference—behavior that is free from struggle, contrivance, or artificiality. It is action that is unaggressive and in accord with the natural tendency of things.

Much of Daoist practice, then, is geared toward maintaining and participating in this harmony and nurturing it. One important means of doing this is communication with the gods—the celestial immortals and other spirits and ancestors. This can happen anywhere, of course, but one important liminal space where this communication takes place in Daoism is the cave. Many immortals are believed to have lived some or much of their lives in caves, and thus caves are seen as repositories of spiritual power. Not unlike other religious traditions, where mountain caves and grottos are seen as places to meet the divine, in Daoism, caves represent "physically and symbolically the secret paths that lead the religious traveller [*sic*] from the ordinary plane of existence to a more transcendent plane."[23]

Aside from particular loci of communication between humans and the heavenly realm, there are two primary means by which humans can facilitate

22. Ibid., 41.
23. Ibid., 47.

communication between all three aspects of life—heaven, humanity, and earth. The first is through practices of self-cultivation and the second is through specific Daoist rituals. Both kinds of practices are meant to further the harmonious flow of energy and power between the three realms, and both sets of practices are fundamentally and inextricably related to the body.

Daoism and the Body

Concern for the body has a long history in China, so it should be no surprise that there is a deep, wide tradition in Daoism of practices that are geared toward holistic physical health. Ute Engelhardt writes, "Keeping the body healthy and preserving its harmonious functions by nourishing and prolonging life has been an important concern for Daoists of all different schools and currents as well as for the practitioners of Chinese medicine."[24] Daoism strenuously resists the mind/body dualism that characterizes so much of Western thought and instead views the human (and everything that exists) holistically. For this reason, almost all Daoist practices—all the different ways Daoists seek to harmonize their own existence with the Dao—involve the body. In fact, it is fair to say that "Daoism is fundamentally a religion that has to do with the whole of one's body."[25]

The holistic understanding of the body in Daoism is part of a larger holistic cosmology in which the body is seen as a microcosmic image of the universe itself. This, too, is a part of traditional Chinese medicine. One text describes the parallelism this way: "In the year there are 365 days; human beings have 365 joints. On the earth there are high mountains; human beings have shoulders and knees. On the earth there are deep valleys; human beings have armpits and hollows in back of their knees . . . in the earth there are veins of water; human beings have defensive *qi*."[26]

All of the practices designed to facilitate and further one's health and longevity center around stimulating and supporting *qi* (pronounced *chi*), usually translated as breath or life energy. In the earliest texts, *qi* simply referred to the vapor that arises when water is heated, but by the second century BCE, it was seen as the universal energy out of which everything in the cosmos is composed.[27] It is believed that upon birth, the *qi* that fills the body of a newborn baby begins to dissolve and dissipate into the surrounding universe. Therefore, it is critical for vitality and longevity to intentionally engage in practices that will conserve and maintain as much *qi* as possible, allowing *qi* to flow freely and naturally in the body.

---

24. Ute Engelhardt, "Longevity Techniques and Chinese Medicine," in *Daoism Handbook*, ed. Livia Kohn (Leiden: Brill, 2000), 74.

25. J. Miller, *Daoism*, 53. For a more detailed examination of this theme, see Kristofer Schipper, *The Taoist Body* (Berkeley: University of California Press, 1993), particularly ch. 6.

26. Engelhardt, "Longevity Techniques," 95.

27. Harold D. Roth, "The Inner Cultivation Tradition of Early Daoism," in *Religions of China in Practice*, ed. Donald S. Lopez Jr. (Princeton, NJ: Princeton University Press, 1996), 125.

The main point here is that the entire understanding of the body—indeed, the understanding of everything from rocks to gods—is centered around *qi*: where and how it manifests, the way in which it circulates, and how the *qi* in the body is related to the larger physical world of seasons, directions, elements, and weather. So, for example, the muscles and the pulse are seen as expressions of yang and related to wood and fire respectively, while skin and bones are seen as expressions of yin and related to metal and water.[28] This demonstrates a much different understanding of the human being than typically seen in the West:

> Things and beings are seen less as specific individual entities, and more in terms of relationships and dynamic interactions. As a rule, the connection between, for example, the liver and the heart is understood as analogous to that between spring and summer, green and red, vision and touch. . . . It places human beings into the network of the cosmos, seeing them as replicas of larger structures and patterning human existence in a wider framework.[29]

There are many practices in Daoism that seek to promote the flow of *qi*, including both breathing and dietary techniques, as well as physical exercise. Related to the latter, two specific practices warrant mention: *Qigong* (Chi Kung) and *Taijiquan* (T'ai Chi Ch'uan). Particularly in the United States, many people are familiar with these and assume that they originated within Daoism itself. This is actually not true; both *Qigong* and *Taijiquan* are best understood as traditional Chinese health practices that some individuals have incorporated into a Daoist framework. These two physical practices continue to gain in popularity, even by people who do not consider themselves Daoist. Qigong literally means "qi exercises" and involves physical postures, breathing exercises, and meditation. Practice typically includes "softer" kinds of physical activities, like the flowing, gentle movements of Taijiquan, but it also can incorporate more vigorous forms of activity, like *Gongfu* (Kung Fu). In either case, the purpose is to facilitate the movement of *qi* to promote circulation, cleansing, or even direct it outward to promote the healing of others. Taijiquan is similar, involving not only a specific choreography of movements but also focused awareness intended to relieve stress and promote mental calm. Advanced practitioners can also be trained to use Taijiquan as a martial art and a form of self-defense. Both of these physical practices have been used to promote the circulation and vitality of *qi*.

In addition to these two physical disciplines, I want to briefly mention three other bodily practices: dietary practices and breathing exercises, the

---

28. Catherine Despeux and Livia Kohn, *Women in Daoism* (Cambridge, MA: Three Pines Press, 2003), 179.

29. Ibid.

practice of alchemy, and ritual practices. Typically these are not practiced exclusively or independently of each other but rather in combination.

DIET AND BREATHING EXERCISES

Given the importance of the body in Daoism, it should be no surprise that what one eats and drinks also has received extensive attention. Daoist dietary practices reflect the traditional Chinese context in which they developed; this means that the focus has been on eating grains, vegetables, beans, and fruit. Dairy products traditionally have not been a part of a Chinese diet, and historically meat was eaten only in moderation. Customarily, food was categorized according to the characteristics of yin and yang: food was either cold/cooling (yin foods) or hot/drying (yang foods). So depending on one's personal constitution, more or fewer hot, spicy foods might be recommended to bring the body into balance. In general, equal amounts of different foods that reflect the five flavors are recommended: spicy, bitter, sour, sweet, and salty.[30] Some Daoists also practice what might be called an ascetic diet, that is, a diet that involves regular fasting and also abstinence from certain foods, including meat.

Breathing techniques are also related to diet in that they too seek to harmonize the body and facilitate vitality and longevity. Interestingly enough, and unlike many breathing techniques found in Buddhism, the standard breathing practice in Daoism involves allowing the body to find its own natural rhythm and breathe in a way that feels comfortable and relaxed. This is "the application of the Daoist principle of *wuwei* to breathing."[31] However, there is also the recognition that breathing reflects a state of mind and state of body, and so there are many different breathing techniques that seek to facilitate relaxation and a sense of calm. Some of these techniques involve holding the breath and envisioning the breath circulating to all parts of the body. Other practices involve breathing in conjunction with stretching exercises. At least one of the objectives here is "to control excessive emotions and harmful outer influences such as 'moisture' and heat.'"[32]

ALCHEMY AND IMMORTALITY

Alchemy has two primary definitions. First and most specifically, it is considered to be a form of prescientific chemistry concerned with transmuting elements—for example, changing baser metals into gold. Second and more broadly, it is the name for a larger category of esoteric practices that have the power not only to change elements but also to create magical elixirs for long life and vitality—that is, changing not only elements but the people who practice alchemy. As part of this larger practice, alchemy "provides ritual and

---

30. Komjathy, "Daoist Tradition," 166. See also Livia Kohn, *Daoist Dietetics: Food for Immortality* (Dunedin, FL: Three Pines Press, 2010).

31. Komjathy, "Daoist Tradition," 192.

32. Engelhardt, "Longevity Techniques," 101.

symbolic support to understanding the origins and nature of the cosmos and gaining access to the forces that govern its functioning, represented either as supernatural beings or abstract notions. Thus the elixir represents both the authentic state of the cosmos and the knowledge acquired by the adept."[33] Alchemy was practiced in societies all over the world, from Asia to Europe to Egypt, and it is still practiced in many places today. In China, the earliest records of alchemy link it with the search for elixirs of immortality, and this is also a component of Daoist alchemy.

Immortality is a concept that one often finds in discussions of Daoism, but which is not always well understood. There is a longstanding belief in Chinese culture, stretching back millennia, that "human life can be prolonged beyond normal limits and that the body can be transcended."[34] This relates to concepts of longevity but pushes beyond them as well. While the idea of immortality circulated broadly in China, it became a particular focus of Daoism, such that "becoming an immortal or transcendent has always been the goal of the Daoist adept."[35] Immortality, then, often points to a transformation of the mortal body and a higher level of celestial consciousness: "a movement from ordinary existence . . . to immortal life, here associated with Daoist sacred realms and spiritual transcendence."[36]

While the *Zhuangzi* (*Chuang Tzu*) emphasizes the ideal of the sage over the immortal, there are several places in this text where a description of an immortal is given. In chapter 1, we read: "there is a Holy Man living on faraway Ku-she Mountain, with skin like ice or snow, and gentle and shy like a young girl. He doesn't eat the five grains, but sucks the wind, drinks the dew, climbs up on the clouds and mist, rides a flying dragon, and wanders beyond the four seas. By concentrating his spirit, he can protect creatures from sickness and plague and make the harvest plentiful."[37] And in another chapter, the following description is recorded: "The Perfect Man is godlike. Though the great swamps blaze, they cannot burn him; though the great rivers freeze, they cannot chill him; though swift lightning splits the hills and howling gales shake the sea, they cannot frighten him. A man like this rides the clouds and mist, straddles the sun and moon, and wanders beyond the four seas. Even life and death have no effect on him, much less the rules of profit and loss."[38]

Both of these exhibit what have become standard descriptors: "a being with a purified body, who uses a special diet without grains and has the ability to fly, to roam afar and to heal."[39] In fact the powers of an immortal are extraordinary and include the ability to transform objects into something else—like making

33. Fabrizio Pregadio, "Elixirs and Alchemy," in Kohn, *Daoism Handbook*, 179.
34. Benjamin Penny, "Immortality and Transcendence," in Kohn, *Daoism Handbook*, 109.
35. Ibid.
36. Komjathy, "Daoist Tradition," 173.
37. Chuang Tzu, *Chuang Tzu*, 27.
38. Ibid., 41–42.
39. Penny, "Immortality and Transcendence," 110.

food from something inedible—and controlling animals, particularly dangerous animals. Immortals also have control over the weather and can cure many kinds of disease. Some of those who became immortals ascended to heaven immediately—simply rising up into the air and disappearing. Others were liberated upon death, like "a cicada shedding its carapace or a snake shedding its skin."[40]

RITUAL

The word "ritual" covers a vast scope of activities that indicate specific behaviors that reinforce membership in a religious community and are often meant to influence one's relationship to God/gods and/or procure some favorable result in the present. In Daoism, rituals are performed for personal purification, communal harmony, divination, communication with the immortals, and individual transformation. The history of Daoist ritual is complicated and still not widely studied, so for the purposes of this chapter, the focus is on two contemporary Daoist rituals.[41]

The first is the ritual of ordination. As already mentioned, the priesthood in Daoism goes back millennia, and Daoist priests continue to have an important role in temple life and in the lives of individual Daoists. Thus ordination rituals continue to be an important form of ritual practice. Both men and women can serve as Daoist priests. At major Daoist temples in China, ordination rituals can be performed for many people at the same time, but there is also a more private form of ordination that involves direct transmission of knowledge from a master to a disciple. The ordination rites typically involve bowing before a Daoist altar and "taking refuge" in the Dao, the scriptures, and the teachers—a rite adapted from the Buddhist practice of taking refuge in the three jewels of the Buddha, the Dharma, and the Sangha.[42] They also typically involve receiving a new name, new robes, and specific texts, and being empowered to perform other rituals, like consecration ceremonies and purification ceremonies. Finally, there is also often a hair-pinning ceremony in which the ordinand's hair is formed into a topknot by his/her master and then a hairpin is inserted.[43]

The second is the combined *zhai* (purification) ritual and the *jiao* (offering) ritual. Originally these were two separate rituals, but today they are typically performed together.[44] The purification rite comes as the first part of the offering ritual. *Zhai* were originally actual physical fasts—including fasting from meat, alcohol, and sexual intercourse—and involved purifying oneself through bathing and meditating in order to approach the gods at a Daoist altar. Today, however, this ritual is performed more communally, with a rite of atonement

40. Ibid., 124.
41. For more information on the historical context, see Komjathy, "Daoist Tradition," 244–62.
42. Ibid., 251.
43. Ibid., 250.
44. Ibid., 249.

that is presented to the gods. Once this is completed the *jiao* can occur. These are typically large-scale events that take place over a series of days, involving the whole community. They are meant to reinforce the relationship between the community and a deity/deities and seek blessings for the community and/or protection from misfortune.

Finally, let me say a word about the role of ritual in the everyday life of Daoists. Again, there are a wide variety of practices here depending on both cultural context and Daoist school, with some traditions practicing more formalized daily rituals and others outlining only the basics. So, for example, in the Quanzhen school, one of the main expressions of Daoism in China, there is a prescribed set of rituals for waking up in the morning, including invocations to recite while washing the face and hands, brushing the teeth, combing the hair, and putting on one's clothes. More generally, however, perhaps the most important ritual is bowing: "the most common and foundational form of Daoist ritual activity."[45] This activity can take the form of a simple *mudra* (hand formation) or can include formal full-body prostration. In addition, many Daoists also make regular visits to altars or even have a private altar at home.

DAOIST TEXTS

There are many sacred texts in Daoism—considered manifestations of the Dao—most of which have not been translated into English. Indeed, most of the major Daoist movements have their own corpus of texts, often with little overlap among them. The word for scripture in Chinese is *jing*, which can also be translated as "canon" or "classic," and is also used to describe sacred Confucian and Buddhist texts. Traditionally, scripture study has been an important Daoist practice, and in the tradition as a whole, scripture holds a central position—even if some individual Daoists regard the practice with indifference. There is a Daoist canon, called the *Daozang* (storehouse of the Dao).[46] It was compiled by Lu Xiujing in the fifth century. A revised edition, called the "received *Daozang*" and created during the Ming dynasty, endured into the twentieth century. This edition is the one still most widely used, and it contains a total of 1,487 texts.[47]

In addition, there is a whole compendium of texts that are used exclusively in Daoist rituals. These texts include petitions to the immortals written by Daoist priests and also those that are chanted in Daoist services. Some texts are believed to have been revealed by Laozi and other immortals, and this tradition of revelation continues. Even today, there are schools of Daoism where a medium (or sometimes a Daoist priest) goes into a trance and receives a revelation from one of the immortals.

There are also many secret texts that are passed down from priest to priest

45. Ibid., 254.
46. Ibid., 237.
47. Ibid.

in the context of their ordination. These texts are powerful talismans, and as part of the ordination process, the priests promise not to reveal their context and only use them in the course of the prescribed liturgies.

LAOZI AND THE DAODEJING

Of the many Daoist texts, by far the two most important are the *Daodejing* (the *Tao Te Ching*) and the *Zhuangzi* (the *Chuang Tzu*). The figure typically offered as Daoism's founder, Laozi (sometimes spelled Lao Tzu), is the author of the *Daodejing*. His traditional dates are usually given as 571–480 BCE. Also known as Master Lao, he casts a long shadow over Daoism and is universally considered to be its most revered individual. He is a figure of legend with little concrete historical data to undergird the picture of him that has grown and expanded over time. Some scholars even doubt that he was a historical person at all.

The core of the biographical data that we possess about him comes from records written by Sima Qian in the first century BCE, in a text called *Shiji* (*Records of the Historian*). Qian writes that the historical figure we have come to know as Laozi was originally an archivist named Lao Dan (or Li Dan or Li Er) who lived during the Zhou Dynasty, sometime during the sixth century BCE. This would make Laozi a senior contemporary of Confucius. The story goes that after retiring from court service, he set off on a journey westward. While on the way, he was stopped and asked to write down his philosophy of life—the resulting text is known as the *Daodejing*. When he was finished, he left and vanished from history's sight. This final image has become a central component of all the stories of Laozi's life: "the old man sitting on his ox cheerfully leaving his homeland."[48] However, even this information is not clear, and many scholars believe that this narrative actually compiles information from several different people—one of whom, or none of whom, might be the historical Laozi.[49]

The wisdom and popularity of this text, as well as the lack of further historical data about Laozi himself, has resulted in an elaborate mythology developing around him. Most noticeably, in some Daoist traditions, he is not viewed as a person at all, but rather as the embodiment of the Dao itself. In many Daoist schools, he has been deified and is worshipped as a god. In these traditions, "Laozi is worshiped as the personification of the eternal Dao, the 'Way,' the ultimate power that makes the universe exist and causes beings to be alive. Known then as the god *Taishang Laojun*, the Most High Lord Lao, he is believed to reside in the center of Heaven and at the beginning of time."[50] So, for example, in one of his biographies, it is recorded that his mother became pregnant when "she was touched by a huge meteor." This is meant to explain

---

48. Livia Kohn, "Laozi: Ancient Philosopher, Master of Immortality, and God," in Lopez, *Religions of China*, 55.

49. Ibid., 53.

50. Ibid.

that Laozi therefore "received his basic energy directly from Heaven," even though he was born on earth into a regular family.[51]

The *Daodejing* is without question the most well-known and well-read text of Daoism—read by many people who know nothing else at all of the religion. This is also the earliest Daoist text, and in China, it is known by the name of its author, *Laozi*. The title can be translated as *Classic of the Way and Its Power*, which comes from a translation of the opening Chinese characters from its two main parts: *dao* (way) and *de* (power)—although the latter can also be translated as "virtue."[52] There is no autograph copy of the text, and the one typically used today, known as the Wang Bi edition, was put together by the philosopher Wang Bi in the third century CE—although it clearly existed for centuries before that date. New manuscripts were found in the early 1970s dating from around 200 BCE, and in 1993, another version of the text was discovered, dating from around the mid-fourth century BCE.[53]

The text is a collection of sayings that are most likely from a variety of Daoist thinkers, which were handed down orally for generations until they were finally transcribed on bamboo or silk. Scholars agree that no single author wrote the text. Instead, it was compiled from various aphorisms by various sources. It was first translated into English in 1868, and now there exists a wide variety of translations, some of which are more scholarly, based more closely on the Chinese text, and others are much freer. Thus the interested reader needs to take caution. Benjamin Penny writes:

> As interest in the *Daodejing* has become more widespread and as its popularity as a text for translation has grown, it has sometimes been considered as a philosophical gem suspended in a historical and cultural void, removed from its ancient Chinese context. Without this context, some translators and writers on the *Daodejing* have dressed it in clothes of their own choosing, often inappropriately.[54]

This is true not only for translations but even more so for all the books that begin: "The Tao of . . ." This means that the wildly popular *The Tao of Pooh*, published in 1982, probably should not be considered the gold standard of commentary, even if the illustrations are very appealing.

The text itself is very short. The Wang Bi edition contains only eighty-one brief chapters, but in the course of its long lifetime it has been read and interpreted from a wide variety of perspectives: as a mystical text, a political guide, a health and wellness manual, and a religious classic. The claim has been made that it is the most translated book after the Bible.[55] Whether or not that is

51. Taken from the *Biography of Spirit Immortals* as quoted in Kohn, "Laozi," 57.

52. Poceski, *Introducing Chinese Religions*, 64.

53. Laozi, *Daodejing*, trans. Edmund Ryden (Oxford: Oxford University Press, 2008), xv, xvii.

54. Ibid., vii.

true, it is clear that its popularity has not waned over time, and it continues to be read by a broad audience. The chapters are divided into two sections. The first section has thirty-seven chapters and comes under the heading *Daojing*, since the opening chapter of this section (and the book as a whole) focuses on the Dao. The second section has forty-four chapters and is titled *Dejing*, since its opening chapter, chapter 38, focuses on the De (power, virtue)—hence the title of the whole collection: *Daodejing* (Classic/Book of the Way and Power).

Here are a few selections from the text that illustrate some of the main overarching themes:

To know others is wisdom;
To know oneself is insight.

To conquer others is to have force;
To conquer oneself is to be strong.

To know what is enough is to be rich;
To forcibly press on is to be ambitious.

To not lose what one has is to last;
To die yet not depart is to be long-lived.[56]

One who knows does not speak.
One who speaks does not know.
. . . .
Thus,
One cannot get him and make him one's kin,
and one cannot get him and keep him distant;
one cannot get him and let him profit,
and one cannot get him and do him harm;
one cannot get him and hold him high,
and one cannot get him and hold him low.
Thus he is held high by the world.[57]

To know that one does not know is the best.
To not know that one does not know is the worst.[58]

Human beings in life are soft and weak, in death are always stretched, stiff, and rigid.

55. Poceski, *Introducing Chinese Religions*, 65.

56. Laozi, *Daodejing*, trans. Ryden, 69, from ch. 33. Another good translation is Lao-Tzu, *Tao Te Ching*, trans. Stephen Addiss and Stanley Lombardo (Indianapolis: Hackett, 1993).

57. Laozi, *Daodejing*, trans. Hans-Georg Moeller (Chicago: Open Court, 2007), 131, from ch. 56.

58. Laozi, *Daodejing*, trans. Ryden, 147, from ch. 71.

The myriad things, grass and plants, in life are soft and pliant,
in death are withered and dry.

Therefore it is said,
"Stiffness and rigidity are indicators of death;
Softness, weakness (tiny and small) are indicators of life."

For this reason,
When an army is rigid it will not win;
When a tree stands erect it will not last;
What is stiff and large lies below ground;
What is soft and weak, tiny and small, stands above ground.[59]

These brief excerpts illustrate several key ideas. The text advocates fluidity and
flexibility over rigidity—thus the ebb and flow of water is often lifted up as
a model for human behavior. It privileges detachment and equanimity in the
face of both success and disappointment, and encourages one to carry a sense
of oneself within, rather than looking for validation from outside. Times and
people change, and therefore in the eyes of the world, one's fortunes will always
change as well. Finally, it is more important to have knowledge of oneself and
be in harmony with nature than to gain power and ascendency over others.
This harmony is contentment, and striving for "more" will only lead to anxiety
and unhappiness.

The *Daodejing* has had a long life, and people continue to find it relevant
and helpful in a variety of contexts all over the world: personal, public, and
philosophical. Joel Kupperman writes that "the Daodejing is both mystical
and political. The mysticism centers on an awe of nature, and a sense that it
is important to be in tune with the natural tendencies of the universe. . . .
The politics of the Daodejing can be appreciated in relation to the idea that
the political is personal. The good Daoist ruler will avoid confrontation with
subjects and officials, and will not push at the world."[60] It continues to offer
wisdom not only for ordering one's own life individually but for living one's
life in public and professional settings.

ZHUANGZI: THE MAN AND THE BOOK

Perhaps the second most important writer in the Daoist tradition is known as
Zhuangzi (Chuang Tzu), also known as Master Zhuang. Like Laozi, we have
little historical information about him, although unlike Laozi, it is believed that
Zhuangzi was a historical person. As with Laozi, much of the information we
have about him comes from chapter 63 of Sima Qian's *Shiji*—written almost

59. Ibid., 157, from ch. 76.

60. Joel Kupperman, *Classic Asian Philosophy: A Guide to the Essential Texts* (Oxford: Oxford
University Press, 2001), 111.

two centuries after Zhuangzi's death. There we read, "Master Zhuang was a Man of Meng and his given name was Zhou. . . . His style and diction were skillful and he used allusions and analogies to excoriate the Confucians and the Mohists. Even the most profound scholars of the age could not defend themselves. His words billowed without restraint to please himself."[61] He is said to have lived in the fourth century BCE, around the same time as Mencius, and he is most famous for the text that bears his own name. And in his case, the connection between the man and the book has greater historical veracity.

The text *Zhuangzi* is made up of thirty-three chapters, and it is believed that only the first seven chapters were written by Zhuangzi himself and are therefore regarded as the most authentic; these chapters are typically referred to as the Inner Chapters. The next fifteen chapters are called the Outer Chapters and the last seven are called the Miscellaneous Chapters. These others were composed by either his disciples or other like-minded thinkers of the time. The *Zhuangzi* is widely regarded as a literary classic and one of China's greatest traditional texts. It contains a variety of anecdotes, clever allegories, beautiful poetic renderings of the natural world, and more than one dig at Confucius; most of the time when Confucius shows up in the text, he is caricatured as "a stiff moralist" and compared unfavorably with the wise Daoist sage.[62] The text is surprising, divergent, spontaneous, and flamboyant. In short, "The Zhuangzi is a philosophical counterpart to fireworks. Brightly colored lines of thought go off in many directions."[63]

Even though the topics of each chapter vary greatly, there are some overarching general themes. One of the most important is the concept of spontaneity and the value of being in harmony with the Dao and with one's own inner nature. So, for example, in the first chapter, "Free and Easy Wandering," there is the story of the big tree called a *shu*. The tree is gnarled, crooked, and bumpy, and therefore its owner complains that it has no use. In response, Zhuangzi says, "Now you have this big tree and you're distressed because it's useless. Why don't you plant it in Not-Even-Anything Village, or the field of Broad-and-Boundless, relax and do nothing by its side, or lie down for a free and easy sleep under it? Axes will never shorten its life, nothing can ever harm it. If there's no use for it, how can it come to grief or pain?"[64] The tree is just what it is; it is for the individual to accept that and live in harmony with it.

This message is reinforced in "Fit for Emperors and Kings" where the Nameless Man offers this advice to T'ien Ken, who asks him how to rule the world: "Let your mind wander in simplicity, blend your spirit with the vastness,

---

61. Victor Mair, "The *Zhuangzi* and Its Impact," in Kohn, *Daoism Handbook*, 31.

62. Poceski, *Introducing Chinese Religion*, 68.

63. Kupperman, *Classic Asian Philosophy*, 127.

64. Chuang Tzu, *Chuang Tzu*, 29–30.

follow along with things the way they are, and make no room for personal views—then the world will be governed."[65]

Another important theme is the cultivation of one's own inner nature and the turn from deep engagement with the social and political life, which can only lead to anxiety and unhappiness. Thus we read in "Mastering Life," "When you're betting for tiles in an archery contest, you shoot with skill. When you're betting for fancy belt buckles, you worry about your aim. And when you're betting for real gold, you're a nervous wreck. Your skill is the same in all three cases—but because one prize means more to you than another, you let outside considerations weigh on your mind. He who looks too hard at the outside gets clumsy on the inside."[66] Caring too much about worldly goals such as success, wealth, and status, and putting too much stock in the opinion of others only distracts from one's own peace and contentment, and obscures one's true nature.

Finally, another key theme in the text is the necessity of equability in the face of both good and misfortune: the Daoist sage "readily accepts constant change as a basic fact of earthly existence and goes along with what life brings to him, remaining composed and equanimous when confronted with pain and pleasure, gain and loss, life and death."[67] So, for example, in "The Sign of Virtue Complete," Zhuangzi is commending to Hui Tzu "a man who has no feelings." Zhuangzi says, "When I talk about having no feelings, I mean that a man doesn't allow likes or dislikes to get in and do him harm. He just lets things be the way they are and doesn't try to help life along."[68] When one lives in harmony with the Dao, one accepts the ebb and flow of life gracefully and without struggle, knowing that nothing is permanent and change is the nature of reality. Thus we see that "not only are all things relative, they are constantly evolving and transforming. Based on this principle, one should follow nature, acquiesce in fate, and avoid all striving, especially for fame or rank. Only then can one be free."[69]

In addition to these themes, there are several stories told in the *Zhungzi* that are quite well known and worth sharing here. This first is the story of Chuang Chou and the butterfly:

> Once Chuang Chou dreamt he was a butterfly, a butterfly flitting and fluttering around, happy with himself and doing as he pleased. He didn't know he was Chuang Chou. Suddenly he woke up and there he was, solid and unmistakable Chuang Chou. But he didn't know if he was Chuang Chou who had dreamt he was a butterfly, or a butterfly dreaming he was Chuang Chou. Between Chuang

65. Ibid., 91.

66. Ibid., 122.

67. Poceski, *Introducing Chinese Religion*, 69.

68. Chuang Tzu, *Chuang Tzu*, 72.

69. Victor Mair, "*Zhuangzi* and Its Impact," 43.

Chou and a butterfly there must be *some* distinction! This is called the Transformation of Things.[70]

In truth, reality is as ephemeral as a dream, and our knowledge of this world is as fleeting as our knowledge of our dreams.

The second is the story of the cook and his knife:

> When I first began cutting up oxen, all I could see was the ox itself. After three years I no longer saw the whole ox. And now—now I go at it by spirit and don't look with my eyes. Perception and understanding have come to a stop and spirit moves where it wants. I go along with the natural makeup, strike in the big hollows, guide the knife through the big opening, and follow things as they are. So I never touch the smallest ligament or tendon, much less a main joint.
>
> A good cook changes his knife once a year—because he cuts. A mediocre cook changes his knife once a month—because he hacks. I've had this knife of mine for nineteen years and I've cut up thousands of oxen with it, and yet the blade is as good as though it had just come from the grindstone. There are spaces between the joints, and the blade of the knife has really no thickness. If you insert what has no thickness into such spaces, then there's plenty of room—more than enough for the blade to play about in.[71]

This story emphasizes the value of not imposing one's own ideas on reality but seeing things for what they are and following the natural movement of things, not forcing a cut where there is "no room" but finding the natural spaces between things and slipping through them. At its core, then, the *Zhuangzi* offers a way of viewing the world and acting in it that will lead to harmony and contentment, regardless of the circumstances in which one finds oneself: "The central theme of the *Chuang Tzu* may be summed up in a single word: freedom. Essentially, all the philosophers of ancient China addressed themselves to the same problem: how is [a hu]man to live in a world dominated by chaos, suffering, and absurdity? . . . Chuang Tzu's answer to the question is: free yourself from the world."[72]

WOMEN AND DAOISM

Before concluding this chapter, a bit should be said about the role of women in Daoism. Like Confucianism, Daoism was strongly influenced by the patriarchal Chinese culture in which it developed, and therefore it also was shaped by male-

---

70. Chuang Tzu, *Chuang Tzu*, 45.

71. Ibid., 46–47.

72. Ibid., 3.

centered Confucian societal norms. Yet as is true in many religions, the role of women in Daoism is complex, and while there certainly are practices and beliefs that are exploitative and oppressive toward women, there are also traditions in which women are elevated and celebrated.

Catherine Despeux and Livia Kohn describe five different major "visions and roles" for women in Daoism, each of which was prevalent during a specific period of Daoist history. In chronological order, these five are:

- The female as mother, the life-giving power of the Dao itself
- Women as representing the cosmic force of yin
- Women as divine teachers of esoteric revelation
- Women as shamans, possessed of healing powers
- The female body as the place of spiritual transformation.[73]

So, for example, in the *Daodejing*, we see the Dao personified as female: the womb of the universe, flowing water, and the soft yielding power of the feminine. This relates to the complementary relationship between yin and yang, where yin is seen as governing the organs of the body that conserve *qi*, such as the liver, heart, and kidneys.[74] This led to the development of sexual rituals that were related to the cultivation of *qi* and based on an understanding of women as representatives of yin. In some of these practices, men and women were equal partners, as through sexual intercourse, yin and yang came together and the participants' own *qi* was harmonized with the cosmic *qi*. However, this also led to some exploitative practices. For example, Despeux and Kohn describe the "sexual vampirism" that encouraged men to withhold their own orgasm (thereby conserving their *qi*) while absorbing the sexual essence of young, healthy women through their orgasms.[75]

Finally, it is important to note the role of goddesses and female immortals in Daoism. There are several important goddesses, including the mother of Lord Lao (the divinized form of Laozi), who is called the Mother of the Dao. Of these, the most well known is the Queen Mother of the West, *Xiwang mu*. She is one of the oldest (with a long history) and one of the most important deities in Daoism. She has great power, particularly over immortality, and she represents the cosmic power of yin.

CONCLUSION: CONTEMPORARY DAOISM IN THE UNITED STATES

Daoism in the United States is very fluid today, and there is an increasing variety of "ways to affiliation," the traditional phrase used to indicate the path to becoming a Daoist. Louis Komjathy uses Livia Kohn's three categories to map the United States Daoist population: the literati (that is, those who focus

73. Despeux and Kohn, *Women in Daoism*, 6.
74. Ibid., 8.
75. Ibid., 9.

on texts and ideas—they are usually highly educated); the communal (those who have a ritual/liturgical orientation, which includes a priesthood and regular prayers to the gods); and the self-cultivators (those who focus on health, peace of mind, and immortality).[76] Overwhelmingly, United States Daoists fall into the third category, not least because it includes those who self-identify with Daoism through the physical practices of Taijiquan and Qigong. In short, more and more people are discovering Daoism through an ever-expanding menu of diverse entry points.

One way to respond to this diversity is to adopt the principle of "self-identification" when it comes to affirming who is a Daoist. Under that principle, "anyone who identifies himself or herself as a Daoist is a Daoist."[77] This may sound hopelessly confusing and entirely unhelpful to Christian ears. However, it makes the point that, at its heart, Daoism is the kind of religion that allows for this flexibility and openness. Far from being resistant to or fearful of such elasticity, Daoism welcomes it. Fluidity, dynamism, change, and growth: this is the way of the universe; this is the Dao.

---

76. Louis Komjathy, "Tracing the Contours of Daoism in North America," *Nova Religio: The Journal of Alternative and Emergent Religions* 8, no. 2 (2004): 8–9. Komjathy has refined and elaborated on this categorization in his *The Daoist Tradition*; see especially ch. 3.

77. Ibid., 6–7.

5

Life, Death, and What Comes After

SOTERIOLOGY: THE WHOLE OF CHRISTIAN THEOLOGY

Soteriology, the doctrine of salvation, stands at the very center of Christian theology. The Christian message flows from the core gospel proclamation "Jesus saves" and aims toward the eschatological promise of the coming kingdom of God. In short, Christianity begins and ends with soteriology. Carl Braaten says it this way: "The chief aim of the church is to proclaim the gospel of salvation. Salvation is the most inclusive term for what the Bible declares that God has accomplished for the world through Jesus the Christ."[1] He goes on to argue that "one reason there is no *specific* doctrine of salvation is that the whole of theology is inherently developed from a soteriological point of view. Salvation is not one of the many topics, along with the doctrine of God, Christ, church, sacraments, eschatology, and the like. It is rather the perspective from which all these subjects are interpreted, for the sake of the church's mission in the world."[2] The point he makes here is that salvation is the beating heart of Christian theology, regardless of how it is parsed, regardless of what specific doctrines are argued, regardless of what specific practices are advocated.

It should come as no surprise, then, that in today's context, there are a wide range of perspectives on salvation, both inside and outside the church. Many of these are places around which Christians come together, places where people hear the good news of forgiveness and meet Jesus Christ. However, it also must be acknowledged that some of these perspectives compromise, rather than facilitate, the church's witness to Jesus Christ; some alienate, rather than unite; some emphasize condemnation, rather than forgiveness. Thus the church must continue to engage in the critical work of reexamining its narrative of salvation, seeking fresh ways to make this fundamental gospel message relevant and compelling to those both inside and outside the church.

THE CHRISTIAN NARRATIVE OF THE ARK

The fact is that while the proclamation of salvation is the most important

1. Carl Braaten, "The Christian Doctrine of Salvation," *Interpretation* 35, no. 2 (April 1981): 117.
2. Ibid.

message Christianity has to offer to the world, this teaching is also the area that often creates the most division between Christians and all of those deemed "other"—whether that is people of other religious traditions, sexual orientations, races, nationalities, and so on. Christians must admit that this central message of God's love has been used as a weapon of hate and exclusion to demonize and punish others and to create strong lines between insiders and outsiders—the "good" vs. the "evil."

Figure 26: "Noah's Ark," by Edward Hicks.

The image of Noah's Ark is one of the best examples of this, and it is highly ironic that what is actually one of the most terrifying stories in the Bible has been so sanitized and "Disneyfied," if you will, that it has become a popular motif for decorating children's nurseries. Certainly, when viewing many traditional representations of Noah's Ark, such as this famous image by Edward Hicks, one can see the appeal: representatives from the whole animal kingdom, people included, rounded up and brought together to be rescued from the coming darkness. However, when a little more consideration is given, that "representatives" part becomes a bit more troubling: it is good for those on the inside, but what about the rest?

The popular story, the story told to children, is focused above the water, not below it, simply because facing the ones in the story who are left out when the door closes is uncomfortable. This is one reason why many found the 2014 Darren Aronofsky movie, *Noah*, so gripping. It does not turn away from that awful, terrifying moment when the sheets of rain start to fall and the cries of the drowning rise up to heaven, unheard and unheeded. It is true that for those on the inside, the ark is an image of protection, warmth, comfort, and love—that is why it has been such a popular motif in both church architecture and theology. However, for those on the outside, the ark is an image of exclusion, rejection, judgment, and death. Much traditional language for salvation has functioned in the same way: great for the insiders, not so great for the outsiders.

BROADENING A CHRISTIAN UNDERSTANDING OF SALVATION

Part of the problem is a misunderstanding about what salvation actually means and how it is received and experienced. Christian conversations around salvation are often narrowly focused on one specific line of argumentation, perfectly exemplified in the image and metaphor of the ark. The argument typically proceeds in three stages.

- In the fall, all humanity has been damned as punishment for sin against God. This sin is typically characterized as rebellion, pride, disobedience, or idolatry.
- In response, Jesus Christ suffered death on the cross in order to save humanity, taking human sin upon himself and suffering the punishment we deserve, thereby redeeming us.
- If an individual believes in Jesus Christ and is baptized, their salvation will be assured, and instead of suffering eternal damnation, they will receive the reward of eternal life in heaven after they die.

This specific trajectory of thought around salvation has played an important role in the belief and practice of Christians all around the world for centuries, and it still continues to play a key role today. The value of this thinking is that it emphasizes the central Christian belief in human sin, our inability to "fix" ourselves on our own, our need for a savior—for Jesus Christ and the promise of eternal life with God where Christians will be reconciled with their loved ones. All of those things are significant, and this line of thinking is one important way of understanding and describing what "salvation" is and means. However, this is not the only way of talking about salvation in the Christian church—nor, perhaps, in today's context, is it even the best way. There are other ways to understand and describe salvation and a wealth of different salvific metaphors and images from Scripture and the tradition that are often neglected.

The beginnings of a new century offer a fresh opportunity for the church to rethink some of its traditional language around salvation, particularly in light of increasing numbers of other religious believers and nonbelievers alike, and reassert the relevance and importance of salvation in Christian life today. In service of that task, this chapter proceeds as follows. After offering a definition of salvation, I provide a cursory examination of salvation in the New Testament, specifically in the life and ministry of Jesus. I then give a brief overview of several of the most well-known and frequently discussed "motifs of atonement" in Christian history: *Christus victor*, *theosis*, satisfaction, and moral example. These are the most common answers to the "how" of salvation: how is it, exactly, that "Jesus saves." Finally, I conclude with the main part of the constructive argument of this chapter: the "so what" of salvation, that is, how salvation matters in terms of life, death, and what lies beyond.

Otherworldly Bureaucracy in Daoism

Like many other religions, Daoism contains descriptions of an afterlife, even if language of "salvation" typically is not used. In this area, Daoism has inherited from earlier Chinese tradition a "bureaucracy" of otherworldly rulers that mimicked the Chinese "this-worldly" governmental system. One might well ask, "What is the function of such a bureaucratic system in the afterlife?" and the question is easily answered: record-keeping—in particular, keeping records of individuals' life spans and their deeds on earth. Daoism thus developed a system in which specific deities have this responsibility of oversight and can engage with individuals either positively or negatively: "These deities, who inspected human behavior, could adversely affect one's life span, prevent advancement in the celestial hierarchy, or relegate one to the tortures of the 'earth prisons' until merit from descendants would set one free."[3] For this reason, an important function of Daoist priests is to help facilitate communication between individuals in this world and the otherworldly deities.

Complementing this bureaucracy of Daoist deities, there is also a multileveled realm into which one is assigned upon death. This realm includes a variety of heavens, with the possibility to move "up the ranks" into realms of greater perfection even after death. This realm also includes a "netherworld" called hell; it is not a place of permanent residence but typically a place of temporary suffering and punishment where certain individuals must go before ascending into the heavenly realms. This is one of the places where Daoism was influenced by Buddhism, which also describes a complex system of hells through which sentient beings migrate. Daoist texts developed that cataloged specific punishments and tortures but also described the various rites that could be completed in order to rescue someone from hell. So, for example, certain Lingbao texts described rites that would "erase the names of the unfortunate from the registers of the dead, inscribe them in the registers of transcendents, and either cause their transfer to the Heavenly Hall or ensure a propitious rebirth."[4] In Daoism, heaven and hell are complicated, regulated, and interrelated, part of an overarching hierarchical system that encompasses both life and death.

What Is Salvation?

The English word "salvation" is derived from the Latin *salvus* (safe/well/unharmed). The English word "soteriology," which is the theological study of salvation, comes from the Greek word *soteria* (deliverance/preservation/safety). According to *The Blackwell Encyclopedia of Modern Christian Thought*, soteriology incorporates two broad concerns: "the question of how salvation is possible and in particular how it relates to the history of Jesus Christ; and the question of how 'salvation' itself is to be understood."[5] Both concepts, then, are obviously wide-ranging. Thus there are many ways to envision what it might mean to be saved.

Grace Jantzen describes it this way:

> "Salvation" . . . implies that there is something to be saved from; what this is varies according to context. A person might be saved from drowning, bankruptcy, starvation, embarrassment, or any number of other things. . . . Schillebeeckx, indeed, has gone so far as to say that from a people's concept of salvation can be traced to the history of their suffering: whatever has caused them the most pain is that from which they will feel the need to be saved. But if the content of salvation varies in accordance with need, it also varies as to method: the way to save a drowning child is not the same as the way to save a student from failure. And if that from which one is saved and the method of salvation vary, the goal—what is obtained by obtaining salvation—varies as well: life, health, solvency, good graces, social equilibrium.[6]

This, then, is one of the reasons there is no single definitive, canonical explanation or image for salvation in the Christian tradition: how one is saved depends on what one is saved from. So, for example, if Christians are imprisoned by the devil, we need Jesus to fight Satan and free us. If Christians are sick with guilt and shame, we need Jesus to heal us and make us whole again. If Christians are turned in on ourselves and unable to be in relationship with God, we need Jesus to come and straighten us up and turn our heads around. Indeed, perhaps the only universally agreed-upon aspect of salvation in the Christian tradition has been the "who" of salvation: it is Jesus Christ who saves; everything else is open for discussion.

It is important to emphasize here that this multiplicity is not a weakness.

3. Amy Lynn Miller, "Otherworldly Bureaucracy," in *The Encyclopedia of Taoism*, vol. 1, ed. Fabrizio Pregadio (London: Routledge, 2008), 68.

4. Amy Lynn Miller, "Hell," in Pregadio, *Encyclopedia of Taoism*, 71.

5. Alister E. McGrath, ed., *The Blackwell Encyclopedia of Modern Christian Thought* (Malden, MA: Blackwell, 1998), 616.

6. Grace Jantzen, "Human Diversity and Salvation in Christ," *Religious Studies* 20, no. 4 (1984): 579–80.

Instead, having many ways to describe salvation is a gift, a precious asset of the church in its mission of proclaiming the gospel. Braaten writes:

> The theology of salvation must be as multi-dimensional as the supreme act of God in Christ surely is, involving the entire spectrum of saving events in the Gospel story of Jesus, his birth, his life and teachings, his death and resurrection, his ascension and session at the right hand of God, and his final coming in glory to judge the living and the dead. Soteriology must be multi-dimensional also because it corresponds to the many dimensions of human existence in the world, individual and corporate, and all sorts of needs and conditions. No one theory of redemption can cover the whole story of the relationship between God and the world in the person of the mediator, Jesus Christ.[7]

Salvation in Scripture: The Witness of the Gospels

New Testament interpreters interested in salvation often focus specifically on the passion narrative—Jesus's death and resurrection. However, when we look specifically at the accounts of Jesus's life in the four Gospels, we discover several overarching characteristics and commitments that directly relate to a Christian understanding of salvation. These are features that figure prominently in Jesus's ministry: they stand at the core of how Jesus related to the world around him and how Jesus himself understood his saving mission. They therefore point to Jesus's distinctive embodiment of salvation and the way he lived out the message of God's love he came to share.

The first aspect of Jesus's ministry that needs to be emphasized is the explicit and strong link Jesus makes between loving God and loving one's neighbor, who, for Jesus, is not first and foremost one's in-group but rather the stranger. For Jesus, these two relationships—what we might call the vertical relationship with God and the horizontal relationship with not only other human beings but the whole creation—are fundamentally linked. Furthermore, this love is a key aspect of salvation. So to the one who asks, "What must I do to inherit eternal life?" the answer is, "Sell all that you have and give the money to the poor" (Luke 18). The point of salvation, for Jesus, is not merely assurance of life after death for the individual, but a transformed relationship with God and others in the here-and-now.

Certainly one of the best illustrations of this is the story of Zacchaeus, found in Luke 19. Most people remember the image of a short man climbing a tree to see Jesus, but not everyone remembers the powerful end of the story. After Jesus invites himself over to Zacchaeus's house—breaking the taboo of socializing with tax collectors—Zacchaeus experiences a radical change of heart, offering to give over half his wealth to the poor and pay back four times the

---

7. Braaten, "Christian Doctrine of Salvation," 124.

amount to anyone he has defrauded. In response, Jesus says, "Today salvation has come to this house, because he too is a son of Abraham. For the Son of Man came to seek out and to save the lost" (Luke 19:9). This story demonstrates that Jesus never understood salvation as purely an after-death idea, but rather, in the same way that hell is certainly a present-moment concept, so also is salvation.

The second emphasis of Jesus's ministry can be seen in Jesus's repeated depiction of himself as a seeker of the lost and a healer of the sick. Jesus continually thwarts the attempts of the insiders to corral him for themselves and their own agenda, and instead leaves their company to seek out those whom everyone else has forgotten. Over and over again, Jesus puts aside all the well-behaved sheep in favor of the one little sheep who is out wandering around lost, the righteous Pharisee who has kept the law in all its aspects in favor of the sinner who recognizes his unworthiness, and those who are well in favor of those who are sick. This preferential treatment for the lowliest, the neediest, and the most vulnerable is a leitmotiv of Jesus's entire ministry.

Perhaps the best example of this is the series of "lost" passages—the lost coin, lost sheep, and lost son (better known as the prodigal) found in Luke 15. In this series of stories, a shepherd, a woman, and a father refuse to be content with "almost"—almost all the sheep, almost all the coins, almost all the sons—and instead actively seek (and hold out hope) for the one that others would have given up on long ago. Jesus tells all three of these parables in response to the grumbling of the Pharisees who are offended that Jesus continually "welcomes sinners and eats with them." In his response, Jesus indicates that this act of welcoming the profoundly unwelcome is not a tangential aspect of Jesus's salvific mission in the world; instead it is its center.

Third, and directly related to the previous point, is Jesus's deliberate and repeated association with outsiders. Purity norms were of critical importance during Jesus's time, and it is difficult for most of us in the United States to imagine the kind of ostracism that resulted when one was considered unclean, either literally, like lepers and menstruating women, or figuratively, like prostitutes and tax-collectors. Those individuals were cut off from their communities, often forced to live in isolation, and excluded from religious gatherings. They were, in many cases, "non-persons"—not in the sense of being invisible, but in the sense of being "contaminants" and thus "hyper-visible," in a way.[8] Jesus, however, coveted their company, and to the chagrin of the Pharisees and the dismay of his own disciples, he continually sought them out. He talked with them, touched them, and ate with them, heedless of the fact that he was defiling himself in the process. There are many examples in Scripture that can be referenced here: his scandalous conversation with the Samaritan woman in John 4, the daring act of the woman with the alabaster jar in Luke 7, and the many lepers and demoniacs he approached and cured. Far from

8. Thanks to my colleague Mark Vitalis Hoffman for this description, personal correspondence with the author, March 8, 2016.

protecting his body from pollution by others, he extended his body outward, encompassing and healing the impure with his own purity.

Women and Death in Confucianism

Confucius himself was much more concerned about life than death and did not regularly speculate on life after death. He believed that the most important thing was to focus on life now, finding meaning in the present rather than worrying about death. At the same time, Confucianism affirms that life and death are integrated, that the living and the dead interact. Therefore, the social order and familial responsibilities that govern this life also relate to the practices that govern mourning and burial rituals. Key to these responsibilities are the overarching requirements of filial piety and, in particular, the demands on a son to properly honor his parents. In this system, one of a son's most important duties to his parents is carrying out the proper funerary rites after death. These rites are directly related to the proper performance of filial piety, and there are multiple texts in Confucianism that detail the various rites, specifically the mourning rites and the burial rites. However, one might well ask what this means for women, and what role women play in the funerary rituals.

In a Confucian worldview, it is important to note that the whole notion of "ancestors" focuses primarily on men and men's families. "Insertion into a family line and becoming an ancestor are indeed essential to the process of identity formation in Chinese culture. To be granted ancestor status one must marry and have male heirs. Thus only men, or women who are wives and mothers of sons, are regarded as socially correct and complete persons who will be granted the status of ancestor in the world of the dead."[9] Therefore, when someone dies who has "ancestor" status, this is considered a "good death" and the funeral rites are concerned primarily with shifting "the discontinuity of their biological death into social continuity in such a way that they become ancestors."[10] This is a symbolic way of transforming death into life, since as an ancestor, the individual will live on with a permanent place in the family lineage and an expected give-and-take relationship in which the ancestors bless the lives of their descendants.

A different situation occurs with the death of a child or an unmarried woman. In the latter case, a woman who dies while still in the house of her father—not yet in the house of a husband—dies "at the wrong time and in the wrong place. . . . Dying without a husband, without being incorporated into a male line as an ancestor, deceased maidens are condemned to become homeless and unidentifiable ghosts, extremely polluting and dangerously powerful."[11] Distinct rituals are thus needed in these cases: sometimes Daoist specialists are brought in or fees are paid to allow the ashes of the person to be lodged in a Buddhist temple or pagoda, where sutras can be chanted for her.[12]

The fourth aspect of Jesus's ministry is Jesus's warnings about the "outer darkness," which we find exclusively in the Gospel of Matthew, specifically Matthew 8:12, Matthew 22:13, and Matthew 25:30. (There are a few other places where Jesus warns specifically of *Gehenna*, most notably in the admonition to cut off one's member if it is a cause for stumbling, found in Matthew 18 and Mark 9.) In her book *The History of Hell*, Alice Turner notes that "it is on the Gospel of Matthew that much of the Christian proof of Hell's existence and purpose depends."[13] It certainly is true that there are more direct references in Matthew to what Christians have come to think of as hell than in any other single book in the New Testament. However, the question about these passages, of course, is: What did Jesus mean by the metaphor "outer darkness"? In each case, it is followed by the phrase "where there will be weeping and gnashing of teeth," so clearly Jesus seems to be indicating a place of sorrow and suffering. Yet, is this a future prediction or merely a hypothetical warning (and a call to repent) for those who do not believe? Is Jesus pointing to a place of eternal torment or is he indicating in a more timeless way the sense of anguish that comes with alienation from God and from others? It is not entirely clear, and the same can be said about his warnings about *Gehenna* (the Greek translation of a specific place, the Valley of Hinnom, a place of idolatry and sacrifice). What can be said, however, is that when it comes to salvation, we must assume that Jesus did have at least some sense of its opposite—damnation—as well.

Finally, we must examine the biblical witness regarding Jesus's uniqueness as savior. The Gospels reiterate this repeatedly: Jesus is the way, the truth, the light (John 14:6); he is the gate (John 10:9); the bread of life (John 6:35); the Messiah (Matt 16:16); and the only way to the Father (John 14:6). This is one specific reason why many Christians separate themselves from non-Christians: either you believe in Jesus Christ as the one and only savior, or you do not; and if you do not, you do not fully understand or appreciate who Jesus is.

It should be noted here that while some Christians interpret these passages literally, there are other ways to interpret this exclusive language. For example, in his book *No Other Name?* Paul Knitter describes this "one and only" way of speaking about Jesus as "love language." He compares it to the language a spouse might use in describing her partner as "the only one for me." This may not be literally true, but it speaks to the depth and passion of her commitment to this one particular individual. Knitter suggests that Christians can read this language faithfully as a measure of the disciples' commitment to Jesus (and their own), rather than as an ontological statement about his exclusive ability

9. Fang-Long Shih, "Chinese 'Bad Death' Practices in Taiwan: Maidens and Modernity," *Mortality* 15, no. 2 (May 2010): 123.

10. Ibid., 124.

11. Ibid., 127.

12. Ibid., 129–32.

13. Alice Turner, *The History of Hell* (New York: Harcourt Brace, 1993), 53.

to save.[14] In any case, regardless of how one chooses to interpret these passages, they certainly cannot be overlooked or shunted aside. Through the centuries, they have provided the strongest rationale for those who insist that salvation is only for Christians and who are convinced that the mercy and forgiveness of God comes only through an explicit relationship with Jesus Christ.

SALVATION IN CHRISTIAN HISTORY:
FOUR CLASSIC THEORIES OF ATONEMENT

In the long life of the Christian church, the agent of salvation, the "who," has never been in doubt, but when it comes to the "how," a wide variety of theological motifs and metaphors have been used, both in Scripture and the tradition, to explain the details. Some of these metaphors have focused on Christ's death, others have emphasized the resurrection, and yet others have looked to his incarnation, life, and ministry—even while keeping together the entire arc of Jesus of Nazareth's complete narrative. There are many reasons for this multiplicity, not least because of the experience of the early Christians themselves. Stephen Need writes, "The first Christians were people whose lives had been radically changed through their experience of Jesus. In his life, death and resurrection they had come to see something fundamentally new about God and their relationship with [God]. In [Jesus] the nature of God had been revealed to them and through him they experienced a new sense of salvation."[15] They thus used a variety of different concepts to try and express this new experience—in liturgy first and then in theology[16]—and indeed, these concepts were not seen as mutually exclusive. Throughout the tradition, many theologians, maybe most, maybe all, have used different theories together, even within the same treatise, to help comprehend, at least in part, the incomprehensible: how humanity is reconciled to God, made new, and given eternal life.

These different explications often are called models of atonement, doctrines that elaborate how it is, exactly, that Jesus's life, death, and/or resurrection brought about human salvation. While there exists a wide variety of theories and no definitive list of them all, there are four models that are widespread and found in a variety of places across the geographical and chronological expanse of the church. In the next few pages, these four motifs are briefly introduced in order to demonstrate the range of possibilities for constructive conversation around the "how" of salvation. These four theories are *Christus victor*, *theosis*, moral influence, and penal substitution.

---

14. Paul Knitter, *No Other Name? A Critical Survey of Christian Attitudes Toward the World Religions* (Maryknoll, NY: Orbis Books, 1996), 184–85.

15. Stephen W. Need, *Truly Divine and Truly Human: The Story of Christ and the Seven Ecumenical Councils* (Peabody, MA: Hendrickson, 2008), 14.

16. Jaroslav Pelikan, *The Emergence of the Catholic Tradition (100–600)*, vol. 1 of *The Christian Tradition* (Chicago: University of Chicago Press, 1975), 146.

CHRISTUS VICTOR

One of the earliest discussions of salvation focuses on the cosmic battle between good and evil, between God and the devil, and the way in which that battle was decisively won by God in the resurrection—hence the name *Christus victor*. For those Christians who come out of liturgical traditions, one needs only peruse the Easter section of the hymnal to find familiar language describing this understanding of salvation: "The Strife is o'er, the battle done. . . . The pow'rs of death have done their worst; Jesus their legions has dispersed"; "Thine is the glory, risen, conquering Son; endless is the victory thou o'er death has won"; "O sons and daughters, let us sing with heav'nly hosts to Christ our king: today the grave has lost its sting"; "Christ is risen! Henceforth never death or hell shall us enthrall"; "Christ has crushed the pow'r of hell; now there is naught but death's gray shell—its sting is lost forever." This language celebrates the final vanquishing of the dread powers of nonbeing that threaten human existence, the evil that chains us and keeps us from God.

From these brief hymn excerpts, the contours of this theory should be clear: through its own iniquity, humanity has come under the power of sin, death, and the devil, and finds itself in prison, in bondage, captive to the devil with no hope of escape. Into this desperate situation comes Jesus Christ, a champion to fight on humanity's behalf. He engages the evil powers of the world and triumphs over them, securing human freedom and bringing us back into the safety and protection of God.

There are many variations on this motif, and this theory has been utilized by a wide variety of theologians. It is discussed here in one of its earliest forms, in the theology of Gregory of Nyssa, and then concludes with a nod to John Chrysostom. In his *Great Catechism*, Gregory of Nyssa begins by discussing the state of fallen humanity and the nature of God. Of particular importance for Gregory is God's justice. He recognizes the logical question that Jews and Greeks ask of Christianity: Why, in the face of sin, does God not just "fix it" and by divine fiat restore the world to order and free humanity from its bondage? Surely for an all-powerful God, this should be possible. Gregory concedes that it is. However, God is more than just powerful—God is also wise, good, and just. These attributes are always present together with God's power, and God chooses to exercise God's power only in and through them.[17]

In particular, Gregory expands on the concept of divine justice. The problem is that humanity has "yoked itself" freely to the "enemy of life."[18] Thus it is clear that human beings are in a terrible position with no defense: they have "sold their own liberty for a price" and "are justly slaves of those that bought them, and it is not right for them or for anybody else to claim liberty on their behalf."[19] For Gregory, then, for God to be just means that God must refuse to

---

17. Anthony Meredith, "Oratio Catechetica," ch. 20 in *Gregory of Nyssa* (London: Routledge, 1999), esp. 76.

18. Meredith, *Gregory of Nyssa*, 78.

"use tyrannical power against him who held us in his grasp."[20] Therefore, the only option left is to "buy back" the captives: "once we had sold ourselves freely, the one who was out of his goodness to lead us back again into freedom must think up a method of recall which was not tyrannical but just, and therefore must be one which hallowed the captor to select any ransom he might choose in return for his captive."[21]

It should be no surprise that the price the devil exacts for humanity is costly. In fact, the devil will only be satisfied with a superlative human being, and to this end, the devil is lured by the eminence of Jesus: his virgin birth, his healing powers, his ability to walk on the water, and his ability to go without food. The devil cannot resist this tempting prize and believes that by trading humanity for Jesus, he will gain more than what he already has. Yet, Gregory is clear: the devil knows not what he asks. He sees Jesus's flesh, not his immense divine power, and therefore the devil does not realize he should be afraid. Gregory describes this with a well-known image: "in order that the exchange might be more easily effected, the divine was concealed by the covering of our nature in order that, after the manner of greedy fish, the hook of the deity might be swallowed down along with the bait of the humanity."[22] And then? What God had intended comes to pass. The devil overreaches in his greedy desire to obtain the prize that is Jesus Christ, and by this act, he is undone. His abdomen is split, hell is broken open, and all the captives are released. Victory indeed.

Two critiques of this concept should be noted. First is the idea that the devil somehow has legitimate rights over humanity. This challenge was made first by Gregory of Nazianzus, who characterized the devil as a robber, taking what was never his to begin with. Therefore, a doctrine that stated that the one who is the very embodiment of deceit would have legitimate rights over humanity was abhorrent: "how shameful that the robber should receive not only a ransom from God, but a ransom consisting of God himself, and that so extravagant a price should be paid to his tyranny."[23] For Gregory of Nazianzus, Peter Abelard, and others, this simply could not be.

The second critique can be found in the idea that God would stoop to subterfuge. Anselm and others entirely rejected the possibility that a shadow of darkness and deceit could shade the one who was light and life eternal. Such a deception was impossible for God and unworthy of the divine. The one who is truth itself cannot deceive anyone; it is incompatible with God's nature and therefore unthinkable. Jaroslav Pelikan describes it this way: "Any amount of critical reflection on the notion of salvation by deception had to lead to its rejection as unworthy of a just and holy God. . . . The idea was self-contradictory and hence self-defeating."[24]

---

19. Ibid.
20. Ibid.
21. Ibid., 79.
22. Ibid., 81.
23. J. N. D. Kelly, *Early Christian Doctrines* (San Francisco: HarperSanFrancisco, 1978), 383.

While in much of mainline Christian theology this language of *Christus victor* has fallen out of favor, it is still prevalent in many other Christian denominations; and in one very specific place it remains lively and vivid. It is still typical today in many Eastern Orthodox congregations to hear John Chrysostom's famous Paschal homily during the liturgical celebration of Easter. While Chrysostom did not use "ransom" language like Gregory of Nyssa, he certainly emphasized the victory Christ won in his descent into hell and his vanquishing the powers of evil. It is a fitting conclusion to this section.

> Let no one fear death, for the Savior's death has set us free. He that was held prisoner of it has annihilated it. By descending into Hell, He made Hell captive. He embittered it when it tasted of His flesh. And Isaiah, foretelling this, did cry: Hell, said he, was embittered, when it encountered Thee in the lower regions. It was embittered, for it was abolished. It was embittered, for it was mocked. It was embittered, for it was slain. It was embittered, for it was overthrown. It was embittered, for it was fettered in chains. It took a body, and met God face to face. It took earth, and encountered Heaven. It took that which was seen, and fell upon the unseen.

> O Death, where is your sting? O Hell, where is your victory? Christ is risen, and you are overthrown. Christ is risen, and the demons are fallen. Christ is risen, and the angels rejoice. Christ is risen, and life reigns. Christ is risen, and not one dead remains in the grave. For Christ, being risen from the dead, is become the first fruits of those who have fallen asleep. To Him be glory and dominion unto ages of ages. Amen.[25]

THEOSIS

The concept of *theosis*, sometimes also translated as "deification" or "divinization," points to an idea that was described first in the New Testament, particularly by Paul in his letter to the Romans, and has been developed most thoroughly in the Eastern Orthodox Church. Basically, *theosis* means becoming God-like, sharing in the divine life by being united with Christ in baptism. A key point to emphasize here is that this is only possible because of the incarnation, in which God willingly and freely took on human flesh in love and united the divine with the human in the person of Jesus Christ. This union is the paradigmatic union that facilitates our divination. Athanasius, one of the early church fathers who utilized this idea, had many different phrases to describe it:

24. Jaroslav Pelikan, *The Growth of Medieval Theology (600–1300)*, vol. 3 of *The Christian Tradition* (Chicago: University of Chicago Press, 1978), 135.

25. John Chrysostom, "The Paschal Sermon," Orthodox Church in America, accessed March 13, 2016, http://tinyurl.com/jc9wu7u.

Figure 27: Christ Pantocrator, the classic icon reflecting the two natures of Christ in the two sides of his face.

"The Word became [hu]man so that we might be deified"; "The Son of God became [hu]man so as to deify us in Himself"; and "Because of the Word in us we are sons and gods."[26] Stated more plainly: "God became what we are so that we might become what God is."

This theological doctrine is present in a variety of places in Scripture; most notably, it has been called "the heart of Romans."[27] Specifically for Paul, it refers to "transformative participation in the kenotic, cruciform character of God through the Spirit-enabled conformity to the incarnate, crucified, and resurrected/glorified Christ."[28] For Paul, in this one person, Jesus of Nazareth, the divine life of Christ spreads through all humanity because of the essential interconnectedness of human nature: just as all have sinned in Adam, all are restored in Jesus Christ. We see this in a variety of places, but particularly in Romans 6:3–8:

> Do you not know that all of us who have been baptized into Christ Jesus were baptized into his death? Therefore we have been buried with him by baptism into death, so that, just as Christ was raised from the dead by the glory of the Father, so we too might walk in newness of life. For if we have been united with him in a death like his, we will certainly be united with him in a resurrection like his. We know that our old self was crucified with him so that the body of sin might be destroyed, and we might no longer be enslaved to sin. For whoever has died is freed from sin. But if we have died with Christ, we believe that we will also live with him.

In the Christian tradition, we find the concept of *theosis* in multiple places, notably in the theology of Gregory of Nazianzus, who serves as exemplar in this section. *Theosis* is Gregory of Nazianzus's central soteriological focus, and it is this focus that shapes his Christology.[29] In his understanding of salvation, the Son does not become incarnate merely to be known—that is, merely as a tool of divine revelation. Instead, the incarnation occurred "so that you may ascend from below to become God, because [God] came down from above us."[30]

In his *Orations*, Gregory discusses this idea in detail using a variety of images, all of which emphasize the main point: God and humanity "became a single whole, the stronger side predominating, in order that I might be made God to the same extent that [God] became [human]."[31] To be clear, this is not to be understood ontologically: "one cannot literally 'become God' since that would be as absurd as if we were to state that God is a 'creature.'"[32] Rather, there

26. Kelly, *Early Christian Doctrines*, 378.

27. Michael J. Gorman, "Romans: The First Christian Treatise on Theosis," *Journal of Theological Interpretation* 5, no. 1 (2011): 14.

28. Ibid., 18.

29. Frederick W. Norris, *Faith Gives Fullness to Reasoning: The Five Theological Orations of Gregory Nazianzen*, trans. Lionel R. Wickham and Frederick Williams (Leiden: Brill, 1991), 180–81.

30. Norris, *Faith Gives Fullness*, 181.

31. Ibid., 257, oration 29.19.

is an "exchange" of properties between the divine and the human, which allows for humans to share in the glory of God through their participation in Christ. Gregory writes that God comes to us in order to "make us like God . . . uniting himself with us, making himself known to us, as God to gods."[33]

To explain how this is possible, Gregory uses the metaphor of yeast and dough, saying "[Jesus] bears the title, '[Human]' . . . with the aim of hallowing [humanity] through Himself, by becoming a sort of yeast for the whole lump. He has united with himself all that lay under condemnation, in order to release it from condemnation. For all our sakes he becomes all that we are, sin apart—body, soul, mind, all that death pervades."[34] Gregory also explains it using the contrast between a rich man and a poor man: "He who is rich is a beggar—for he goes begging in my flesh, that I might become rich with his godhead! He who is full has emptied himself—for he emptied himself of his own glory for a while, that I might have a share of his fullness."[35]

Another church father who described salvation this way was Maximus the Confessor, whose work in the seventh century helped solidify orthodox Chalcedonian theology about Christ's two natures. In his introduction to Maximus's work, Jaroslav Pelikan emphasizes the assertion that "the chief idea of St. Maximus, as of all Eastern theology, [was] the idea of deification."[36] Pelikan goes on to offer his description of Maximus's view of salvation: "having been transformed into 'children of God' in this life, believers could anticipate yet a further transformation in the life to come, into a participation in the very nature of God."[37] Maximus's most famous analogy for this process is using a sword thrust into the fire. He writes:

> For it is just like the way the cutting-edge of a sword plunged in fire becomes burning hot and the heat acquires a cutting edge (for just as the fire is united to the iron, so also is the burning heat of the fire to the cutting-edge of the iron, and the iron becomes burning hot by its union with the fire, and the fire acquires a cutting-edge by the union with the iron). Neither suffers any change by the exchange with the other in union, but each remains unchanged in its own being as it acquires the property of its partner in union. So also in the mystery of the divine Incarnation.[38]

---

32. Donald F. Winslow, *The Dynamics of Salvation: A Study in Gregory of Nazianzus* (Cambridge, MA: Philadelphia Patristic Foundation, 1979), 186.

33. Brian E. Daley, *Gregory of Nazianzus* (London: Routledge, 2006), 120, oration 38.7.

34. Norris, *Faith Gives Fullness*, 277, oration 30.21.

35. Daley, *Gregory of Nazianzus*, 124, oration 38.13.

36. Maximus the Confessor, *Maximus Confessor: Selected Writings*, trans. George C. Berthold (New York: Paulist Press, 1985), 10.

37. Ibid.

38. Andrew Louth, *Maximus the Confessor* (London: Routledge, 1999), 178, Difficulty 5, 1060A.

Like Gregory, Maximus makes it clear that *theosis* does not point to a merging or mixing of natures such that there is confusion between the divine and the human: God does not become other than God, nor does the human become other than human. Rather, in the incarnation, God envelops humanity and transforms it from the inside out, pervading every aspect of created nature with God's very being.

Important to note here is that this unification has salvific consequences for more than just humanity. Certainly the question of whether or not creation as a whole needs salvation is contested. Holmes Rolston argues persuasively that if salvation—he uses the language of redemption—can be understood using ideas of regeneration, then the answer is definitively "yes." He writes, "Whatever is in travail needs redemption, whether or not there is any sin to be dealt with."[39] And in Jesus Christ, we see and experience that redemption that occurs for all creation: "seen in the paradigm of the cross, God too suffers, not less than God's creatures, in order to gain for the creatures a more abundant life."[40]

In light of this expectation and this promise, the concept of *theosis* suggests that we can justifiably hope for the salvation and resurrection of the whole creation in that in the incarnation, the divine has been united with the finite, spirit with flesh, heavenly with earthly. Insofar as humanity is physically imbedded in the whole of creation, what is united with the human is united with the earthly—there can be no hard and fast separation here. Thus the salvific, restorative transformation that humanity experiences, all creation experiences as well. Nonna Harrison describes it this way: "When we die our bodies are dissolved and their biological substance is given to other organisms and to the earth. On a biological level, the life that was ours is then given away freely to other beings. This process unites us physically with the creation around us. Hence we can hope that when God raises our bodies from the dead on the last day, the biological and physical world with which they are commingled will be raised with us."[41]

THE HAPPY EXCHANGE

The concept of *theosis*, in that it focuses on Christ's indwelling in us and the transformation of our nature (μεταμορφοω ["be transformed"], Romans 12:2), relates to a number of other important soteriological doctrines, another of which warrants mention here: the concept of the "happy exchange," particularly as it is found in the theology of Martin Luther. In the last few decades, the scholarship of the "Finnish School" of Lutheran theology, led by Tuomo Mannermaa, has emphasized the role of *theosis* in Luther's soteriology, which Mannermaa describes this way: "It is a central idea of Luther's theology

39. Holmes Rolston III, "Does Nature Need to Be Redeemed?," *Zygon* 29, no. 2 (June 1994): 218.
40. Ibid., 220.
41. Nonna Verna Harrison, "Theosis as Salvation: An Orthodox Perspective," *Pro Ecclesia* 6, no. 4 (Fall 1997): 439.

that in faith human beings *really* participate in the person of Christ, and in the divine life and victory that comes with him."[42] For Luther, as with the early church fathers, the foundation of this concept is based on and stems from the *communicatio idiomatum*—the communication of attributes we find between the divine and human natures of Christ.

The paradigmatic place in Luther's work where he elaborates this idea is in his *Treatise on Christian Liberty*. Here, Luther discusses the image of an exchange in the context of the benefits of faith. He writes that one of the central benefits of faith is that "it unites the soul with Christ as a bride is united with her bridegroom."[43] In paralleling the relationship between the believer and Christ to that of a married couple, Luther is making several points. First, the two are one flesh; they are joined together by the power of God, and a mystic union exists between them. Second, everything they have is shared in common, both the good and the evil. By Christ's own choice, the debts of the one are the debts of the other. The merits of the one are the merits of the other. Finally, the marriage is one of love and devotion, and there is only good will and mercy on Christ's side when he joins himself to us. Here, Luther uses the imagery found in Hosea: "this rich and divine bridegroom Christ marries this poor, wicked harlot, redeems her from all evil, and adorns her with all his goodness."[44]

For Luther, all that humanity can lay claim to is "sin, death, and damnation," and the only way humans can obtain "grace, life and salvation" is through an exchange with Christ, in which Christ freely takes on what is ours and gives us what is his. Only in this way can we be said to have justification, righteousness, and reconciliation with God. What we require before God we cannot obtain ourselves. Only because God in Christ gives us what we need do we possess it at all, and only to the degree that we are united to him in faith.

So, to sum up: in the atonement motif of *theosis*, humanity is alienated from God because of corruption or sin and cannot reconcile itself on its own. In divine love, God descends into the human experience and is born there in Jesus Christ. Because of this, Christ's divine nature is also born in us, and each one of us is united with God in loving relationship and empowered through the Holy Spirit to live a Christ-like life, glorifying God and in service to the neighbor. *Theosis*, then, points to a dynamic relationship between God and humanity: "Although we and God are separated as creature and Creator, the gulf in between is not absolute, the distance not infinite. From the time of creation, [hu]mankind and the Creator have been bound together, first by God's creative goodness which called us into being, and subsequently by

---

42. Tuomo Mannermaa, *Christ Present in Faith: Luther's View of Justification*, trans. Kirsi Stjerna (Minneapolis: Fortress Press, 2005), 16.

43. Martin Luther, *A Treatise on Christian Liberty*, trans. W. A. Lambert (Philadelphia: Fortress Press, 1957), 14.

44. Ibid., 15. One salient critique of this metaphor is the way it reifies traditional hierarchical interpretations of marriage and associates women with sexual sin. As with all biblical metaphors, it should be used with care.

the divine *oikonomia* which has ever sought to guide us toward our ordained destiny. . . . This abiding relation between God and humankind is also part of our created nature."[45] Humanity was created for life in and with God; in this metaphor of salvation, that life is realized for us in Jesus Christ.

MORAL EXAMPLE

There is another theory of atonement that also relies on Christ's indwelling presence in the human being and the subsequent transformation this presence creates in us. This theory is typically called "moral example," although that designation is somewhat of a misnomer. The main interpretive problem comes through the word "example," which suggests that the way Jesus saves is by living a morally exemplary life, giving us the "perfect person" on which we should model our own lives, such as by asking the question, "What Would Jesus Do?" when faced with a challenging situation. While there is nothing wrong with viewing Jesus as a model for right human behavior, the problem comes in thinking that a good model is enough to save us. Christian theology has been emphatically clear about this from its very inception: humans cannot save ourselves, even with the very best model as an exemplar. Only God can save. Therefore, to bring about salvation, it is not enough for Jesus to simply show humanity how to live rightly: he has to enable right living, above and beyond our power to do so alone.

One of the first names associated with this theory is Peter Abelard, and one of the places where he explores this idea most clearly is in his commentary on Romans. In this work, Abelard rejects both the idea of God the Father ransoming the Son to the devil for humanity and also Anselm's doctrine that a sacrifice was necessary to restore God's honor (more about that shortly). Instead, Abelard emphasizes God's love as the sole motivation for human salvation and describes Christ's entire history—life, death, and resurrection—as a demonstration of God's love. In his introduction to Abelard's Romans commentary, Steven Cartwright notes that "[Abelard] speaks of Christ's death as a demonstration of the love of God that binds us to [God] through love and that kindles love and causes us to love God more."[46] In his discourse on Romans 3:26, Abelard writes, "Therefore, our redemption is that supreme love in us through the Passion of Christ, which not only frees us from slavery to sin, but gains for us the true liberty of the sons [and daughters] of God, so that we may complete all things by his love rather than by fear."[47] For Abelard, there is one reason and one reason only for Christ's death, the gift and growth of love in our hearts: "he died for us, not for the sake of anything else, unless it was on account of that true freedom of charity to be enlarged in us, namely through

45. Donald F. Winslow, *Dynamics of Salvation*, 187–88.
46. Peter Abelard, *Commentary on the Epistle to the Romans*, trans. Steven R. Cartwright (Washington, DC: The Catholic University of America Press, 2011), 71.
47. Ibid., 168.

this highest love which he showed to us, just as he says, 'No one has greater love than this.'"[48]

This divine love, then, which is within us, cultivates love in us and deepens our own love for God and for others, insofar as we love God in loving them. In his explication of Romans 7:6, Abelard emphasizes that "love of neighbor" necessarily includes love of God, "since we should understand no one more rightly as neighbor or friend than our Maker and Redeemer, from whom we have both ourselves and all good things."[49] The saving love God first has for us, which God has implanted in us, always bears fruit in the world and finds expression in the loving life of a Christian.

For Abelard, it is first and foremost the presence of the Holy Spirit that makes possible acts of love and the cultivation of Christian virtues. Richard Weingart, in his discussion of Abelard's soteriology, writes, "The Holy Spirit gives the Christian all the good obtained by Christ's incarnation and atoning death, sustains him in the participation in that goodness, and provides the means for the perpetual application of Christ's benefits through the sacramental life of the Church."[50] Here we see a connection with a doctrine of *theosis*: for Abelard, this divine love that is infused into the human being and both restores and transforms the soul is not something other than God Godself. Thus this love is "participation in the divine life. . . . The fullness of love poured into [the human] heart is Jesus Christ indwelling the soul."[51] It is this indwelling of Christ that radically re-creates the human soul, inspires the Christian to strive for a life of Christian discipleship, and consoles us with loving intimacy with God.

The primary critique of this theory, and one that persists still today with Abelard's work, is that it is "subjective." This suggests that salvation ends up being at least in part a work of human action; while salvation is a gift from a loving God, it is up to us to realize it in our own lives. Certainly, some of Abelard's language suggests this interpretation. His writing is full of exhortations to put on Christ's virtues, walk in Christ's ways, imitate the good, fight against the devil, and suffer with Christ. When read in isolation, it can sound like Abelard is putting the responsibility for human salvation on us, turning what should be gospel into law, such that what is intended as an inspired response to God's prior love becomes a demand for sinful humanity to fulfill on its own.

However, a persuasive argument can be made that when seen in toto, Abelard's theology does not justify such an interpretation. Weingart states it clearly: "It cannot be repeated too often that Abailard [*sic*] is not a Pelagian. Although he denies that Christ's work is one of appeasement or substitution, he never moves to the other extreme of presenting the atonement as nothing

48. Ibid., 206.

49. Ibid., 247.

50. Richard E. Weingart, *The Logic of Divine Love: A Critical Analysis of the Soteriology of Peter Abailard* (Oxford: Clarendon Press, 1970), 153.

51. Ibid., 157.

more than an inducement for [humanity] to effect [its] own salvation. God in Christ does for [the human] what he cannot do for himself; [God] lifts him from the predicament of sin."[52] The atonement motif of moral influence relies on the transformative power of God's indwelling in human beings in Jesus Christ, who makes it possible for us to live differently, in right relationship with God and others, through participation in the divine life.

SATISFACTION

Some decades before Abelard (1079–1142) came Anselm of Canterbury (1033–1109), a giant in medieval theology, whose articulation of another common model of atonement remains dominant in many Christian denominations still today. The model, called "penal satisfaction," "blood atonement," or "substitutionary atonement," is grounded on one basic idea: humanity has sinned against God (particularly through disobedience), staining God's good, well-ordered world and violating God's honor. Because of this, all humanity deserves to die. Therefore, something is demanded of humanity to make this right: a sacrifice must be made, a debt must be paid, God's honor must be restored. However, humanity has nothing additional to offer to this end, as everything humans are and have already comes from God and belongs to God. How, then, can this rending in the relational fabric of creation be mended?

This is the exact problem that Anselm takes up in his famous treatise *Cur Deus Homo, Why Did God Become Human?* He was seeking to make a rational explanation for the incarnation that anyone would understand, even those who were not Christians. Jaroslav Pelikan explains it this way: "Read as an essay in speculative divinity, the treatise [*Cur Deus Homo*] was a virtuoso performance with few rivals in the history of Christian thought, Eastern or Western; for it proposed to show, 'without paying attention to Christ (*remoto Christo*),' that salvation was impossible except through someone who was simultaneously true God and true [hu]man."[53]

This theory depends on an elaborate, orderly picture of the universe. For Anselm, the universe has a moral order that is dependent upon right relationship with God, and human sin violates that order. Because of this link between our relationship to God and the greater cosmic order, Anselm insists that sin cannot simply be forgiven. There are two reasons for this: First, were sin to be remitted without correcting the fault that it created through some form of payback, the universe would remain in a state of imbalance and estrangement. Second, were humans simply to be forgiven freely, this would create further disorder, and disorder in God's creation suggests a deficiency in either God's power or God's justice.[54] Therefore, there must be a reckoning, and a sacrifice is required.

So, using the language of *Cur Deus Homo*, we are left with the following

---

52. Weingart, *Logic of Divine Love*, 150.
53. Pelikan, *Growth of Medieval Theology*, 107.

Figure 28: A crucifixion scene from an illuminated manuscript, the Ethiopian Gospels, from the Walters Art Museum.

dilemma. There has been a breach in the cosmic order that humans cannot fix because they have nothing more to offer to God than what they already owe, that is, everything. However, the reparation must come on their behalf—God's honor must be restored by an offering on the part of humanity. At the same

54. R. W. Southern, *Saint Anselm and His Biographer* (Cambridge: Cambridge University Press, 1963), 98.

time, this is impossible for humanity and must be accomplished by God because only God can offer something commensurate with the offense that was committed: only God can compensate God. Therefore, the main conclusion is as follows. "Satisfaction for sin can be made only by a God-[Hu]man, able, by His divinity, to give something worthy of God, yet able, by His humanity, to represent [hu]mankind. In other words, salvation and human happiness are possible only through Christ."[55]

Central to Anselm's whole theory of atonement is Christ's full obedience to God's will, even to his death on a cross. Clearly, Christ did not deserve the punishment of death nor was it required of him by God. However, he willingly accepted it for our sake in order to restore God's honor, and it was this free gift that creates that abundance of merit that then cancels out the stain of human disobedience. Alister McGrath argues that the foundation of Anselm's argument is as follows. First, "[Humanity] was created in a state of original justice for eternal felicity." Second, "This felicity requires the perfect and voluntary submission of [hu]man's will to God – i.e. *iustitia*."[56] What Christ did, then, in his submission to God's will, was restore to right balance the order and beauty in God's kingdom. Without Christ's submission, God's honor remains tarnished and God's kingdom cannot be realized. Pelikan writes that what gives Christ's death such great worth was "the utterly voluntary and spontaneous character of Christ's suffering, which was motivated not by any debt but by the honor of the Father and the plight of [hu]mankind. The Father did not force him to undergo such suffering and death, but Christ took it upon himself. His 'obedience' in doing so was addressed to the justice of God, which could not prevail without his dying, not to any necessity imposed upon him."[57]

Anselm uses an interesting metaphor to describe Christ's redemptive act, explicating its comprehensive salvific efficacy. I quote him in full here.

> Suppose, for instance, that there is some king and suppose the whole population of one of his cities, with the exception of a single person, who is nevertheless a member of their race, committed such offences against the king that none of them would be able to escape condemnation to death. Suppose, too, that the one innocent person has such favor with the king that he has the ability, and such love for the guilty ones that he has the desire, to reconcile with the king all those who have confidence in his plan, by means of some service which is most agreeable to the king, and which he will perform on a day set by the decision of the king. And since not all who need to be reconciled are able to assemble on that day, the king, having regard for the great value of that service, grants forgiveness from

---

55. Anselm of Canterbury, *Cur Deus Homo*, trans. Joseph M. Colleran (Albany, NY: Magi Books, 1969), 27.

56. Alister McGrath, *Iustitia Dei*, vol. 1 (Cambridge: Cambridge University Press, 1986), 60.

57. Pelikan, *Growth of Medieval Theology*, 143.

every past fault to all who, before or after that day, acknowledge their desire to seek pardon through that action performed on that day, and to give consent to the agreement that was made there. And should it happen that they again give offence after this pardon, they may obtain pardon anew through the efficacy of the same agreement, on condition that they are willing to make adequate satisfaction and to correct their conduct. No one, however, may enter his palace until the condition of the remission of his faults is fulfilled. Parallel with this illustration, since not all [people] who were to be saved have been present when Christ effected that redemption, so great was the efficacy in His death that its effect reaches even to those who live in other places and times.[58]

While Anselm's personal view is far from universal salvation, the theory itself is quite expansive and recognizes the effectiveness of Christ's salvific work across both time and space. Indeed, if we take his metaphor literally, there is a way in which the act of the one innocent person has completely altered the entire fabric of the city and changed forever the relationships of the people to their king. Once the act has occurred, it becomes the axis around which their lives turn, around which the entire city centers itself. It is, to some degree, an ontological change in the lives of the people: they go from being condemned to being forgiven, from being outcasts to being welcome guests in the king's palace. And, not only is the change good for them, it is good for others, too, even those "who live in other places and times"—their children and their grandchildren, their parents and their grandparents. Anselm recognized that what Christ did, to some degree, reconciled all creation to God, in that it restored the cosmos to order and brought harmony back to the universe.

FEMINIST AND WOMANIST CRITIQUES

There have been significant challenges to this theory, most notably from feminists, womanists, and others who reject the idea of a God who requires the sacrifice of God's own son as appeasement for God's honor. Perhaps the strongest articulation of this idea comes in the work of Rebecca Parker and Rita Nakashima Brock, who charge that such a view is akin to "divine child abuse" and only perpetuates violence, particularly violence against women and children, by implying that such violence is sanctioned by Christian theology.[59] Monica Coleman describes this particular critique this way: "the idea of a father sacrificing a child (on the cross or on an altar) for a greater good, offers

---

58. Anselm, *Cur Deus Homo*, 144–45.

59. Rita Nakashima Brock and Rebecca Ann Parker, *Proverbs of Ashes: Violence, Redemptive Suffering, and the Search for What Saves Us* (Boston: Beacon Press, 2001). See also Joanne C. Brown and Carole R. Bohn, eds., *Christianity, Patriarchy and Abuse: A Feminist Critique* (New York: Pilgrim, 1989).

an example of divine child abuse and domestic violence that contributes to centuries of theological acceptance of abusive patriarchal relationships."[60]

Another problem with this view of salvation is that it valorizes suffering and sacrifice, suggesting that the best way to follow Christ is to suffer, even when that suffering is inflicted unjustly and has nothing to do with one's faith. Mary Streufert argues that this can lead to a "sacrifice of glory, in which sacrifice for its own sake is glorified or the endurance of pain or loss is viewed as an end in itself."[61]

Finally, womanists have argued that putting Christ in the position of a "surrogate" (suffering the death we deserve) recalls the surrogacy experiences of black women during slavery. Delores Williams writes, "Jesus represents the ultimate surrogate figure standing in the place of someone else: sinful humankind. Surrogacy, attached to this divine personage, thus takes on an aura of the sacred. It is therefore altogether fitting and proper for black women to ask whether the image of a surrogate God has salvific power for black women, or whether this image of redemption supports and reinforces the exploitation that has accompanied their experience with surrogacy."[62]

These critiques are valuable and significant, and should stand as a warning against anyone who would too easily embrace the idea that there is "power in the blood." To close this section with a return to hymnody—this time from the Lenten section of the hymnal—the Christian church must state only with care that "through your suff'ring, death and merit life eternal I inherit"; that "in the cross of Christ I glory"; and it "was for sins that I had done he groaned up on the tree." This all-too-familiar language can have devastating consequences if not properly interpreted.

THE "SO WHAT" OF SALVATION:
LIFE, DEATH, AND WHAT COMES AFTER

With these models of salvation as background it is now time to return to the pressing concern that opened this chapter: the desire for a fresh articulation of salvation that addresses the practical "So what?" question: "How does salvation really matter in the daily life of a Christian?" It is a critical question and the one addressed in this final section of the chapter. Certainly, there are some Christians who emphasize the answer that has dominated practical Christian soteriological reflection for centuries: first and foremost, "being saved" means "being saved from hell"; the primary benefits of salvation come after death, when one receives the reward of heaven rather than the punishment of hell.

60. Monica A. Coleman, "Sacrifice, Surrogacy and Salvation: Womanist Reflections on Motherhood and Work," *Black Theology* 12, no. 3 (November 2014): 203.

61. Mary Streufert, "Maternal Sacrifice as a Hermeneutics of the Cross," in *Cross Examinations*, ed. Marit Trelstad (Minneapolis: Fortress Press, 2006), 64.

62. Delores S. Williams, "Black Women's Surrogacy Experience and the Christian Notion of Redemption," in Trelstad, *Cross Examinations*, 27–28.

However, for many people today, this answer is unsatisfactory; more specifically, it is "meaning-less"; not in the sense that it is worthless but rather that it literally has no meaning—makes no sense—for countless numbers of people today who do not even believe in hell, let alone fear it. It has contributed to the idea that Christianity is a relic of a past era and has no constructive bearing on one's life in the here-and-now, no purpose, no function beyond an insurance policy against a possible negative future reality.

Therefore, a reinterpretation, a reimagining of a Christian doctrine of salvation is in order. What I suggest here, then, is a new narrative of salvation, which goes something like this:

- All humanity is separated from God, each other, and the whole creation, due to both a fundamental orientation toward and specific actions of disdain, indifference, selfishness, and cruelty—all expressions of sin.
- Jesus Christ came into the world, lived, died, and was resurrected to bring humanity and the whole world into the relational being of God, thereby restoring and revitalizing the bonds of love between God, humanity, and creation.
- In Christ's eternal, vibrant abiding with us—and with the whole creation—through the power of the Holy Spirit, humanity is transformed, making possible a new life that is grounded in the welcome of the stranger, the love of the neighbor, and the work for justice and peace for all.

This retelling of a Christian narrative of salvation not only has the potential to make the gospel message that "Jesus saves" more relevant in a twenty-first-century context, it also makes possible creative, positive dialogue with people of other religious traditions and no religious tradition, while still remaining faithful to the core narrative that stands at the heart of Christianity. It is welcoming instead of exclusionary, it is loving instead of judgmental, and it is expansive rather than limiting. I now explore the contours and consequences of this narrative under three related headings: life, death, and what comes after.

LIFE: SALVATION IN THE HERE AND NOW

One of the most important ramifications of this new narrative is the way in which it makes salvation a present reality, not merely a distant promise. Too often, a Christian doctrine of salvation has led to quietism and passivity in the face of injustice: "You are suffering now? Bear your cross, and trust that you will be rewarded in heaven." Heaven, then, becomes a panacea for all that is wrong with the world now and encourages a disregard for life today in favor of an exclusive focus on life tomorrow. This is a false choice. Instead, the promise of the coming resurrection gets its power from the in-breaking of the kingdom of God, an in-breaking embodied in Jesus himself. In this view, heaven is not merely something we experience after death, but a reality that comes to us today.

This is not a new idea. Instead, it finds its inception (at least in a New Testament context) in the Gospel of Luke. Mark Allan Powell argues that "Luke emphasizes salvation as a reality to be experienced here and now,"[63] and he goes on to elaborate his argument persuasively. He writes that most of the time,

> the focus of salvation in Luke's Gospel is on the quality of life that God enables people to have in the present. Many scholars have said that Luke envisions salvation as primarily liberation (4:18). People need to be set free from certain things in order to experience life as God intends. Some people are ill and need to be healed; others are possessed by demons and need to be exorcized. Luke's Gospel uses the Greek word for "salvation" in describing what Jesus does for these people (e.g., 6:9; 8:36, 48, 50; 17:19; 18:42). Likewise, when Jesus tells Zacchaeus that salvation has come to his house (19:9), his main point is probably not that Zacchaeus will go to heaven when he dies, but rather that Zacchaeus has been set free from slavery to mammon and is now able to experience life as God intends.[64]

Let me reiterate the point Powell is making here: for Luke, salvation is not an after-death reality, but rather the real-life, real-time experience of being healed, being set free, and most importantly, encountering Jesus as savior. Furthermore, this proffered restoration is not only for the individual, but for the whole community. So, like the hemorrhaging woman in Luke 8, whose salvation comes not merely in the cessation of the flow of blood but in her ability to take her rightful place in her community, for all people, salvation is a communal reality that creates and reinforces bonds of love between the whole human family and all of creation. It makes possible "life together" in a radically new way that is both surprising and grace-filled. What was true for Luke's audience, then, is still true today: "Christians should experience the consequences and manifestations of God's saving power here and now rather than simply waiting for Christ to rescue them from an imperfect world or longing for bliss in a life to come."[65]

THE CONCEPT OF PROLEPSIS

Theologically, one of the most helpful categories for thinking about this is the concept of prolepsis, which is a central theological locus for twentieth-century theologian Wolfhart Pannenberg. In a theological context, prolepsis points to

---

63. Mark Allan Powell, *Introducing the New Testament: A Historical, Literary, and Theological Survey* (Grand Rapids: Baker Academic, 2009), 161.

64. Ibid., 161–62.

65. Ibid., 162–63.

an anticipatory experience of a future reality: a "foretaste of the feast to come," a vision of something "now" whose fullness awaits in the "not yet." Pannenberg utilizes this concept of prolepsis in his understanding of salvation, describing salvation in Jesus Christ as both present already in the dawning rule of God but also still to come in a future consummation that is linked with reconciliation and deliverance. In his description of the biblical witness, Pannenberg writes, "In and by Jesus future salvation is opened up for believers and can be attained now."[66]

Thus for Pannenberg, eternal life with Christ involves the "interlacing of historical future and hidden present in the eternity of God."[67] In accordance with the biblical witness, even while we anticipate a life after death, in the meantime we can indeed trust the proclamation of Jesus Christ that in him the kingdom of God has drawn near, and we participate in salvation insofar as our lives are joined with his. This is a reality that happens now, a transformation that has occurred and does occur in our lives today. We do not have to wait for this transformation or question its veracity. Our new life has dawned in Jesus Christ now.

However, there is another dimension to salvation as well. Pannenberg writes, "As we praise God for the dawning of his eschatological salvation in Jesus, so also we yearn and pray for the completion of that salvation."[68] It is not too difficult to realize that the full consummation of the promised salvation has not yet happened. We look around and we see a world that is still broken, lives and relationships that are still bound by the power of sin. Thus we recognize that the fullness of salvation is yet to come. What happened to Jesus will happen to us, but not right away. We still have our lives to live and our deaths to experience. We cannot bypass our history. We live in a present that has been transformed by God's great act of love for the world, and yet we also live in hope for the future, when that act will finally be fully realized and perfected. Again Pannenberg: "salvation is linked to the future of God, which is already present in this world in Jesus Christ, though its consummation is still ahead."[69]

HOPE, LOVE, AND THE STRUGGLE AGAINST INJUSTICE

One of the most important ramifications of this idea is the way it empowers us to struggle against injustice, oppression, and the forces of evil, even when the odds seem overwhelmingly stacked against us. The Christian hope in which we live sees not merely the incompleteness of life as it is now but also what is to come, and so it infuses us with the confidence that life will be transformed.

66. Wolfhart Pannenberg, *Systematic Theology*, vol. 2, trans. Geoffrey W. Bromiley (Grand Rapids: Eerdmans, 1994), 400.

67. Wolfhart Pannenberg, *The Apostles' Creed in the Light of Today's Questions*, trans. Margaret Kohl (Philadelphia: Westminster Press, 1972), 173.

68. Wolfhart Pannenberg, *Theology and the Kingdom of God* (Philadelphia: Westminster Press, 1969), 92.

69. Pannenberg, *Systematic Theology*, 2:402.

Hope looks to the promise of new life in Christ and takes strength from that promise, enabling us to envision something better, something greater, not only for ourselves but for the whole world. In that sense, true Christian hope has a universal focus.

Christian hope is hope for humanity and hope for creation. Therefore, "Christian hope, then, is not such as individuals cherish only for themselves. The imparting of hope by faith in Jesus Christ frees us from this imprisonment in self and lifts us above the self. Faith thus gives rise to a hope that is concerned not merely about one's own well-being but is bound up with the cause of God in the world that has the salvation of all humanity as its goal and embraces the believer's I only in this broad context."[70] For this reason, every time we are moved to action by the suffering and oppression in the world, every time our hearts stir with righteous indignation, and every time our spirit sighs, knowing there must be more than this, we recognize that hope that lives within us, giving us courage in the struggle both through the presence of salvation now and the trust in the salvation that is to come.

Hope, then, also is related to love, and love is perhaps the most universal and most common way we experience this promised salvation in our existence now. This experience comes primarily in two ways: in the love of neighbor and the love of God. To be sure, these are not two separate experiences, only two different ways of living out the same reality. Even though we can never enter into perfect communion with another because of human sin, we still retain the ability to sustain deep, meaningful relationships that have the power to transform our lives. While it is true we both possess and exercise the capacity to hurt the very ones we love the most, in Christ we also have been given the capacity to give ourselves wholeheartedly to another and receive another wholeheartedly as well. Through the power of the Holy Spirit, we have the capacity to put ourselves at risk, physically and emotionally, for the well-being of both friends and strangers.

As God first loved and continually loves us, we then can and do love across all borders and nationalities, across boundaries of race and class, and our capacity to include more and more people in our love is endless. This love that encompasses us is the very being of God, and through our love, we experience God both as present reality and promise. Both our love of neighbor and our love of God reveal this dual aspect of our salvation. "In love of God, as a response that the Holy Spirit makes possible to the love received from God, we have a part in the intratrinitarian life of God, in the mutuality of fellowship between Father, Son, and Spirit. By love of neighbor we take part in the movement of the trinitarian God toward the creation, reconciliation, and consummation of the world."[71] Love motivates our actions and our prayers and is the most powerful form our participation in our salvation takes in the here and now—a

70. Pannenberg, *Systematic Theology*, vol. 3, trans. Geoffrey W. Bromiley (Grand Rapids: Eerdmans, 1998), 179.
71. Ibid., 193.

love so strong that it enables us to lay down our lives for friends, for strangers, and, of course, for God.

Martyrdom in Sikhism

Many, if not most religions have some concept of martyrdom: "heroic death with the hope of posthumous recognition and anticipated reward."[72] Martyrs offer a witness to others and a spur to others' fidelity, and they galvanize a religious community and solidify a group identity. What is important, then, is not the means of death but the reason: "martyrdom depends not upon the fact or the manner of one's death, but rather on the cause for which the martyr died."[73]

Sikhism is no different, and since at least the late seventeenth century, the idea of martyrdom has been described and elaborated in various Sikh texts. In Sikhism, the first text to explicitly include the concept of martyrdom is the *Bachitar Natak*, written by Guru Gobind Singh. In describing the death of the ninth guru, Guru Tegh Bahadur, the text affirms that a person will enter heaven if he sacrifices himself for the "sake of righteousness."[74]

It can be argued that martyrdom has a special place in the Sikh religion, where bravery and strong resistance against all odds, even to death, are central values.[75] The specific Indian context in which Sikhism developed played no small part in that valuation, given that Sikhs have experienced extreme persecution by both Muslim and Hindu governments over the centuries. Thus for Sikhs, martyrdom is linked to the protection of the Sikh community, the Khalsa Panth, and the defense of *dharam*, righteousness, morality, and religious duty.

Still today in many Sikh communities, the martyr (*sahid*) is highly revered: "an unambiguous exemplar of virtue, truth, and moral justification."[76] Similarly, the idea of martyrdom (*sahadat*) established very early in the tradition by Guru Nanak, is considered to be one of the founding components of the faith. Traditionally, the first and foundational Sikh martyr is considered to be Guru Arjan, who was martyred in 1606 by the Mughal emperor Jahangir. The story is told that Guru Arjan refused to convert to Islam in spite of repeated torture, and he is said to have recited hymns even while hot sand was being poured over his body as he sat on a steel plate in the scorching Indian summer. The importance of this event, and the narrative that has grown up around it, cannot be overstated: "It is this notion of the Sikh martyr calmly embracing death, attributed to Arjun Dev, which looms large in the Sikh imagination."[77]

---

72. Louis E. Fenech, "Martyrdom and the Execution of Guru Arjan in Early Sikh Sources," *Journal of the American Oriental Society* 121, no. 1 (January/March 2001): 22.

73. Ibid., 30.

74. Ibid., 25.

DEATH: SALVATION IN THE FACE OF SUFFERING

If anything seems to repudiate a Christian doctrine of salvation, it is death, and perhaps even more, the pain and suffering that often accompany it. Yet, in St. Francis of Assisi's famous Canticle of the Sun, the fifth verse reads as follows:

> And you, most gentle sister death,
> waiting to hush our final breath:
> Alleluia! Alleluia!
> Since Christ our light has pierced your gloom,
> fair is the night that leads us home.
> Alleluia! Alleluia! Alleluia! Alleluia![78]

How can Francis call death a "gentle sister"? Is there a way that Christian theology can affirm such a claim, in light of the dominant train of thought that argues otherwise?

Throughout the Christian tradition, and certainly in Scripture, the argument is repeatedly made that death is a consequence of sin and one of the enemies to be overcome in salvation. Thus many Christians have presumed that in creation—in the metaphorical "garden"—the intention was that humanity would be immortal. However, it is worth interrogating this idea and asking whether or not immortality actually is "natural" for human beings.

Asking if immortality is natural is another way of asking if humans were created that way, if that was God's intent for humanity. That is, is immortality part of our created goodness? In his analysis of sin and death, Wolfhart Pannenberg makes a very interesting and helpful distinction: he distinguishes "death" from "finitude."[79] Pannenberg notes that "the inner logic of the link between sin and death as Paul stated it arises on the presupposition that all life comes from God. Since sin is turning from God, sinners separate themselves not only from the commanding will of God but also from the source of their own lives."[80] So, the biblical view, and the one developed most consistently and thoroughly in the Christian tradition, emphasizes that it is our alienation from God that results in our death, and thus death is the punishment we have earned through our disobedience and waywardness. What logically stands behind this, then, is the idea that we were created *not* to die—that is, we were created to live

75. Paul Brass, "Victims, Heroes or Martyrs? Partition and the Problem of Memorialization in Contemporary Sikh History," *Sikh Formations* 2, no. 1 (June 2006): 20.

76. Fenech, "Martyrdom," 625.

77. Rory G. McCarthy, "Martyrdom and Violence in Sikhism," in *Religious Innovation in a Global Age: Essays on the Construction of Spirituality*, ed. George N. Lundskow (Jefferson, NC: McFarland, 2005), 264.

78. Evangelical Lutheran Church in America and Evangelical Lutheran Church in Canada, *Evangelical Lutheran Worship* (Minneapolis: Augsburg Fortress, 2006), hymn #835.

79. This argument takes shape in Pannenberg, *Systematic Theology*, 2:265–75.

80. Ibid., 2:266.

forever, and it was only because of the sin of our first parents that death entered human existence.

However, what Paul refers to as death seems to encompass more than a final extinguishing of breath, and in fact, that final last breath may be more symbolic than literal here. For Paul, "death" refers to what we experience every day as we choose darkness over light, falsehood over truth, money over God, selfishness over altruism, and so on. Death is something that we bring on ourselves as we try to save ourselves, secure ourselves, preserve ourselves at the expense of our true life with God and with others. As "the wages of sin," then, death is not first and foremost a final punitive end of human life but rather a daily reality, a constant temptation, a looming shadow that always seeks to pull us back into the gloom of our own miserly misery. Thus death is less about the natural end of our mortal lives and more about the power of sin to drain away life from us at every moment and to make us fear and resist that which is an inherent aspect of all life on earth, including human life. Pannenberg writes, "only the nonacceptance of our own finitude makes the inescapable end of finite existence a manifestation of the power of death that threatens us with nothingness. The fear of death also pushes us more deeply into sin."[81]

This reorientation of a Christian understanding of death is particularly important in the twenty-first century in light of what we know about humanity and the world from science, specifically from the theory of evolution. Again, Pannenberg says it well: "For death seems to be an ineluctable consequence of our finitude, not our sin. All multiple-cell life must die. It is not just that organisms age and wear out. They also must make way for future generations. Life cannot go on without the death of individuals."[82] In this respect, humans are not different from every other creature God has made in goodness and love. With us, as with them, finitude is hardwired into our very existence. God is immortal—better said, God is timeless—but we are not. We are not the Creator, we are the creation, and creation is inherently bound by the limits of both time and space. Our finitude, then, the simple fact of our mortality, is not the result of sin, it is the result of God's ongoing creative process that brought us, together with the whole universe, into being and has sustained the universe through billions of years of evolution.

DEEP INCARNATION

One helpful theological formulation that reiterates how humans stand within creation, not over and above it, is Niels Gregersen's concept of "deep incarnation." Gregersen describes this idea as follows:

> "Deep incarnation" is the view that God's own Logos (Wisdom and Word) was made flesh in Jesus the Christ in such a comprehensive

81. Ibid., 2:273.
82. Ibid., 2:271.

manner that God, by assuming the particular life story of Jesus the Jew from Nazareth, also conjoined the material conditions of creaturely existence ("all flesh"), shared and ennobled the fate of all biological life forms ("grass" and "lilies"), and experienced the pains of sensitive creatures ("sparrows" and "foxes") from within. Deep incarnation thus presupposes a radical embodiment that reaches into the roots (*radices*) of material and biological existence as well as into the darker sides of creation: the *tenebrae creationis*.[83]

This concept of "deep incarnation" reminds us that, in Christ, God entered into the whole of creation and united all beings with God, redeeming the entire material universe in the process. This vision of incarnation, then, radically changes how we view human identity. Elizabeth Johnson describes it this way: "The landscape of our imagination expands when we realize that human connection to nature is so deep that we can no longer completely define human identity without including the great sweep of cosmic development and our shared biological ancestry with all organisms in the community of life."[84] Humanity shares cosmic finitude as a part of our creatureliness—not as a result of our sin.

The theological implications of this are profound and stand firmly against all human attempts to set itself over and against the rest of creation, declaring some human exceptionalism that would hold us apart from all other created life. This insistence on privileging humanity, and an ideal of human immortality, above the rest of creation is an expression of sin: an unwillingness to be dependent, a refusal of relationship, and a rejection of God's grace that comes to us through our nonhuman brothers and sisters. It also contributes to the unfounded idea that while death is the natural end for all the rest of creation, it is not the natural end for humanity. Darwin's theory of evolution strongly suggests otherwise, and here a theological engagement of that theory provides an additional avenue into a rethinking of a Christian understanding of death.

DEATH AND EVOLUTION

In her book *Ask the Beasts: Darwin and the God of Love*, Elizabeth Johnson emphasizes that death is an integral component to life as we know it on earth; life and death are inextricably bound in a symbiotic relationship. She writes, "Like pain and suffering, death is indigenous to the evolutionary process. . . . The time-limit that ticks away in all living organisms and ends with their death is deeply structured into the creative advance of life."[85] Evolution simply cannot

83. Niels Henrik Gregersen, "The Extended Body of Christ: Three Dimensions of Deep Incarnation," in *Incarnation: On the Scope and Depth of Christology*, ed. Niels Henrik Gregersen (Minneapolis: Fortress Press, 2015), 225–26.

84. Elizabeth Johnson, *Ask the Beasts: Darwin and the God of Love* (London: Bloomsbury, 2014), 195–96.

happen without death—countless deaths of individuals, even deaths of species; the creation both of new forms of life and also advanced forms of life demands it. The ramifications for humanity are clear: "Historically speaking, once life emerged there never was a literal garden of Eden or a paradise on this planet where death did not exist."[86] Or, perhaps another way to say it is that the metaphor of the Garden of Eden, as a moment of perfect relationship outside of time, may work well for describing sin and alienation from God, but it does not work well for describing the ongoing creative work of God present in gene mutation, natural selection, and environmental adaptation. When seen from the perspective of sin, death certainly seems malevolent, but when seen from the perspective of evolution, death is "morally neutral."[87]

Of course, there are aspects of death that are not neutral: violent death at the hands of a friend or stranger, death that comes too early in the form of a car accident, death caused by environmental degradation and pollution, death from starvation caused by war—all of these certainly have a component of human sin. Undoubtedly, insofar as death comes by human carelessness, neglect, evil, and selfishness it is to be strenuously combated. But these terrible experiences do not justify the conclusion that death in and of itself is an evil to be avoided at all costs. To live is to die, every moment, and all life stands on the bones of the dead. One day, when sister death comes for us, our bones will be added to this foundation and life will go on, both for those still to come on earth and for us, too, beyond the grave.

Death and the Navajo People

All religions have particular beliefs around death, which include the relationship between the living and the dead, and the means by which one moves from life to death to what comes after. Typically, these beliefs relate directly to human origin stories and also the views about the overarching rules and regulations that govern human life. So, for example, in the creation story of the Navajo (Diné) people, it is said that Coyote, a trickster figure, subverted the attempt of the first humans to live forever by substituting a stone for a piece of wood in a planned water ritual. The stone sank, and by this action the cycle of life as we know it today, including death, became a reality. One thing that the Diné take from this story is that "this world is perilous, and the potential for illness and death is great."[88]

One of the most important principles that shape the life of the Diné is hózhó, which points to a state of balance, a harmonious existence that encompasses all aspects of life. This is the state people work to achieve, as it brings order, peace, and beauty—both for individuals and for the community.

---

85. Ibid., 184.
86. Ibid.
87. Ibid., 185.

Hózhó also incorporates and includes specific rites and rituals around death and dying, which typically are not talked about among the *Diné*, as it is believed that doing so actually can create a pathway by which disease and death might occur: "*Diné* are taught to avoid talking about these topics to prevent any disease becoming overly familiar with the discussants or with those they care about."[89]

Traditionally, once a person died, the burial rites were to take place quickly. There was a sense of apprehension when someone died and the fear that the spirit of the person would return back to this world. Thus upon death, the person was to be dressed in their finest clothes and prepared for a journey, along with any possible possessions they might need. In the past, a horse was also killed, which the spirit could ride on their journey to the next world. The person was buried quickly and the rest of their clothes were burned. Those who took part in the burial had to go through a purification process before they could return to their homes. Additionally, there was a four-day mourning period, after which the person's name was no longer spoken to ensure that their spirit would not be called back into the lives of the living.[90]

In the twenty-first century, however, the *Diné* incorporate a variety of different rituals that have come to them through Christianity, Judaism, and Buddhism. For example, many *Diné* belong to the Native American Church (NAC), which combines Protestant and traditional beliefs and practices and includes the use of peyote. Thus today, there is often a longer period between death and burial, which can include a time of storytelling, a wake, and/or a public funeral service.

WHAT LIES BEYOND: SALVATION AND ETERNAL LIFE

What is going to happen to us after we die, and more specifically, what will heaven be like? This question has proved irresistible for many Christians, and it is the subject of countless books, movies, and television shows. We get hints in Scripture but nothing definitive. There are some suggestions, of course, some of which have become very well known: the image of the Peaceable Kingdom in Isaiah 11, with the wolf and the lamb living together and a straw-eating lion being led by a little child; the picture of a New Jerusalem in Revelation 21, a golden, jeweled city, with a river flowing through its center lined by bountiful fruit trees; and finally, Isaiah's vision of God enthroned in heaven, surrounded by angels singing God's praise. However, even while offering a tantalizing variety of attractive descriptions, Scripture clearly cautions us against excess certitude as well. What we can know about what awaits us after death

88. Lawrence Shorty and Ulrike Wiethaus, "Diné (Navajo) Narratives of Death and Bereavement," in *Bereavement and Death Rituals*, vol. 3 of *Religion, Death, and Dying*, ed. Lucy Bregman (Santa Barbara, CA: Praeger, 2010), 174.

89. Ibid., 178.

90. Ibid., 180.

pales in comparison to what we do not know, and we are repeatedly reminded that there are undoubtedly surprises in store.

For example, in 1 Corinthians 15, Paul speaks about our resurrection with confidence but also with some qualifications. He talks about a "spiritual body," an inherently contradictory term that is meant to signal deep disjunction with the bodies we have now; to be sure, we will have a body, but at the same time, "flesh and blood cannot inherit the kingdom of God" (1 Cor 15:50). How does Paul explain this? "Listen, I will tell you a mystery! We will not all die, but we will all be changed, in a moment, in the twinkling of an eye, at the last trumpet. For the trumpet will sound, the dead will be raised imperishable, and we will be changed. For this perishable body must put on imperishability and this mortal body must put on immortality" (1 Cor 15:51–53). Surely we will be raised, surely we will live again, but what that new life in heaven will look like is almost beyond our imagining now.

Related to this, and more generally, we might think of Jesus's kingdom proclamations, which also manage to combine optimism with surprise in almost equal doses. In Matthew, Mark, and Luke (and a few times in John), Jesus speaks generally about the "kingdom of God." But thirty-one times in the Gospel of Matthew, Jesus talks specifically about the "kingdom of heaven," and uses a wide array of surprising similes to imagine it. The kingdom of heaven is like the master of a household (Matt 13:52), a merchant in search of fine pearls (Matt 13:45), a net thrown into the sea (Matt 13:47), a sower of seed (Matt 13:24) and the seed itself (Matt 13:31), yeast (Matt 13:33), a hidden treasure (Matt 13:44), a king (Matthew 22), a landowner (Matthew 20), and a wedding banquet with five foolish and five wise bridesmaids (Matthew 25).

In these images, we are given to understand that Jesus sees as an important part of his mission the announcement of a new reign of God, a reign that paradoxically has both already come near and yet still will come in fullness after death. And, insofar as this kingdom proclamation reveals something about how Jesus understood salvation, we can surmise that he wanted to convey both the surprising nature of heaven and also the surprising character of the people who would be found there. Whatever heaven is like, according to Jesus, it upends all traditional religious assumptions and all traditional patterns of social interaction. It is a party like no one on earth has ever thrown or ever attended, a wedding feast with the most expansive, creative seating chart imaginable.

"WHEN DEATH COMES"

What then are we to think? Or, perhaps better yet, what is the disposition, the posture we are invited to assume around these future possibilities? How do we walk the fine line between overweening certitude and hopeless ignorance? A rich, provocative poem by Mary Oliver titled "When Death Comes" suggests one such disposition.

When death comes
like the hungry bear in autumn;
when death comes and takes all the bright coins from his purse

to buy me, and snaps the purse shut;
when death comes
like the measle-pox;

when death comes
like an iceberg between the shoulder blades,

I want to step through the door full of curiosity, wondering:
what is it going to be like, that cottage of darkness?

And therefore I look upon everything
as a brotherhood and a sisterhood,
and I look upon time as no more than an idea,
and I consider eternity as another possibility,

and I think of each life as a flower, as common
as a field daisy, and as singular,

and each name a comfortable music in the mouth,
tending, as all music does, toward silence,

and each body a lion of courage, and something
precious to the earth.

When it's over, I want to say: all my life
I was a bride married to amazement.
I was the bridegroom, taking the world into my arms.

When it's over, I don't want to wonder
if I have made of my life something particular, and real.
I don't want to find myself sighing and frightened,
or full of argument.

I don't want to end up simply having visited this world.[91]

Oliver begins her poem imagining the moment "when death comes": like a
ravenous bear, like a greedy merchant, like a ravaging disease, like a stabbing,

---

91. When Death Comes - from *New and Selected Poems,* by Mary Oliver, published by Beacon Press,
Boston, Copyright © 1992 by Mary Oliver. Reprinted by permission of the Charlotte Sheedy Literary
Agency Inc.

icy blow. Then, she postulates how she wants to greet this moment, and, given the unpleasantness of the shock she envisions, her response is amazing. Rather than resisting or running away, she describes a stepping forward, a letting go that is full of wonder and anticipation: "I want to step through the door full of curiosity, wondering: what is it going to be like, that cottage of darkness?" And then the poem takes a beautiful, startling turn: from being poised to step across the threshold into another realm, the poet turns back, and describes what this hopeful curiosity means for her life now, today. "And therefore I look upon everything as a brotherhood and a sisterhood." In the shadow of the doorway into death, she sees the preciousness of each ordinary life, the familiar melody of each individual name, and the beauty of each strange and wonderful body. Musing on death, she sees life, and the whole world is full of delight, full of treasure, full of miracle.

What is clear in the poem is that it is her thoughts on death and the uncertainty that awaits, even in the face of her curious confidence, that spurs her love for life, her desire to drink it all in, taste everything, feel everything, rejoice in everything: "When it's over, I want to say all my life I was a bride married to amazement. I was the bridegroom, taking the world into my arms." In the face of death, there is really only one fear, only one regret she voices: "I don't want to end up simply having visited this world." That would be the greatest mistake: to have used death and what comes after as an excuse to merely pass through this life, rather than building a home in this world and enjoying it to the fullest.

For Oliver, imagining life after death does not lead to a disparagement or a disregard for life now, in fact, it is just the opposite. She translates any hope she has for the future into love and care for the present, any inquisitiveness about what lies ahead into tenderness and affection for what lies around her now. This combination of future optimism and present loving engagement seems to be the best course of action a hopeful Christian can take—and aren't all Christians hopeful Christians, by definition? Presuming so, it is with "hope" that I conclude this chapter.

CONCLUSION: DARE WE HOPE?

Certainly, serious questions remain around many aspects of salvation, most notably, perhaps, the scope of salvation, or more specifically, the possibility of "universal salvation," what the tradition has called *apokatastasis*. Since the very inception of the church, there have been theologians who have argued this possibility on the grounds of God's loving nature, the insistence of God's grace, and a literal interpretation of the biblical witness that "every knee shall bow" at the name of Jesus Christ. At the same time, of course, there have been theologians who have argued just as strongly against this possibility, citing God's respect of human freedom to reject God, the depth of human sin that warrants the damnation of all humanity, and the scriptural witness that seems to threaten nonbelievers with eternal punishment. And, even with those who argue for a "populated" hell (as opposed to a theoretical, empty one), there are varying opinions: Are those in hell conscious of their punishment? Are unrepentant sinners annihilated, such that they simply cease to exist upon death? Is one's time in hell permanent or after a period of punishment, are some "translated" into heaven?[92] None of these questions is easily answered.

In the midst of what can often become extremely contentious debates, and in light of the fact that absolute knowledge on this side of the veil eludes us all, it is both justifiable and most appropriate to conclude on a note of hope, specifically the tone sounded in the work of theologian Hans Urs von Balthasar. In *Dare We Hope "That All Men Be Saved"?*, Balthasar does not attempt to lay out a comprehensive doctrine of universal salvation, simply because he believes that no one can know for sure about anyone's salvation: these "last things" are solely under the purview of God. However, what he does argue is that even if Christians cannot know definitively about the salvation of another, they can and should hope that everyone is saved. Hoping, he makes clear, is different from knowing: "Certainty cannot be attained, but hope can be justified."[93]

His argument proceeds as follows. First, he challenges the assumption that it is an irrefutable ontological fact that hell both exists and that it is populated—whether to a greater or lesser degree. He argues that it is Augustine who first interpreted the biblical witness to mean that Christians know for certain the outcome of divine judgment, which is that some people must be in hell. This is different, obviously, from considering the possibility that hell exists, and the possibility that some people might end up there. Balthasar says that with Augustine, "real possibility" became "objective certainty," and for this, Balthasar argues, there is no theological justification. He writes, "How does Augustine know that there are [people] who are damned? God has revealed nothing of the sort to us, has given us no list of names. Jesus teaches us only, but clearly and plainly, indeed ardently and persistently, that damnation is possible, that we have to fear it, especially we, his friends, who are in danger of betraying him."[94]

Related to this, then, Balthasar believes that the biblical language that has been interpreted as a factual description of hell "should not be understood literally, as if it were a divine report about a future that God already knows."[95] Rather, this language is meant to emphasize the demand for Christians to love as Jesus loved and to confront the hearer with the new situation revealed in Jesus Christ. Balthasar cites Rahner, who says that "either/or" passages like

92. For a specific discussion of some of these options within Evangelical theology, see John Sanders, "Raising Hell about Razing Hell: Evangelical Debates on Universal Salvation," *Perspectives in Religious Studies* 40, no. 3 (Fall 2013): 267–82.

93. Han Urs von Balthasar, *Dare We Hope "That All Men Be Saved"?*, trans. David Kipp and Lothar Krauth (San Francisco: Ignatius Press, 1988), 72.

94. Ibid.

95. Donald W. Musser and Joseph L. Price, eds., *A New Handbook of Christian Theologians* (Nashville: Abingdon, 1996), 502.

Matthew 25 are "*not to be read as an anticipatory report* about something that will someday come into being but rather as a disclosure of the situation in which the person addressed now *truly* exists."[96] In this way, the scriptural language that suggests eternal punishment should be viewed as warning language rather than predictive language.

Balthasar's argument is powerful and persuasive, and it is worth reading in full. But let me end where he does, with the belief that Christian faith in the boundless, unconditional love of God that comes to everyone, bidden or unbidden, which does not discriminate on the basis of gender, race, ethnicity, economics, or even moral fitness, leads us to rejoice that God's love is not only for "us" but for all. And our love of neighbor that is inspired by God's own love inspires us to hope confidently in the salvation of that same neighbor, whatever that might look like for her or him. "The whole of Scripture is full of the proclamation of a salvation that binds all [people] by a Redeemer who gathers together and reconciles the whole universe. That is quite sufficient to enable us to hope for the salvation of all [people] without thereby coming into contradiction with the Word of God."[97] Why not?

QUESTIONS FOR FURTHER DISCUSSION AND REFLECTION:

1. In many aspects, Dante's *Divine Comedy* has been very influential on Christian thinking about the afterlife. Do you think there are various levels in hell and/or heaven? Does the idea of an organized bureaucracy governing the dead make sense in any way to you? How do you think people's destination after death is determined?

2. Do you believe that God keeps a record of our deeds, in a manner similar to what is found in Daoism? (For example, is there a heavenly book with our names inscribed in it?) Why or why not?

3. What constitutes a "bad death" in Christianity? Are there different views about death for women and men? For adults and children? Do you believe in the possibility of being haunted by the dead?

4. Not only in Confucianism but in other religions as well, men are privileged over women and it is important to have a son to carry on the family name. Is this true in Christianity also? Are there differences between the expectations of sons and daughters when parents become ill and die?

5. The Christian church has a long history of venerating martyrs. What do you think about the idea of martyrdom? Do you think Christianity is in agreement with Sikhism on its understanding of martyrdom?

---

96. Balthasar, *Dare We Hope*, 32, emphases von Balthasar's.
97. Ibid., 113.

6. Traditionally for the *Diné*, the ideas of harmony and balance include both death and life, but at the same time, death is also to be avoided, and contact with the dead is thought to be polluting. How do these ideas relate to the changing practices around death and dying in the United States?

7. Is it possible to be a Christian and believe in reincarnation? Is it possible for people to "change location" once they are dead?

8. If salvation is for all and the whole universe, then what does this mean for the church in its relationship with other religions and with nonbelievers?

6

Trinitarian, Troubling, Tangible Spirit

Pluralism and Secularization in the Twenty-First Century

In the contemporary US context, two inescapable realities call out for a fresh articulation of the Holy Spirit: pluralism and secularization. The first, of course, points to the ever-increasing diverse religious population in the United States, in no small part due to immigration. According to the latest data from the Pew Research Center, compiled in the report "America's Changing Religious Landscape," from 2007 to 2014 the number of Christians in the United States declined by 7.8 percent, while "non-Christian" adherents grew 1.2 percent (this includes growth in the Hindu, Muslim, and Buddhist populations). At the same time, the number of the "unaffiliated" is also growing: from 2007 to 2014 that number increased by 6.7 percent.[1]

What is important to note about that latter category, however, is that it includes not only people who are avowedly atheistic or agnostic but also those who, even while rejecting affiliation with any specific religion, still affirm that religion is either "very important" or "somewhat important" in their lives (30 percent of all "nones").[2] What this means is that the Christian church in the United States is experiencing two things simultaneously: an increasing amount of religious diversity, and a steady, if not growing, amount of religious seeking. If these two realities are viewed in light of a Christian understanding of the Holy Spirit, we recognize that on the one hand, they are quite different phenomena: the kaleidoscopic manifestations of some form of "spirit" in a wide variety of different religious beliefs and practices; and the seeking for some kind of "spiritual" connection with a higher and greater power—what we might call a deepened spiritual life. However, what both phenomena share is the demand they make on Christianity to articulate a doctrine of the Holy Spirit that is both theologically flexible and creative, and also theologically faithful and consistent. These demands form the backdrop of the Christian pneumatology articulated in this chapter.

---

1. "America's Changing Religious Landscape," *Religion and Public Life*, Pew Research Center, published May 12, 2015, http://tinyurl.com/jzc528b.
2. Ibid.

ONE OR MANY?

Regarding the challenges of religious diversity, one of the first questions that presents itself in a Christian discussion of the Holy Spirit is whether there is just one Spirit or if there are many spirits. Even looking solely at Christianity, the answer doesn't seem to be quite so clear. Of course, there is only one Holy Spirit, that is, one divine Spirit that shares the essence of God with the Father and the Son. So, on the one hand, it is fair to say that there is one Spirit in the Christian tradition. On the other hand, both Scripture and the tradition clearly speak of angels (to say nothing of demons)—are these spirits of some sort? Are they different spiritual manifestations of the divine presence? How are we to understand these messengers of God, like Gabriel, who clearly speak on God's behalf and even bear God's presence at some points? Is it then also fair to say there are "spirits" in the Christian tradition?

When we turn to other religious traditions, the question becomes even more complicated. In many religions, the distinction between the one and the many is not neatly upheld, and the issue of whether or not there are many spirits or just one is often deemed irrelevant. Instead, what is important is the simple *fact* of many manifestations of spirit, all of which engage in significant and regular ways with humanity. Those different spirits are dealt with individually, often in very pragmatic ways, without much concern for settling the question of whether or not the same singular spirit is in and/or behind them all.

One place where we see this ambiguity very clearly is in the African context. John Mbiti writes that "the spiritual world of African peoples is very densely populated with spiritual beings, spirits and the living dead."[3] He goes on to explain how some spirits are associated with God—he calls these "divinities." However, natural phenomena (rivers, mountains, etc.) are also believed to be/ have spiritual beings, and these are considered to be divinities of a different class. Finally, there are the spirits who represent the continued existence of human beings after their physical death.[4] All of these dimensions of spirit are present in varying degrees among different African peoples, and they play a role not only in indigenous African religions but also in African Christianity.

Regardless of how the question about the one and the many is answered, in all cases what is indisputable is the power of the Spirit/spirits, a power experienced in the vast majority of the world's religions, even if the experience of that power is understood and explained in vastly different ways. From a Christian perspective, Rudolf Otto can be helpful here, particularly his discussion of the experience of the Divine in his classic text *The Idea of the Holy*. Without delving too deeply into his argument, what is relevant is his

---

3. John S. Mbiti, *African Religions and Philosophy* (New York: Praeger, 1969), 74. Another good resource here is Osadolor Imasogie, *Guidelines for Christian Theology in Africa* (Achimota, Ghana: African Christian Press, 1993).

4. Mbiti, *African Religions and Philosophy*, 74–89.

emphasis on the experiential and "non-rational" aspects of the Divine. Otto argues that the "numinous" is an experience of being grasped by something undefinable, outside oneself, and in his view, the most appropriate expression for this experience is "*mysterium tremendum*."[5] This is how he describes it:

> The feeling of it may at times come sweeping like a gentle tide, pervading the mind with a tranquil mood of deepest worship. It may pass over into a more set and lasting attitude of the soul, continuing, as it were, thrillingly vibrant and resonant, until at last it dies away and the soul resumes its "profane," non-religious mood of everyday experience. It may burst in sudden eruption up from the depth of the soul with spasms and convulsions, or lead to the strangest excitements, to intoxicated frenzy, to transport, and to ecstasy. It has its wild and demonic forms and can sink to an almost grisly horror and shuddering. It has its crude, barbaric antecedents and early manifestations, and again it may be developed into something beautiful and pure and glorious. It may become the hushed, trembling, and speechless humility of the creature in the presence of—whom or what? In the presence of that which is a *mystery* inexpressible and above all creatures.[6]

Whether or not one agrees with Otto's universalizing tendency here—the attempt to ground all religions in some universal, shared experience—his argument that in a majority of religions there is a manifestation of something superhuman, full of awe, and overpowering continues to merit consideration. Even if Christians do not recognize that "something" as the Holy Spirit—or even divine in any sense of the word—it must be conceded that Christians share with other religious traditions the powerful experience of a divine or superhuman "Other," and the recognition that this experience cannot be explained, controlled, ignored, or dismissed.

The *Ori* in Santería

The concept of spirit is very important in Santería, a religion that developed in Cuba and has its roots in the Yoruba religion of Nigeria. In Santería, there is a spiritual component to the entire physical universe, and spiritual forces, good and bad, permeate one's life and constantly need managing.

One specific example of this can be seen in the concept of *ori*. The word literally means "head," but in function, it is more like the concept of the soul in Christianity. However, humans are not the only ones who possess *ori*. Instead,

---

5. Rudolf Otto, *The Idea of the Holy: An Inquiry into the Non-Rational Factor in the Idea of the Divine and Its Relation to the Rational*, trans. John W. Harvey (Oxford: Oxford University Press, 1967), 12.

6. Ibid., 12–13.

"All forces of nature have it: trees, plants, minerals, winds, mountains, animals. Every element and force of nature is spiritual and self-aware."[7] *Ori* also carries with it something of Olodumare, the supreme being; this means that every aspect of the universe possesses something of the divine and is thus sacred.

In human beings, it is believed that one's *ori* lives on after death and can be reincarnated, often in the body of one's descendants. Each *ori* has a specific destiny, set for it at the beginning of time by Olodumare, which unfolds through the course of many lifetimes. However, one's destiny also can be changed by petitioning one of the many *orishas* who rule various aspects of the world, including the forces of nature. Humans and *orishas* are in a vital, dynamic relationship that governs much, if not all, of human existence, and humans regularly make sacrifices to the *orishas* for blessing and protection. *Orishas* are complex beings with multifaceted personalities. For example, they can possess human beings, sometimes for good and sometimes not. In addition, they are also said to be the spiritual "parents" of humans, and each individual is encouraged to discover their specific *orisha* mother/father and develop a special relationship with that *orisha*.

"SPIRITUAL, BUT NOT RELIGIOUS"

While the use of the term "nones" has become common in Christian vernacular, there is another name that is also widely used to describe this group of people in the United States who do not identify with any organized religion, and that is "spiritual but not religious." While the distinction has become a common one in the context of the United States, it is worth emphasizing that both "spiritual" and "religious" have multiple definitions, and there is significant overlap between them. However, it is generally true in a twenty-first-century US context that people use "spiritual" to denote one's inner life and disposition, and "religious" to describe external, outwardly behaviors. Thus the former is much more about the self and the latter is more about the community—or at the very least, the self in relationship to a larger community.

The growth of people in this category is a pressing concern for religious communities, particularly Christian churches. One of the most important questions this raises for those who remain in the church in one form or another is whether the "spiritual but not religious" represent the new face of the American religious landscape or whether they are a temporary anomaly: Are they the destination or a detour? A further question is how best to define and describe them. In her book *Belief without Borders*, Linda Mercadante uses five different categories.[8]

---

7. Miguel De La Torre, *Santería: The Beliefs and Rituals of a Growing Religion in America* (Grand Rapids: Eerdmans, 2004), 19.

8. In the appendix, Mercadante notes that "the main criterion for interviewees was to self-identify as a 'spiritual but not religious' person. Even if interviewees did not personally use the term, they needed to

First are the Dissenters, those who "largely stay away from institutional religion." She notes that they can be "protesting" dissenters or "drifting" dissenters. Second are the Casuals, those who seek out and engage in a variety of spiritual and religious practices only insofar and for as long as they are practically helpful. Mercadante writes that theirs is a "therapeutic" spirituality that focuses on "personal well-being." Then there are Explorers, those who have a spiritual "wanderlust" and are on a "destination-less, almost touristic, journey, with no plans to settle anywhere." Fourth are the Seekers, those who are actually looking for a spiritual home, some with "a spiritual longing they could just barely define or articulate." The last group is the Immigrants, those who "had moved to a new spiritual 'land' and were trying to adjust to this new identity and community"—that is, they were "trying to live in a new spiritual home."[9]

Among all five categories, even in spite of the differences, Mercadante discovered a cluster of overarching themes common to them all: a rejection of religious exclusivism, the acceptance of an internal "locus of authority," a liberative social/moral standpoint, a belief in some form of Universal Truth, a "therapeutic orientation" to religious/spiritual practices, a "positive thinking" approach to the world and a corresponding rejection of a doctrine of sin, and finally, the understanding of nature as a key source of spiritual experiences.[10]

In the course of her research, Mercadante returned repeatedly to the core question, "Why did they insist on being 'spiritual but not religious'?"[11] She found there were different reasons, including that, for many people, it meant that "they were 'alive' spiritually, rather than being confined by arbitrary rules, needless denominational identity, dry dogma, and pointless ritual."[12] Others Mercadante characterizes under the heading "The Righteousness of Not Belonging." Many in this category operate out of the assumption that "spirituality is an individualistic pursuit, one that is not necessarily supported—and may even be hindered—by group membership."[13] For these individuals, joining a specific religion is limiting and closes off other options.

There are many aspects of this phenomenon that are interesting, but in the context of theological reflection on the Holy Spirit, it is the use of the word "spirituality" that is most relevant, and more specifically, the challenge it poses to Christians about how to understand and describe the work of the Holy Spirit in community and individually. Mercadante notes how before the twentieth century, spirituality was seen as an aspect of religion, not divorced

---

resonate and agree with it." Linda A. Mercadante, *Belief without Borders: Inside the Minds of the Spiritual but not Religious* (Oxford: Oxford University Press, 2014), 265. It is also worth noting that her research pool consisted almost exclusively of those who came from a European, Judeo-Christian background. Ibid., 268.

9. Ibid., 52–67.
10. Ibid., 74–75.
11. Ibid., 33.
12. Ibid.
13. Ibid., 164.

from it. In fact, spirituality went "hand-in-hand" with religion, "designating a variety of practices that fostered faith, devotion, and connection with God."[14] However, in the current context, the two are being increasingly opposed, often with spirituality touted as something "purer" or "truer," or "more authentic" than religion, which is then characterized as hypocritical, rigid, and unfeeling. Yet, a precise definition of "spiritual" can be hard to come by and proves both elusive and deeply subjective. So, for example, spirituality can refer to the invisible or deeper world vs. religion as mundane, material reality. Another way of opposing spirituality and religion are with the categories "heart-felt" vs. "head knowledge."

What seems very clear, however, is that for many people in this category, "spirituality" is seen as something very individualistic, concerned primarily with the self—and, significantly, this is viewed as positive. Mercadante writes that the "detraditioning" that happens with those who are rejecting traditional religion creates a vacuum with the "revoking of religious authority in favor of personal decision."[15] Into the vacuum steps a new ethos, which includes "an impersonalization of transcendence, a sacralization of the self, a focus on therapeutic rather than civic goals, and a self-needs orientation to community and commitment."[16] The assumption here seems to be that the work of the Spirit is exclusively, or at least primarily, on a one-to-one basis; that is, the Divine engages primarily with individuals and only secondarily, if at all, through communities.

In her conclusions, Mercadante notes that this new phenomenon of the "spiritual but not religious" is not wholly negative. She argues that many people in this category have important concerns and values to which the church needs to attend: the desire for mystery and awe, the need to care for creation, the importance of a practical morality, and an awareness of and great sensitivity to diversity. However, she also challenges the "inward turn" of many in this group and the rejection of a group identity. Ultimately, she says, "Separating spirituality from religion is not the answer. At the least, it is an artificial dichotomy. If taken to extremes, it can also make people reluctant to form healthy long-term personal commitments in all sorts of arenas. Yet such commitments are a necessary component of change. . . . To deal with the magnitude of the problems we face, we need an 'engaged spirituality' rather than simply a privatized one. In fact, spiritualty actually may be a smaller, not larger, category than religion."[17]

14. Ibid., 4.
15. Ibid., 231.
16. Ibid.
17. Ibid., 237–38.

Ainu Shamanism

The Ainu are an example of an indigenous group that utilizes shamans; this should be no surprise given their proximity to Siberia in particular, which has the closest original association with shamanism. As in other indigenous cultures, shamans have a particularly important role in relating to the spirit world. Shamans are believed to be boundary crossers of sorts, such that they can ascend to the spirit world or spirits can descend into their bodies, facilitating communication between the human and superhuman realms.

In Ainu societies, both men and women can be shamans, and in contemporary Ainu culture, their main role is as healers. (Though it should be noted that the role of the shaman differs among the different Ainu peoples.) Shamans often participate in group rites that can last all night, and it is in the course of these rites that the shaman becomes possessed by a spirit (or perhaps several spirits) who conveys messages from either gods or ancestors to the people.[18] These spirits are often animal spirits, such as the spirit of a fox, for example, and they offer guidance and instruction, both for individual problems and for decisions involving the whole community.

In addition, the Ainu also recognize the presence of evil spirits, which also can take possession of a person and cause illness. An important aspect of a shaman's work is being able to drive out these evil spirits and cure the person of the illness.

OPENNESS AND FLEXIBILITY

In this current context of multiple and sometimes vaguely defined spirits, one might conclude that the Christian response that is needed is one of retrenchment and repristination—both reinforcing traditional church doctrine and refuting anything that threatens it. However, there is another way to respond as well, grounded not in fear and mistrust but rather the belief that a plurality of interpretations of Spirit and spirituality—this diversity and even this challenge to traditional Christian understandings of the Holy Spirit—is a good thing. This disposition sees in others—non-Christian and nonreligious alike—an opportunity for Christians to experience God in a new way and to have our relationships with others across boundaries of nation, creed, ethnicity, and age strengthened and deepened.

Particularly in the context of interreligious dialogue, a fresh articulation of a doctrine of the Holy Spirit is quite helpful. As Roger Haight writes, "the doctrine of the Spirit and Spirit-language can help us thread the narrow passage between the traditional demands of faith and a new respect for the autonomous value of other religious traditions."[19] And, to be clear, this is not only for the

18. Kan Wada, "Ainu Shamanism," in *Ainu: Spirit of a Northern People*, ed. William W. Fitzhugh and Chisato O. Dubreuil (Washington, DC: Arctic Studies Center, National Museum of Natural History, 1999), 261.

sake of the other. Haight goes on to say, "the Spirit is at work abroad in the religions. Therefore, dialogue with other religions can influence the church: the church can learn new things and be changed by other religions because of the Spirit."[20]

One of the best articulations of this attitude can be found in the World Council of Churches document "Religious Plurality and Christian Self-Understanding." There, the authors write:

> The Holy Spirit helps us to live out Christ's openness to others. The person of the Holy Spirit moved and still moves over the face of the earth, to create, nurture, sustain, to challenge, renew and transform. We confess that the activity of the Spirit passes beyond our definitions, descriptions, and limitations in the manner of the wind that "blows where it wills" (Jn 3:8). Our hope and expectancy are rooted in our belief that the "economy" of the Spirit relates to the whole creation. We discern the Spirit of God moving in ways that we cannot predict. . . .
>
> We believe that this encompassing work of the Holy Spirit is also present in the life and traditions of peoples of living faith. People have at all times and in all places responded to the presence and activity of God among them, and have given their witness to their encounters with the living God. . . . This ministry of witness among our neighbors of other faiths must presuppose an "affirmation of what God has done and is doing among them."[21]

This powerful expression of hope and confidence in the unpredictable yet trustworthy activity of the Holy Spirit, which always reveals the presence of the loving and living God, is a model for what a Christian witness can and should be in the contemporary context.

METAPHORS FOR THE HOLY SPIRIT IN SCRIPTURE AND THE TRADITION

Before beginning this section, and indeed, as a lead-in to the rest of the chapter, an explanation of nomenclature is necessary. Following many others in the Christian tradition—both in Scripture and church history—I use feminine pronouns to refer to the Holy Spirit. While there is good precedent for doing so, the fact remains that the majority of theologians have used "he," or even worse, "it" to describe the Spirit. However, there are several reasons why "she"

---

19. Roger Haight, "Holy Spirit and the Religions," in *The Lord and Giver of Life: Perspectives on Constructive Pneumatology*, ed. David H. Jensen (Louisville: Westminster John Knox, 2008), 56.

20. Ibid., 59.

21. World Council of Churches, "Religious Plurality and Christian Self-Understanding," *Current Dialogue* 45 (July 2005), http://tinyurl.com/zdkj7zc.

is both a faithful and appropriate designation for the Holy Spirit. First is the fact that *ruach*, the Hebrew word for "breath/spirit," is a feminine noun, and this reflects the genitive, creative work of the Spirit we find in both the Old and New Testaments—the "birthing" work of the Holy Spirit both in the creation of the universe and also in the pregnancy of Mary. More will be said about this shortly.

Second is the connection between the Spirit and "Woman Wisdom" found in Proverbs 8, where she recounts her role in the creation of the universe as "master worker" alongside the Lord and emphasizes that those who find her, find life. Third, the practice of referring to the Spirit as "it" is extremely unhelpful as it perpetuates subordinationism, where the Spirit is seen as somehow not an equal person in the Trinity but some *thing*, derivative of both the Father and the Son. As a person, the Spirit warrants a personal, not an impersonal, pronoun. Finally, and perhaps most simply, there just is no reason not to: either of the other divine persons could just as well be referred to as "she"—after all, it is a grammatical, not an ontological designation. We call the other two divine persons "he" first and foremost because the two words used in Scripture describe a paternal/filial relationship of a Father and a Son. For most people, then, using "she" for the Holy Spirit is a reminder that all three divine persons are either beyond gender or inclusive of all genders, or both.

WAITER, WINE, HAND, AND KISS

In the accounts of the early church, the Holy Spirit was a direct experience of God before she was a theologically articulated person of the Trinity. In fact, according to Jaroslav Pelikan, no treatise was written specifically on the person of the Holy Spirit until the second half of the fourth century.[22] He notes that at least part of the reason stemmed from the relative lack of clarity around the person of the Holy Spirit found both in the liturgical practices of the early church and in Scripture. Prior to the fourth century, we see from the writings of the early church fathers, as they were attempting to articulate doctrine from the experience of the biblical witnesses, that what is most decisive about the Spirit is her work: "The Holy Spirit was God because [s]he did what only God could do."[23] Pelikan cites Cyril of Alexandria, who said that because the Holy Spirit was able to make alive, the Spirit could not be a creature but had to be God. That is, the Holy Spirit does what is appropriate "only to the divine and supremely exalted nature."[24]

To a large degree, it is still true today that descriptions of the *person* of the Holy Spirit continue to be subsequent to experiences of her presence and work. Bishop Kallistos Ware describes the Spirit this way: "There is a secret

---

22. Jaroslav Pelikan, *The Emergence of the Catholic Tradition (100–600)*, vol. 1 of *The Christian Tradition: A History of the Development of Doctrine* (Chicago: University of Chicago Press, 1975), 211.

23. Ibid., 216.

24. Ibid.

and hidden quality about the Holy Spirit, which makes it hard to speak or write about him. As St. Symeon the New Theologian puts it: He derives his name from the matter on which he rests, for he has no distinctive name among [people]."[25] Perhaps it is because of her inherent enigmatic nature that in both the Bible and throughout the Christian tradition there have been a wealth of interesting, vivid metaphors used to describe her person and work. Let me offer just a few of these.

One of the earliest and most well-known depictions of the Spirit in the context of the triune God is Irenaeus's characterization of the Son and the Spirit as the "two hands" of God, which Irenaeus uses repeatedly in his master work *Against Heresies*. Ambrose describes the Holy Spirit as an "abundant River," "the oil of gladness," and the "ointment of Christ."[26] Augustine, whose theology here, like in many other places, was very influential on the Western church as a whole, repeatedly called the Holy Spirit "Love" and "Gift." Symeon the New Theologian describes the Spirit as the "key" to the door that is the Son.[27]

Catherine of Siena has one of the most evocative images of the Spirit, set in the context of the heavenly banquet table. She writes, "For you see, the Father is for us a table bearing everything there is. . . . The Word, God's Son, is made our food, roasted over the blazing fire of charity. And that very charity, the Holy Spirit, is our waiter, who with his hands has given and continues to give us God. He is constantly serving us every grace and gift, spiritual as well as material."[28] Bernard of Clairvaux calls the Holy Spirit the "kiss" of the Father and Son: "Thus the Father, when he kisses the Son, pours into him the plenitude of the mysteries of his divine being, breathing forth love's deep delight."[29] Finally, another mystic, John of the Cross, describes the Spirit as "spiced wine" in a beautifully elaborate description:

> This spiced wine is another much greater favor which God sometimes grants to advanced souls, in which He inebriates them in the Holy Spirit with a wine of sweet, delightful, and fortified

25. Bishop Kallistos Ware, *The Orthodox Way* (Crestwood, NY: St. Vladimir's Seminary Press, 1979), 90. As quoted in Veli-Matti Kärkkäinen, ed., *Holy Spirit and Salvation* (Louisville: Westminster John Knox, 2010), 285.

26. Saint Ambrose, *The Holy Spirit, Nicene and Post-Nicene Fathers*, vol. 10, ed. Philip Schaff and Henry Wace (Buffalo, NY: Christian Literature Publishing Co., 1896), 113–14. As quoted in Kärkkäinen, *Holy Spirit and Salvation*, 85–86.

27. Symeon the New Theologian, *The Discourses*, trans. C. J. De Catanzaro (Mahwah, NJ: Paulist Press, 1980), 124–25. As quoted in Kärkkäinen, *Holy Spirit and Salvation*, 110.

28. Catherine of Siena, *The Letters of Catherine of Siena*, vol. 1, ed. Suzanne Noffke, OP (Binghamton, NY: Center for Medieval and Early Renaissance Studies, 1988), 161. As quoted in Kärkkäinen, *Holy Spirit and Salvation*, 122.

29. Bernard of Clairvaux, *The Works of Bernard of Clairvaux*, vol. 2, part 1, *On the Song of Songs*, sermon 8, trans. Kilian Walsh, OCSO, and Irene Edmonds (Kalamazoo, MI: Cistercian Publications, 1976), 2:46–50. As quoted in Kärkkäinen, *Holy Spirit and Salvation*, 128.

love. . . . As this wine is seasoned and strengthened with many diverse, fragrant, and fortified spices, so this love, which God accords to those who are already perfect, is fermented and established in them and spiced with the virtues they have gained. Prepared with these precious spices, this wine gives such strength and abundance of sweet inebriation in these visits granted by God to the soul that they cause her to direct toward Him, efficaciously and forcefully, flowings or outpourings of praise, love, and reverence, etc., which we have mentioned.[30]

It is unfortunate that much of the richness of these lush, vibrant images has been lost in much twenty-first-century pneumatologic reflection.

VIVIFIER, NOT GHOST

One of the helpful linguistic changes in English that has come in more recent pneumatologic language is the shift away from the name "Holy Ghost." This nomenclature has ceased to be the norm in both Catholic and mainline Protestant churches, although some individuals and churches still use it, and of course, this is the language found in older versions of both the Apostles' and Nicene Creeds. In his book *Finding God in the Singing River*, Mark Wallace emphasizes why this change is a good thing. "Ghost," he argues, perpetuates the image of the divine Spirit as "a heavenly phantom—immaterial and unreal (and perhaps a bit scary as well!)."[31] This is not the intent of Scripture, where instead the Spirit is "God's all-pervasive presence and energy within the universe."[32] Wallace rejects the spirit/body, God/nature dichotomies the language of "Holy Ghost" perpetuates, arguing instead that "not only do the scriptural texts not divorce the spiritual from the earthly, but, moreover, they figure the Spirit as a creaturely life-form interpenetrated by the material world."[33] He emphasizes the organic metaphors of "animating breath," "healing wind," "living water," "cleansing fire," and "divine dove," all of which emphasize the Spirit's earthen identity.[34]

Certainly, he has a point. The dominant images in Scripture for the Holy Spirit are the dove that descends upon Jesus in his baptism; the fire that descends upon the gathered crowd in Acts; the breath/wind from God that animates creation, the first human creature, and the dry bones in Ezekiel; and the living water in John 7 that Jesus promises to those who believe. All of

---

30. St. John of the Cross, *Collected Works of St. John of the Cross*, trans. Kieran Kavanaugh (Washington, DC: Institute of Carmelite Studies, 1991), 508. As quoted in Kärkkäinen, *Holy Spirit and Salvation*, 184.

31. Mark I. Wallace, *Finding God in the Singing River: Christianity, Spirit, Nature* (Minneapolis: Fortress Press, 2005), 7.

32. Ibid.

33. Ibid., 8.

34. Ibid., 8–9.

these organic metaphors connect to and reinforce one of the most important names of the Holy Spirit, that of vivifier—the one who gives and sustains life. Elizabeth Johnson writes, "Of all the activities that theology attributes to the Spirit, the most significant is this: the Spirit is the creative origin of all life. In the words of the Nicene Creed, the Spirit is *vivificantem*, vivifier or life-giver. This designation refers to creation not just at the beginning of time but continuously."[35]

This is why the person of the Holy Spirit provides a focus point for thinking about and describing God's work and presence in creation. This is true not only in the images used to describe the Holy Spirit specifically, but also in those used to describe the persons of the triune God. In her book *Women, Earth and Creator Spirit*, Elizabeth Johnson cites several trinitarian images that have been present in Christian thinking since the early church. She writes:

> If the great, unknowable mystery of God is pictured as the glowing sun, and God incarnate as a ray of that same light streaming to the earth (Christ the sunbeam), the Spirit is the point of light that actually arrives and affects the earth with warmth and energy. And it is all the one light. Again, the transcendent God is like an upwelling spring of water, and a river that flows outward from this source, and the irrigation channel where the water meets and moistens the earth (Spirit). And it is all the one water. Yet again, the triune God is like a plant with its root, shoot, and fruit: deep, invisible root, green stem reaching into the world, and flower that opens to spread beauty and fragrance and to fructify the earth with fruit and seed (Spirit). And it is all one living plant.[36]

Her point is compelling and unmistakable: "Speaking about the Spirit signifies the presence of the living God active in this historical world. The Spirit is God who actually arrives in every moment, God drawing near and passing by in vivifying power in the midst of historical struggle."[37]

This creative work and presence of the Holy Spirit has also been depicted in "mothering" images. Martin Luther described the Holy Spirit as "brooding" over the waters and used feminine imagery to describe this generative activity of the Holy Spirit: "As a hen broods her eggs, keeping them warm in order to hatch her chicks, and, as it were, to bring them to life through heat, so Scripture says that the Holy Spirit brooded, as it were, over the waters to bring to life those substances which were to be quickened and adorned. For it is the office of the Holy Spirit to make alive."[38] Catherine of Siena spoke explicitly of the Spirit

---

35. Elizabeth Johnson, *Women, Earth, and Creator Spirit* (New York: Paulist Press, 1993), 42.

36. Ibid., 41.

37. Ibid., 42.

38. Martin Luther, *Lectures on Genesis, Chapters 1–5*, vol. 1 of Luther's Works, ed. Jaroslav Pelikan (St. Louis: Concordia, 1958), 9.

as a mother, writing, "Such a soul has the Holy Spirit as a mother who nurses her at the breast of divine charity."[39] Leonardo Boff writes that "theological reflection saw the feminine dimensions in the Holy Spirit very early, more so than with reference to the Father and the Son—beginning with the name Holy Spirit, which in Hebrew is feminine."[40] He offers many examples in Scripture where the activity of the Holy Spirit is described in "characteristically feminine terminology," reminding us of biblical metaphors for God as a knitter (Ps 139:13), a woman in labor (Isa 42:14), and a midwife (Ps 22:9–10).

At the same time, care must be taken to avoid gender stereotyping, unintentionally giving divine sanction to the idea that women are warm and men are aloof, women are soft and men are strong, and so on. These stereotypes both restrict the kind of language and imagery we can use for all three persons of the triune God and also restrict the kinds of models we humans can envision for ourselves. So, while the church should welcome a broad range of female images for God, these should never be restricted to one narrow range of characteristics (nurturing) or one specific kind of relationship (mother).

Deities, Immortals, and Spirits in Daoism

There is no straightforward equivalent in Daoism for what Christians call Spirit. Instead, there is an enormous, diverse spiritual world, that includes myriad categories of superhuman beings. There are, of course, gods: two of the earliest and most important gods are Laojun (the deified version of Laozu) and the Queen Mother of the West. Later, a trio of primordial deities was recognized: *Yuanshi tianzun, Lingbao tianzun*, and *Daode tianzun*—the Three Pure Ones (*tianzun* [Lord of Heaven] is an honorific title for specific Taoist deities). There is also a large pantheon of lesser, more localized deities that is very fluid and varies from place to place. These deities often relate to various natural phenomena or have a special relationship with people in a specific occupation.

In addition to gods, since at least the third century BCE, Daoism has also included descriptions of what are called immortals, and this still continues to be an important category of spiritual beings today. Typically, it is believed that these beings were originally human, but they excelled on the path of perfection to such a degree that they became immortal or "transcendent"—either before death or after it. There are different types of immortals, but all of them have surpassed the ordinary limitations of physical life and have extraordinary abilities—to fly, to become invisible, to heal others, and so on.

Daoists also recognize a variety of what we might call "spirit beings," the spirits of the dead, who either dwell in heaven where they can reward and protect their descendants or who wander on the earth where they can cause

---

39. Catherine of Siena, *Dialogue*, trans. and ed. Suzanne Noffke (New York: Paulist Press, 1980), 292. As quoted in Kärkkäinen, *Holy Spirit and Salvation*, 121.

40. Leonardo Boff, *Holy Trinity, Perfect Community* (Maryknoll, NY: Orbis Books, 2000), 92.

mischief and illness. These latter beings are sometimes also called ghosts, and it is believed that their state is a temporary one, perhaps caused by an unfortunate death, which can be reoriented by proper rituals.

Twenty-First Century Descriptors of the Holy Spirit

Presupposing all that has already been said about the person and work of the Holy Spirit, and in light of the specific characteristics of the twenty-first-century US context described in the beginning of the chapter, there are three characteristics of the Holy Spirit that are particularly relevant and fruitful for contemporary theological reflection. These descriptors provide a strong foundation from which to make a Christian exploration of and engagement with different understandings of spirits and spirituality, while at the same time presenting a compelling picture of who the Holy Spirit is from a Christian perspective to those who are seeking a richer spiritual life. These three characteristics are "trinitarian," "troubling," and "tangible."

Trinitarian

Perhaps it goes without saying, but it is worth emphasizing nonetheless that one of the first things that should be accentuated in any Christian doctrine of the Holy Spirit is that in Christianity, the Holy Spirit is not a free agent. That is, the Holy Spirit is not just any spirit; the Holy Spirit is the spirit of Christ, the spirit of God the Father. This means that the Holy Spirit never works alone. Instead, the three persons of the triune God always and everywhere work together—all works of God are works of all three persons. Gregory of Nyssa says it this way: "Every operation which extends from God to the creation . . . has its origin from the Father, and proceeds through the Son, and is perfected in the Holy Spirit."[41] This was true in creation, when God the Father brought the universe into existence through the Word and the Spirit; this was true in the crucifixion, when God the Father suffered the death of God the Son while God the Spirit bound them together in dynamic love; and it will be true in the consummation, when God the Son will come in fullness and truth, through the power of God the Spirit, to return all things to God the Father. The church has confessed this reality since its inception with the ancient rule "*opera Trinitis ad extra sunt indivisa*"—that is, "the works of the Trinity outwardly are indivisible."[42] Roger Haight notes that Aquinas emphasized the same point, arguing that "when God acts outside of God's self, the whole or essential Godhead acts, not a single 'person.'"[43]

---

41. William C. Placher, *The Triune God: An Essay in Postliberal Theology* (Louisville: Westminster John Knox, 2007), 146–47.

42. Veli-Matti Kärkkäinen, *The Holy Spirit: A Guide to Christian Theology* (Louisville: Westminster John Knox, 2012), 61.

43. Haight, "Holy Spirit and the Religions," 63.

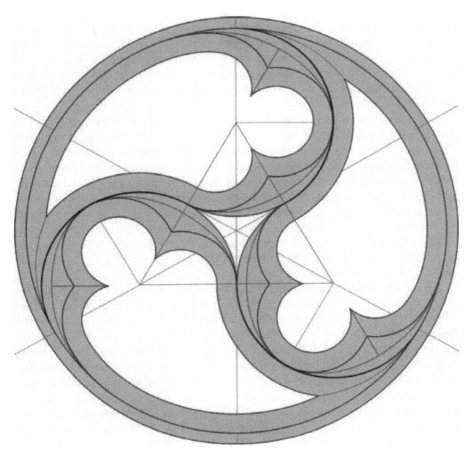

Figure 29: An image of divine perichoresis, the dynamic interplay of the three persons of the triune God.

Part of the challenge with understanding and appreciating this reality, at least in the West, is the word "person," used to translate the Western *persona*, which comes from Tertullian ("There are in God 'three persons' [*personae*] who are 'of one substance' [*unius substantiae*]"[44]), and the Eastern *hypostaseis*, which comes from the Cappadocians ("one being [*ousia*] of God in three hypostases [*hypostaseis*]"[45]). The problem, of course, exacerbated by the Enlightenment, is that "person" suggests an independent individual; and when the concept of a "person" is taken from human experience and applied to the divine life, what is immediately envisioned is three discrete, separate divine beings wandering

44. Robert Jenson, "The Triune God," in *Christian Dogmatics: Volume 1*, ed. Carl E. Braaten and Robert W. Jenson (Philadelphia: Fortress Press, 2011), 122.
45. Ibid., 135.

around, each of whom can go his or her own way, leaving the other two behind, as it were. One of the main problems with this theological construction is that it invites a high degree of ambiguity in trying to experience and evaluate the work of the Spirit in the world. Without the intrinsic connection to God the Father and God the Son, who is to say where and how the Holy Spirit is at work? All Christians can do is shrug their shoulders and say, "The Spirit blows where she wills."

Certainly, an attitude of freedom and openness is helpful when it comes to the Holy Spirit. At the same time, emphasizing her Trinitarian character allows Christians to "test the spirits" where they appear. Sometimes Christians feel a little helpless in the face of what seem to be spiritual manifestations that they don't understand, and this helplessness can lead to theological paralysis—the inability to say anything or make any concrete judgments or reflections. However, this is both an abdication of responsibility and also an erroneous assumption. The fact is, Christians do have a basis on which to engage and even judge purported activity of the Holy Spirit, and on which to stand against the manifestation of evil spirits, including structural powers and principalities: the life and ministry of Jesus Christ.

Kirsteen Kim emphasizes that "for the Christian, the criteria for discernment of the Spirit cannot be other than christological. What defines Christians as Christians is that they understand the Spirit of God to be the Spirit of Jesus Christ, who is revealed in the Bible. This is the only criterion for discernment on which Christians can agree."[46] If Christ said that he came that we might have life and life abundant, and if indeed Scripture bears witness to the Holy Spirit as the agent of that life, then Christians can safely assert that whatever is contrary to that life, whatever is death-dealing, whatever isolates and violates, is not the work of the Holy Spirit. Veli-Matti Kärkkäinen articulates this same point using the theology of Jürgen Moltmann. He writes, "Moltmann sees the Spirit of God at work everywhere there is promotion of life, growth, inclusivity, and a reaching for one's potential; conversely, whatever destroys, eliminates, frustrates, and violates life is not from the Spirit of God."[47] Only a Trinitarian understanding of the Holy Spirit makes such a judgment possible.

TROUBLING

The second characteristic of the Holy Spirit is "troubling," and at first glance, this might seem a suspicious word to use in the context of the Holy Spirit—after all, it sounds quite negative: Who wants trouble? And does Christianity really want to promote a doctrine of the Holy Spirit that includes the bringing of trouble to God's people? However, the concept actually can be extremely

---

46. Kirsteen Kim, *The Holy Spirit in the World: A Global Conversation* (Maryknoll, NY: Orbis Books, 2007), 167.

47. Kärkkäinen, *The Holy Spirit*, 86.

constructive, just not in the sense it is often used—that is, to indicate something adverse or damaging. Instead, we need to look at "troubling" in its biblical context—specifically the troubling of the waters: the Spirit stirring up what is inert and bringing life to what is lifeless.

There are three specific places in Scripture where we see the Spirit troubling the waters. The first instance comes in the very first words of the Bible, where we read, "In the beginning when God created the heavens and the earth, the earth was a formless void and darkness covered the face of the deep, while a wind from God swept over the face of the waters" (Gen 1:1–2). Commenting on this passage, one Old Testament scholar writes that in the "hovering" or "sweeping" (or troubling) of the Holy Spirit, "God is present and active." The verb suggests an "ever-changing velocity and direction, and because God is involved this movement is purposeful. This use of the language of movement rather than static categories . . . suggests creative activity in this verse, a bringing of something new out of a chaotic situation."[48]

The second example, which is theologically related to the previous one, is the account of the Israelites' escape from Egypt, when, in Miriam's account of the Red Sea crossing, God drove back the waters with "a blast of [God's] nostrils" (Exod 15:8). Finally, and most specifically, is the story of the healing of the paralytic, which takes place in Bethsaida, by pools of water that are "stirred up"—by God or by an angel—and imbued with healing power.

Thinking of it this way, we see how "troubling" is actually another way of describing the creative work of the Holy Spirit: the stirring of seeds underground and the disturbance of the soil as the sprouts burst through, the tremors and tearing that accompany all birth pains, and the pulling away from the past and wrenching toward something new that a divine call can demand. This creative work, which is one of the signature activities of God's Spirit in the world, always troubles the status quo, the current state of things, because it inaugurates something new and it requires change: a break from what is, and an embrace of what might be. And, make no mistake, this is often unpleasant. Humans characteristically do not like change; even when the current situation is not working so well we often cling to it, simply out of familiarity. The Holy Spirit does not allow for such safe conventions.

Finally, this characteristic also serves as a reminder that the church does not know everything about the Holy Spirit and always has something new to learn as the Spirit continues to reveal novel aspects of God's creative work and will every day. The Spirit of God cannot be limited either to what Christians say and have said about the Sprit, or what the Bible tells us. As Amy Plantinga Pauw writes, "The universal edge of the Spirit's work cuts against the church's perennial attempts to cage the Spirit, restricting its role to granting a seal of divine approval to the church's established structures and teachings."[49]

---

48. Bruce C. Birch, Walter Brueggemann, Terence E. Fretheim, and David L. Petersen, eds., *A Theological Introduction to the Old Testament*, 2nd ed. (Nashville: Abingdon, 2005), 42.

Figure 30: Paul and the Ethiopian Eunuch.

TANGIBLE

The final characteristic is one of the most important, and that is the tangible, physical character of the Holy Spirit, whom we can touch (or more accurately, who touches us), and the physical evidence we have of her work and presence. Simply put, the Spirit is not averse to matter and the physical world but instead always works in and through bodies to accomplish the divine will. David Jensen says it best when he bluntly declares that the "Holy Spirit seeks bodies."[50] This, too, often runs counter to Christian understanding, and again, language is part of the problem. Moltmann makes clear that Western Christians must be particularly careful in their use of "spirit," in light of the spirit/body dichotomy we have inherited from Greek philosophy. He writes:

> The Greek word πνώυμα, the Latin *spiritus*, and the Germanic *Geist*/ghost were always conceived as antitheses to matter and body. They mean something immaterial. Whether we are talking Greek, Latin, German or English, by the Spirit of God we then mean something disembodied, supersensory and supernatural. But if we

---

49. Amy Plantinga Pauw, "The Holy Spirit and Scripture," in *The Lord and Giver of Life: Perspectives on Constructive Pneumatology*, ed. David H. Jensen (Louisville: Westminster John Knox, 2008), 31.

50. David H. Jensen, "Discerning the Spirit: A Historical Introduction," in Jensen, *Lord and Giver of Life*, 1.

talk in Hebrew about Yahweh's *ruach*, we are saying: God is a tempest, a storm, a force in body and soul, humanity and nature.[51]

From the beginning of the scriptural witness, the Spirit has not hidden herself away in heaven but rather persistently—one might even say relentlessly—pursues, indwells, and empowers bodies: all kinds of bodies, human and nonhuman. Elizabeth Johnson says it this way, "For the Spirit creates what is physical—worlds, bodies, senses, sexuality, passions—and moves in these every bit as much as in minds and ideas. About the Creator Spirit this can be said: loves bodies, loves to dance. The whole complex, material universe is pervaded and signed by her graceful vigor."[52]

This has important ramifications not only for physicality in general but also for sexuality. David Jensen does not avoid these considerations, but faces them head on, arguing that "the Spirit embraces sexuality."[53] Jensen's emphasis of this point is particularly valuable because sexuality is another aspect of physical existence that is often—and often pointedly—set in opposition to the spirit and the spiritual. Speaking about Mary and Jesus's birth in particular, Jensen writes, "Holy Spirit does not avoid the body, but enters the body of a young woman who bears within her womb the life of the world. Sexuality is not avoided here, but is claimed and blessed by God. . . . In the incarnation, and in Mary, Spirit rests on sexual bodies."[54]

Another place in Scripture where Jensen sees evidence of this subversive work of the Spirit is in the story of the Ethiopian eunuch, "a cultural outsider whose very body is an icon of gender subversion. Spirit manifests a queer presence here, blessing a body that does not conform to conventional sexual expectations. Spirit here proves boundary-breaker. . . . In the strange movement of Spirit's grace, even Gentiles and eunuchs are welcome."[55] Here we see the Holy Spirit not only embracing bodies, but also "troubling" traditional cultural understandings about them and their role in religious life.

This point has particular relevance for the "spiritual but not religious" in the United States. The assumption that there is some generalized "spirit" floating around in the ether with whom one can have an entirely interiorized, individualized relationship is categorically ruled out by a Christian understanding of the Holy Spirit. Among the serious problems with this interpretation of spirit are first, the complete reliance this places on one's own interpretation and experience of spiritual presence; second, the disconnect this fosters between the life of the spirit and the life of the world; and third, the

---

51. Jürgen Moltmann, *The Spirit of Life: A Universal Affirmation*, trans. Margaret Kohl (Minneapolis: Fortress Press, 1992), 40.

52. E. Johnson, *Women, Earth, and Creator Spirit*, 60.

53. Jensen, "Discerning the Spirit," 4.

54. Ibid., 4–5.

55. Ibid., 7.

assumption it promotes that spirituality is an entirely individualized aspect of life that neither requires nor even values community, life together.

One of the strengths of Catholic and mainline Protestant articulations of the work of the Holy Spirit is their emphasis on her visible manifestation in the sacraments and in preaching. For example, in the Lutheran tradition, this is apparent in Luther's emphasis on the sacraments in general, but on word and sacrament in particular, specifically in terms of God's use of them to be in relationship to humanity. One of Luther's strongest assertions in this regard can be found in the Smalcald Articles. After discussing the different ways in which God conveys the gospel, Luther writes, "In these matters, which concern the spoken, external World, it must be firmly maintained that God gives no one [God's] Spirit or grace apart from the external Word which goes before. . . . We must insist that God does not want to deal with us human beings, except by means of [God's] external Word and sacrament. Everything that boasts of being from the Spirit apart from such a Word and sacrament is of the devil."[56] Here he is arguing against the "enthusiasts," who believed that they could interpret and discern the work of the divine Spirit on the basis of their own understanding and wisdom, without any external manifestation of the Spirit's presence. He goes on to cite the example of Moses and the burning bush, John leaping in Elizabeth's womb at the sound of Mary's voice, and the Old Testament prophets receiving the Spirit through the Word to emphasize that God always works through visible means—not through intangible feelings or inchoate sensations.[57]

Now, while in our twenty-first-century global context we might desire to relax the degree of rigidity of Luther's understanding, the point he is safeguarding remains important to highlight: the emphasis on tangible manifestations of the Spirit's work and presence keeps the focus on what God is doing, rather than what an individual is thinking or feeling. If assurance of the presence of the Holy Spirit rested only on one's sense of her presence, or on one's belief in her presence, we could never be sure of it, and we would always doubt, even despair, that she is really with us. The fact that the Holy Spirit always shows up where she has promised to be reminds the Christian community that God is trustworthy even when God's people are not, and God will continue to abide with them no matter what, even when they choose not to abide with God.

The tangible character of the Spirit also emphasizes the importance of discerning the Spirit in community. Since its inception, the Christian witness has stressed the work of the Holy Spirit in community. Thus the idea of an exclusively personalized relationship between an individual and the Holy Spirit is unthinkable from a Christian perspective. Certainly, the Holy Spirit reveals herself in and relates to individuals—but that is never the end goal. The Holy Spirit works in individuals not exclusively for their own sake but for the sake

56. Martin Luther, "The Smalcald Articles," in *The Book of Concord*, ed. Robert Kolb and Timothy Wengert (Minneapolis: Fortress Press, 2000), 323.

57. Ibid.

of the community and for the sake of the world; this is particularly true in the church. Pauw writes, "A central role of the Spirit in Christian community is to bind believers to God and to each other in loving union."[58] The Holy Spirit is the bond of love not only among the three divine persons but also among the human community and, indeed, the whole creation.

Love: The First and Last

This leads to the last characteristic that bears elaboration here, which actually incorporates and overarches the other three, and that is the understanding of the Holy Spirit as love. One of the most important monikers of the Holy Spirit down through the centuries in the Christian church has been "love"; this connection is made in multiple places throughout Scripture: where the Spirit is, there is love. In perhaps the most oft-cited example, 1 Corinthians 12–13 makes clear that it is love, the gift of the Spirit par excellence, that makes prophecy, faith, and Christian service possible. Love undergirds and nurtures all, and only love abides to the end of time. As New Testament scholar Rick Carlson states so clearly, "Love is the highway on which all gifts of the Holy Spirit travel."[59]

Augustine is one of the most important proponents of this idea; he elaborates upon it in his larger discussion of the Trinity in his text *De Trinitate*. There, in book 15, the culmination of his explication of the Trinity, he emphasizes that it is the Holy Spirit who is "distinctively called by the term charity [a synonym for love in this context]."[60] He says further that it is the Holy Spirit that allows us to abide in God and facilitates the abiding of God in us, and "this is precisely what love does."[61] It is also because the Holy Spirit is love that we can call her the "gift" of God; Augustine writes definitively: "So the love which is from God and is God is distinctively the Holy Spirit; through [the Spirit] the charity of God is poured out in our heart, and through it the whole triad dwells in us."[62] Therefore, it is also the gift of the Holy Spirit, the gift of divine love, which makes possible human love—more specifically, Christian love. Augustine writes, "So it is God the Holy Spirit proceeding from God who fires [a person] to the love of God and neighbor when [the Spirit] has been given to [a person], and [the Spirit] himself is love. [A person] has no capacity to love God except from God."[63]

What requires clarification here, however, is a proper Christian understanding of love. In popular usage, love is often described as a feeling—either romantic or otherwise—that one has for another person, a place,

---

58. Pauw, "Holy Spirit and Scripture," 28.

59. This phrase is from my colleague Rick Carlson, shared in an email in October 2015.

60. Augustine, *The Trinity (De Trinitate)*, ed. John E. Rotelle, OSA, trans. Edmund Hill, OP (Hyde Park, NY: New City Press, 1991), 420.

61. Ibid., 421.

62. Ibid.

63. Ibid.

a sports team, a job, or something else favorable in one's life. That is, it is primarily an emotional, internal experience that may or may not have any outward expression, and furthermore, it is typically elicited from someone due to some inherent quality of the beloved (beauty, intelligence, kindness, etc.). However, in a Christian context, love means something quite different.

For Christians, love actually has less to do with my personal, individual disposition toward someone (or something) and much more to do with how I treat her—how I act toward her. That is, Christian love is not about warm and fuzzy feelings but about actions of justice and mercy. When Christians describe the Holy Spirit as love, they are not talking about a little cherub flying around and shooting darts into hearts to make us "feel good" about other people. Instead, the Holy Spirit inspires *works* of love; she motivates and moves us to compassionate action: to healing and feeding, to visiting and listening, to helping and holding. As the power of love in the world, the Holy Spirit inspires bodies to engage other bodies such that love is manifest among people, nations, and indeed all beings.

The Guru Granth Sahib

Here is a good place to be reminded about the way Sikhs view their sacred text, the Guru Granth Sahib. The text is considered to be the embodiment of the same divine spirit that inspired all ten of the human Sikh gurus. Thus it is more than simply a sacred text; it is, in fact, the eternal living guru and the reason why there will be no more human gurus in Sikhism—none are needed. Instead, the tenth guru, Guru Gobind Singh, declared that the Guru Granth Sahib would exist in perpetuity as the final and definitive guru for Sikhs. This took place on October 20, 1708, and this day is still celebrated by Sikhs worldwide as *Guru Gadi Divas* (Enthronement Day). Guru Gobind Singh declared the book the "visible body" of the guru, the same divine word that had incarnated itself in each of the previous ten human gurus. Thus the book provides ultimate guidance for all aspects of Sikh life.

This is the reason why the Guru Granth Sahib is treated with such respect; it is, in fact, honored in the same way a human guru would be honored. As such, it is kept on an elevated platform during Sikh ceremonies while all the worshippers sit below it, on the floor. It is covered by a canopy and constantly fanned with a whisk. It rests on pillows and fine cloths appropriate to the season of the year. Worshippers who are in the same room with the text are to cover their heads and remove their shoes. There are special services for the morning installation of the book in the *Darbar Sahib*, or hall (*Prakash*), and an evening service for putting the book to bed (*Sukhasan*). In both cases, the Guru Granth Sahib is transported from room to room on the head of the *granthi*, the caretaker of the book, accompanied by other Sikhs singing devotional hymns.

THE SPIRITUAL LIFE

The place to conclude this chapter is with what we might call "the spiritual life": life in the Spirit to which Christians are called. Bishop Kallistos Ware writes that "the whole aim of the Christian life is to be a Spirit-bearer, to live in the Spirit of God, to breathe the Spirit of God."[64] Christians believe that the Holy Spirit is demonstrably active in their lives, and there are ways of living—specific behaviors and attitudes—that Christians can practice in order to help facilitate the Spirit's work. While there are many ways of thinking about and describing the spiritual life, one of the best explanations comes from Marjorie Thompson, who defines the spiritual life as "the increasing vitality and sway of God's Spirit in us. It is a magnificent choreography of the Holy Spirit in the human spirit, moving us toward communion with both Creator and creation."[65]

The point here is that the spiritual life is entirely dependent on the constant, guiding presence and work of the Holy Spirit. At the same time, human beings do have the capacity to respond to this work, to allow ourselves to be formed and conformed to Christ. And in the process of this formation, the synchronization and harmonization of the Holy Spirit and the human person deepens and grows, like two dance partners who have been dancing together for years, or two lovers who have been in a relationship for decades. With this in mind, then, Thompson proposes the following definition of spirituality: "the *capacity* for a spiritual life . . . *the way we realize* this spiritual potential. It involves conscious awareness of, and assent to, the work of the Spirit in us. Spirituality points to a path—to choices of belief, value commitments, patterns of life, and practices of faith that allow Christ to be formed in us."[66]

Obviously, this begs the question: What are these "practices of faith" that further Christian formation? Throughout the Christian tradition, these practices have been called "spiritual disciplines," and the foundational three disciplines are mentioned in Matthew 6: almsgiving, prayer, and fasting. Thompson defines spiritual disciplines as "certain practices that help us attend to the work of grace in our lives and our times."[67] While the Matthean disciplines are still considered the core Christian spiritual practices, the list has expanded to include many, many more, and these practices vary from denomination to denomination, culture to culture. In his classic text *Celebration of Discipline*, Richard Foster lays out a set of spiritual disciplines in the following categories: the inward disciplines of meditation, prayer, fasting, and study; the outward disciplines of simplicity, solitude, submission, and service; and the corporate disciplines of confession, worship, guidance, and celebration.[68]

---

64. Bishop Kallistos Ware, *The Orthodox Way* (Crestwood, NY: St. Vladimir's Seminary Press, 1979), 90. As quoted in Kärkkäinen, *Holy Spirit and Salvation*, 285.

65. Marjorie J. Thompson, *Soul Feast: An Invitation to the Christian Spiritual Life* (Louisville: Westminster John Knox, 2005), 6.

66. Ibid., 7.

67. Ibid., 9.

As a way of introducing these practices, Foster offers a series of reasons for engaging in spiritual disciplines; of the list, several are worth emphasizing. First, Foster argues that spiritual disciplines help us fight superficiality. He writes that superficiality is "the curse of our age," and in an age of superficiality, the spiritual disciplines call us to the depths. They invite us to explore and dwell in the depths of human existence, the depths of our relationship with God, and the depths of our own humanity. They call us to examine what is really important, what we value, where we have stored up our treasure, what our lives mean, and how we embody our life with God.

One of the most common complaints around spiritual disciplines is that we are too busy for them—we simply do not have the time. However, Foster emphasizes that spiritual disciplines are not meant only for those in religious orders or for those who are retired or single—people we often imagine as having a less scheduled life. Instead, Foster writes that "God intends the Disciplines of the spiritual life to be for ordinary human beings: people who have jobs, who care for children, who wash dishes and mow lawns. Disciplines are best exercised in the midst of our relationships with our husband or wife, our brothers and sisters, our friends and neighbors."[69] This is why Foster says that another function of spiritual disciplines is to deepen our joy: joy at living with God, joy at living with others, joy at living in the world God made. Contrary to what we sometimes think (and what the language of "discipline" sometimes connotes), spiritual disciplines are not cheerless drudgeries, boring mechanics, or burdensome mandates. Instead, they are freeing practices of love and grace, practices that give life meaning and purpose, practices that support and nurture the relationships that make us who we are.

THE SPIRIT IN ACTION: LOVING GOD, LOVING THE WORLD

In his *Confessions*, Augustine has a famous reflection that begins with a question directed to God: "But what do I love when I love you?" The beautiful answer he gives is that in loving the whole world—a light, a sound, a perfume, and an embrace—he is, at the same time, loving God. Loving creation and loving the world are not two different things but two forms of the same love. Roughly fifteen centuries later, Moltmann also offers an answer to Augustine's question. It is with his answer that I conclude this chapter, because it is the Holy Spirit that makes this love possible, and it is the Spirit that connects these two expressions of love—love of God and love of creation. "But what do I love when I love God?"

> When I love God I love the beauty of bodies, the rhythm of movements, the shining of eyes, the embraces, the feelings, the

---

68. Richard Foster, *Celebration of Discipline: The Path to Spiritual Growth* (London: Hodder & Stoughton, 1989).

69. Ibid., 2.

scents, the sounds of all this protean creation. When I love you, my God, I want to embrace it all, for I love you with all my senses in the creations of your love. In all the things that encounter me, you are waiting for me. For a long time I looked for you within myself, and crept into the shell of my soul, protecting myself with an armour of unapproachability. But you were outside—outside myself—and enticed me out of the narrowness of my heart in the broad place of love for life. So I came out of myself and found my soul in my senses, and my own self in others. The experience of God deepens the experiences of life. It does not reduce them, for it awakens the unconditional Yes to life. The more I love God the more gladly I exist. The more immediately and wholly I exist, the more I sense the living God, the inexhaustible well of life, and life's eternity.[70]

QUESTIONS FOR FURTHER DISCUSSION AND REFLECTION:

1. What do you think about the "one vs. many" discussion of Holy Spirit/spirits? What might Christians learn from other traditions on this topic?

2. Santería argues that all beings possess a spirit or soul. From a Christian perspective, do you think that animals have a soul? How might you argue either for or against such a position?

3. The Daoist belief in spirit beings might remind you of a Western belief in ghosts. Do you believe in ghosts? If so, who/what are these beings? What categories in Christianity might you use to describe them? What Christian arguments might you make against a belief in ghosts?

4. Do you still feel that you have a relationship with people who have died? How do you experience that relationship? What Christian categories exist for describing/understanding that relationship?

5. What does it mean to you that the Bible is an "inspired" book? How is that similar/different from the way Sikhs view the Adi Granth?

6. The Ainu believe that there are individuals who can cross the boundary between life and death. Do you believe that there are people who can contact the dead? Is there room for such a belief in Christianity? How might that be articulated?

7. What you do think about the category "spiritual but not religious"? What might they learn from Christians about the Spirit? What might Christians learn from them?

---

70. Moltmann, *Spirit of Life*, 98.

A Relevant, Vibrant Church for the Twenty-First Century

The Relevance of the Church in the Twenty-First Century

On the one hand, the answers to the two most basic questions about the church are very simple: *"What is the church?"* The church is the body of Christ. *"What is the purpose of the church?"* To witness to the gospel of Jesus Christ for the sake of God's mission in the world. If only it were that simple. The reality is that in spite of Jesus's own pleas for "oneness," the body of Christ is riven by innumerable fissures—some of them very deep, almost to the point of sunder—and questions about who is "in" and who is "out" are strenuously—sometimes violently—debated. The relationship of the church and the world, the relationship between Christians and "others," the standards for church membership and the standards for church leadership, the visible signs by which a church—and a Christian—can and should be identified: all of these things vary dramatically from denomination to denomination and from context to context.

Yet the crux of the problem isn't actually complexity, it is relevance. That is, in the midst of challenges and contention, the church is called upon to demonstrate and defend its relevance perhaps like never before. While the Christian church is growing explosively in the Global South, particularly in Africa, in the Global North, the church is in rapid decline—particularly among mainline Protestant denominations.[1] This has been true in Europe for some time, but the trend has become alarming to many in the United States. Thousands of those who were raised in the church and continue to love it even in spite of its flaws find themselves asking, with no small amount of dejection, "What happened?"

Therefore, one of the central overriding concerns for a contemporary Christian ecclesiology, especially one written in the United States, is to tell the story of the church in a way that demonstrates its continued vibrancy and

---

1. For statistics from 2014, see Michael Lipka, "Mainline Protestants Make Up Shrinking Number of U.S. Adults," *Fact Tank: News in the Numbers*, Pew Research Center, May 18, 2015, http://tinyurl.com/h7nvm7w.

significance in the diverse, global, multicultural context in which it exists. I argue in this chapter for the continuing vitality of the church by demonstrating the following four points. First, while many Christians become disheartened by conflicts and disagreements—locally, nationally, and internationally—the fact is that such conflicts are unavoidable in the church, and while they are challenging, they also are the means of growth and change. This is illustrated through a discussion of the nascent church in the New Testament and a brief description of the Donatist controversy. Second, while people both inside and outside the church are both bewildered and frustrated by the many different ecclesial bodies, diversity in belief and practice can be a gift and has the potential to strengthen the church overall and better serve God's mission. This is exemplified in the development of the Eastern and Western churches, the Reformation, and in Vatican II. Third, while some people seek a church full of people that look and sound like them, the church is not merely another social organization or club. Rather, the church is the body of Christ on earth, and therefore it offers something unique that cannot be found in any other form, and it serves a distinct purpose. This is illustrated through a discussion of the concept of the "marks" of the church. Finally, the church exists only in and through the power of the Holy Spirit and not through any power of its own. In the explosive growth of the church around the world, we see evidence of the Spirit's continuing creative, genitive work and can find hope for the future in that work.

Before going further, a note of terminology is helpful here. When talking about the church as a whole—in the words of the Nicene Creed, the "one, holy, catholic and apostolic church"—small "c" church is used. When discussing specific denominations or church bodies, like the Catholic Church, large "C" is used. Finally, "church" is not a synonym for "congregation," which is the term for one specific gathering of Christians in a particular building or space.

The Church of the New Testament: Conflicts and Growth

Perhaps it is no consolation, but complexity and contention have always characterized the church, even from its very inception. We need only examine the New Testament to see how early tensions developed among the early Christians and how contested some of those early ecclesial issues were for the communities. The early Christians were trying to figure out who they were as followers of Christ, how they should be organized, and how they should act. Their struggles are not removed from Christians today, who can continue to find wisdom in their solutions.

One example is the question of wealth and ownership—more specifically, what was owed to the church from one's own resources and what, if anything, an individual had the right to keep for him/herself. Acts 4 declares that, among the early Christians, no one was to own any property independently; rather it was all to be shared. And to be clear, this was no mere aspirational ideal. Acts

5 records that sneaky Ananias fell down dead when he violated this principle, so apparently it was important. These issues of communal living, communal property, and communal responsibility continue to be debated today. The role of tithing, the definition of stewardship, and, indeed, even the norms around wealth and lifestyle vary greatly among denominations, with some Christians advocating very simple living and others seeing material wealth as a sign of God's blessing. These questions serve as an ongoing reminder that the church is more than just a collection of individuals; the church is a community, a family, and therefore issues of communal accountability and the sharing of resources are important to the life of the church and require tending.

Passages addressing another issue related to community responsibility, the character of proper Christian behavior, can be found in a variety of places in the New Testament Epistles. So, for example, 1 Corinthians catalogs a long list of prohibited behaviors: sexual immorality, greed, excessive drinking, and theft. And the punishment for such activities is clear: such people are to be driven out of the church. In addition, it is in this letter where we read that women are to cover their heads in church (1 Cor 11:5), but men most certainly are not to cover theirs. Also in this letter, Paul describes proper procedure when one member has a grievance against another. Paul feels strongly that a court of law is not the best place to resolve a dispute among believers, but instead, Christians should be able to settle disagreements among themselves.

Further, very early on, the church had to address the question of Jewish customs, specifically whether the early Christians (many of whom were Jews) would adopt those customs as their own. So, for example, in Acts 10, Peter has a vision of a sheet filled with "unclean" animals. When he resists killing and eating them, a voice from God insists that "what God has made clean, you must not call profane." As another example, Acts 15 describes what might be considered the first official church council, in which the question about circumcision was definitively answered: circumcision would not be a requirement for Christians. These questions of what constitutes appropriate Christian behavior continue to promote constructive dialogue about how one's faith in Jesus Christ should impact the whole of one's life: Is it right for a Christian to serve in the military? Should Christians be vegetarian? What about political affiliation? Are there any jobs that are off-limits to Christians? While Christian denominations answer these questions very differently, they are important means of ensuring that the church continues to be in active dialogue with the society in which it exists while emphasizing that one's faith cannot be compartmentalized from the rest of one's life but rather is the source out of which all other aspects of life flow.

Finally, in the New Testament, the question of the role of women in the church—particularly the possibility of women's leadership—is somewhat ambiguous. Jesus himself actively, shockingly even, welcomed women among his followers and repeatedly and insistently supported and affirmed them—even and especially those women who were outcast or marginalized in any way. Two of the most famous examples of this are the Samaritan woman at the well, whose testimony brought many Samaritans to faith, and the Syrophoenician woman, who seems to best Jesus in a theological debate about the radical reach of God's grace. Further, even though he did not officially call a woman as one of his twelve apostles, certainly women were disciples: first and foremost Jesus's mother Mary, of course, as well as Mary Magdalene, who not only stayed with Jesus at his crucifixion but was also one of the first witnesses of the resurrection and proclaimers of the gospel. Not for nothing has Mary Magdalene been called "an apostle to the apostles." Joanna and Susanna are also mentioned in the Gospels as important followers who supported him financially. In addition, Mary the Mother of James and several other unnamed women witnessed the resurrection along with Mary Magdalene and reported it to the apostles.

In Paul's letters, we have unequivocal evidence that women were serving the early churches in a variety of leadership positions. So, for example, Priscilla/Prisca is counted as a missionary and disciple along with her husband, Aquila, and Paul praises them both for their work in the church they held in their house. In Philippians 2, Paul lauds Euodia and Syntyche as "women who have struggled beside me in the work of the gospel"; and in Colossians, Paul greets Nympha and the church in her house. Finally, there are the women mentioned at the end of Romans, where Paul records a long list of church leaders he wants to greet with admiration and affection. Included in this group are the following: Junia, who is "prominent among the apostles"; Mary, "who has worked hard"; and Tryphaena, "worker in the Lord."

At the same time, Christians cannot avoid the many passages in both the authentic letters of Paul and the Deutero-Pauline and Pastoral Epistles where women's roles in both the family and the church seem radically constrained. In 1 Corinthians, Paul writes that "man is the head of a woman," and that woman was created for the man's sake (1 Cor 11:3–10). Paul also forbids women from speaking in church, counseling instead that they be tutored by their husbands at home (1 Cor 14:33–35). Women are to be subject to their husbands (Titus 2:3–5), dress modestly, and "learn silence in full submission. I permit no woman to teach or to have authority over a man; she is to keep silent" (1 Tim 2:9–15). This passage also includes the unnerving sentence indicating that women will be "saved through childbearing, provided they continue in faith and love and holiness, with modesty" (1 Tim 9:15). Apparently damnation threatens the childless and cheeky alike.

WOMEN'S LEADERSHIP IN THE CHURCH TODAY

Today many different church bodies still wrestle with women's leadership in the church—to say nothing of those who explicitly forbid it in one form or another. This continues to be a contested issue even for those denominations who ordain women, where plenty of individual congregations still insist on male pastoral leadership. This is one place where it is incumbent upon church authorities to continue to facilitate conversation around all the issues that relate to women's leadership: questions of *imago Dei*, societal and theological norms around marriage and gender roles, heteronormativity and sexuality, diversity, models of authority and pastoral identity, expansive and inclusive language, and biblical authority. These kinds of conversations are desperately needed in the church and can also help model healthy discourse in society more broadly.

In addition, and perhaps even more critically, the church must also wrestle with the way these passages have been and continue to be used to oppress women in their own homes and in their own bodies. Prohibitions on birth control, for example, can sentence women to lives of poverty and self-sacrifice; public condemnation of out-of-wedlock pregnancies and abortion can ostracize women from the church at precisely the moment when they need a loving community the most; and strong disapproval of divorce can condemn women to years of debilitating abuse. Women who are lesbian, bisexual, or transgender also can be excluded from the church, and even from church-going families, leaving them vulnerable and alienated from key avenues of support and care. Here, perhaps the church can take its cue from Pope Francis, who, it should be noted, takes his own cue from Jesus as he emphasizes the need for the church to be like a "field hospital," healing wounds first before talking about anything else, acting as a "mother and shepherdess" rather than a bureaucrat or government official.[2]

DONATISM: AN EXAMPLE FROM EARLY CHURCH HISTORY

These areas of conflict and debate occurred up through the development of the church and continue still today. In many instances, we look back on the controversies of the early church and wonder what all the fuss was about; the issues at stake seem trivial or self-evident, and it is hard to imagine why they were fought over so passionately. However, there are also issues that, far from being relics of the past, seem to have been ripped from today's ecclesial headlines, and not only are today's Christians sympathetic, they also see these very same issues rocking their own churches. One such example is the Donatist controversy of the fourth century, which ultimately ended up involving Augustine, Bishop of Hippo (located in modern Algeria) and one of the formative theologians of the Western Christian tradition.

The Donatist controversy had its roots in the Christian persecution by the Roman Emperor Diocletian, which lasted from 303 to 311. Diocletian had issued an edict demanding, among other things, that the Christian scriptures be burned and places of worship destroyed, and he also prohibited Christians from meeting together. During that time, while some were martyred for their faith, others did compromise in one way or another with the ban, including members of the clergy who handed over Christian scriptures to the authorities—these were called *traditores*, from the Latin "to hand over" and from which we get the English words "traitor" and "tradition." Once Constantine became emperor in

---

2. Antonio Spadaro, SJ, "A Big Heart Open to God," *America*, September 30, 2013, http://tinyurl.com/h49g9mu.

306, and particularly after the Edict of Milan in 313, which declared tolerance for Christians all across the Roman Empire, those who had lapsed in one form or another sought to be brought back into the church. However, some were not eager to have them. The Donatists were perhaps the most extreme of that latter group.

Shortly after the persecutions ended, the bishopric of Carthage came open and Caecilian was elected in 311. However, the more rigorous Christians in North Africa rejected him, in no small part because one of those who had consecrated him, Felix of Aptunga, had been a *traditor*. For this reason, in their minds, the sacramental actions that Felix had performed were not valid; more specifically, in the rite of laying on of hands, he could not convey the Holy Spirit. Thus in their minds, Caecilian did not stand in the chain of succession leading back to the apostles and was therefore not a true bishop of the church.[3] This group of Christians then elected a counter bishop, Majorinus, who died shortly thereafter. In his place, Donatus was elected, and it is by his name that these Christians came to be known. Constantine supported Caecilian and so did many bishops in different parts of the Roman Empire, but Donatism was not formally outlawed and disbanded until 405. Nevertheless, the community lingered, as did the theological issues it had raised, which is why Augustine got involved. At the time Augustine became bishop of Hippo in 396, there were more Donatists than Catholics in North Africa, and modern excavations have shown that "the Donatist church in Hippo . . . was larger than Augustine's basilica."[4]

There are several reasons why this controversy is so significant and still resonates in many ways today. The first relates particularly to sacramental acts and the holiness of the presider. The Donatists were convinced that the theological validity of a sacrament was directly tied to the worth of the officiant. Logically, then, if the priest or bishop was morally or theologically deficient, then so were the ordinations, baptisms, communions, and so on that he performed. This also meant that if any other Christians wanted to join the Donatists, they would have to be rebaptized by a pure and untainted priest. The point here is that for the Donatists, these tangible experiences of God's mercy and grace only could be mediated by someone whose own personal holiness was above reproach; if the individual's holiness was compromised, so was the validity of the sacraments.

These questions about the holiness and purity of the clergy naturally relate to more general questions about both the purity of individual Christians and the holiness of the church itself. Margaret Miles describes the controversy this way: "two different images of the Church emerged. Donatists understood the Church as the pure 'bride of Christ,' 'without spot or wrinkle,' a 'shut-in garden.' Augustine, who spoke for Catholics, saw the Church as a community

---

3. Vince Evener, personal correspondence with the author, April 29, 2016.

4. Margaret R. Miles, *The Word Made Flesh: A History of Christian Thought* (Malden, MA: Blackwell, 2005), 99.

of imperfect people defined by their love of God."[5] This debate is still with us today: Is the church an island of salvation in a sea of damnation, or is it a motley gathering of filthy beggars sharing with other beggars where to find bread? In his biography of Augustine, Peter Brown describes it like this:

> "This is the door of the Lord," they [the Donatist Christians] wrote on the lintel of a church in Numidia, "the righteous shall enter in." "The [person] who enters," however, wrote Augustine, "is bound to see drunkards, misers, tricksters, gamblers, adulterers, fornicators, people wearing amulets, assiduous clients of sorcerers, astrologers. . . . He must be warned that the same crowds that press into the churches on Christian festivals, also fill the theaters on pagan holidays."[6]

The contrast is between two starkly different visions of the church and its members: either a church that is set apart from the world and preserves the distinct identity of its members, an identity that is uncontaminated by and superior to the society that threatens it from all sides, or a church that sees its identity as based fundamentally on the holiness of God and the presence of the Holy Spirit instead of on the quality of individual Christians. As Brown characterizes this latter view: "This Church was hungry for souls: let it eat, indiscriminately if needs be."[7]

These questions about the moral worth of a minister, the individual purity of a Christian, and the holiness of a church community are not dead. There are still today Christian churches that practice rebaptism, particularly those that only recognize believer's baptism, not infant baptism, and those that demand rebaptism after a specific kind of conversion experience. Even more, larger questions of moral purity and theological fidelity continue to divide the church, specifically around issues of who can and cannot serve as a public minister (women, members of LGBTQ communities, those who are married, etc.) and whether or not there are ethical offenses that would bar someone from church leadership. Finally, questions of the moral purity of the church itself remain, with individuals being excluded—or at the very least unwelcome—for a variety of offenses, depending on the context.

All of these issues push the church to continue to reassess its fundamental orientation to the world, an orientation that is always changing. In addition, they encourage the church to keep asking itself how it defines itself, what it expects of individuals in terms of membership and participation, and how it positions itself in relationship to those outside the church. These are critical, fruitful questions that help the church more faithfully serve God's mission in the world and assist Christians in our own self-understanding and the positive expression of our baptismal vocation in all the contexts in which we live.

5. Ibid.
6. Peter Brown, *Augustine of Hippo* (Berkeley: University of California Press, 1969), 213.
7. Ibid., 214.

The Sikh *Gurdwara*

As noted in a previous chapter, the place of worship for a Sikh community is called the *gurdwara*, which, in Punjabi, means "the residence of the guru." The particular guru in question is not a living human being, but the Guru Granth Sahib, the holy book of the Sikhs. A building cannot be called a *gurdwara* unless it houses a copy of that book, and any building that does house a Guru Granth Sahib is, by definition, a *gurdwara*. The book is the physical embodiment of Divine wisdom, and while Sikhs believe that God is everywhere, they also believe through recitation/singing and hearing the words of the Guru Granth Sahib one is brought into the presence of God.

The *gurdwara*, then, is the heart of the Sikh community, and the people gather there for a variety of reasons. They come specifically to worship God but also to celebrate religious holidays, educate their children in the faith, and share aspects of Punjabi culture. The *gurdwara* also functions as a sanctuary of sorts, where people can find shelter, food, and refuge. There are no images in the *gurdwara* because Sikhs are clear that God has no physical form. In addition, Sikhs do not use candles or incense in their services. There is one focus and one focus only during a Sikh service, and that is the book.

Gurdwaras are designed as intentionally welcoming spaces, with no discrimination on caste or gender. This is symbolized in the four doors of a *gurdwara*: the Door of Peace, the Door of Livelihood, the Door of Learning, and the Door of Grace. These doors are meant to always be open. When entering the hall where the sacred book resides, everyone covers his or her head and takes off their shoes—this is in order to come into the presence of the Guru Granth Sahib with reverence. Typically, people bow before the book when first entering, and women and men usually sit on the floor on opposite sides of the room. A typical service has two main parts: the *kirtan*, the singing of hymns, and the *katha*, the talk on a theme from the gurus' teachings and Sikh history. The service concludes with prayers and the *hukamnama*, a randomly selected "text for the day." Any competent person, male or female, can lead the service and singing. At the close of the service, the *parshad* is distributed, a sweet bite of sugary dough that represents God's sweetness and blessing. After the service, the *langar* is served to anyone and everyone, a simple vegetarian meal that everyone eats together sitting on the floor.

THE GIFT OF DIVERSITY IN BELIEF AND PRACTICE

Today, the church has a bewildering array of manifestations around the world, some of which are no more than a few congregations, others of which have millions and millions of members. It is easy to see this diversity as a drawback, an obstacle to the church's participation in God's mission in the world, and, to be sure, sometimes it is. If we think of the church as one massive, messy, contentious family, we can easily understand how internal quarrels can involve the worst kind of discord: no one fights like family. At the same time, this diversity is also a blessing, as different ecclesial denominations have different gifts, and, much like Paul's metaphor of the body of Christ in 1 Corinthians 12, the whole is enhanced by unique characteristics of each different part. In what follows, I look at three large members of the universal church body—Eastern Orthodoxy, Protestantism, and the Catholic Church—and suggest something about them that continues to be a gift to the universal church and strength of the whole.

THE BREAK BETWEEN THE EAST AND WEST

In the early centuries of its life, there was, of course, only one church, with multiple locations and multiple centers of power. The Christian church had spread quickly from Jerusalem out around the Mediterranean and beyond: Ephesus, Alexandria, Antioch, Constantinople, Athens, and Rome, and then into Spain, Saxony, France, and Great Britain. As the church grew geographically, political and theological divisions also grew and a gulf opened between the Greek-speaking church in the East and the Latin-speaking church in the West. The former was centered on the bishop of Constantinople, who today is called the Ecumenical Patriarch of Constantinople and is considered *primus inter pares*—the first among the heads of several different autocephalous churches that make up the Eastern Orthodox Church. The latter was centered on the bishop of Rome.

After the fall of the Roman Empire and the ensuing waves of what were called the barbarian invasions—the Huns, the Vandals, and the Goths—the Western church then looked to the pope in Rome as a visual sign of Christian unity. The fifth-century pope Leo I, "the Great," is often considered to be the first pope in modern use of the term. In the sixth century, Pope Gregory I, also called "the Great," solidified the ecclesial supremacy of the bishop of Rome.[8] The split between the churches deepened in 800 when Pope Leo III crowned Charlemagne the first Holy Roman Emperor, in effect creating two competing Christian empires.

In contrast to the West, in the East, Constantine's empire had continued unbroken as the Byzantine Empire and lasted until the Turkish Ottoman Empire captured Constantinople in the fifteenth century. However, the Eastern Church was marked by serious christological controversies, which also weakened the relationship between the East and the West, fed in no small part by the two streams of Antiochene and Alexandrian thought. The declaration of Christ's "two natures in one person," promulgated at Chalcedon in 451, became the definitive christological statement in the West, but in the East, controversies still reigned.

8. Justo L. González, *The Story of Christianity*, vol. 1 (San Francisco: HarperSanFrancisco, 1984), 242, 246.

Figure 31: The icon of the "Triumph of Orthodoxy," which depicts an image of the Theotokos surrounded by famous leaders in the Eastern Church.

This formed the background to what became one of the most serious theological controversies in Eastern Christendom, the dispute over the use of icons in worship. This controversy divided the Empire between "'iconoclasts'—destroyers of images—and 'iconodules'—worshippers of images."[9] This issue was finally settled at the Seventh Ecumenical Council of

Nicaea in 787 with the affirmation of the distinction between *latria* (worship), which was appropriate only for God, and *dulia* (veneration), which could be offered to images. In 842, the use of images in worship was finally and permanently restored, and this event is still celebrated in Eastern churches today on the first Sunday in Lent as the Feast of Orthodoxy.

This was not the only breach between East and West; there were others: the *filioque* controversy first and foremost, of course, which was the "double procession" clause added to the Nicene Creed in the Western church at the Council of Toledo in 589; the rejection of celibacy for the clergy in the East; and the use of unleavened bread in the Eucharist in the West. These all contributed to the final schism between the churches, which occurred in the eleventh century. In 1054, Cardinal Humbert, on behalf of Pope Leo IX, walked into the cathedral of Saint Sophia and laid the bull of excommunication on the altar, an action that was promptly reciprocated by Patriarch Michael Cerularius. These mutual excommunications were not lifted until the Second Vatican Council in 1965 by Pope Paul VI and Patriarch Athenagoras I.

Since the twelfth century, Western theology has all but ignored the East, and it is only in the past few decades that the treasures of Eastern doctrine and practice have been recognized and celebrated. One of the most valuable of these is the use of icons in worship. Icons are not idols; instead they are windows into a spiritual world and points of connection with the Divine. Their use and function stem from a theology of the incarnation in which Christ is understood as the *eikon* of God. They provide a focus for prayer and meditation, and a visual reminder of the presence of God in the world. They call humanity into relationship with God.

Particularly for Protestants, icons can seem not only unfamiliar but even threatening and heretical, and when walking into an Orthodox church for the first time, the sight is dizzying and dazzling. Hardly a space is empty; icons cover the walls and ceiling from top to bottom in every direction: images of saints, Orthodox festivals, biblical figures, Mary and Jesus Christ. In addition, one immediately notices what is called an *iconostasis*—a wooden panel separating the sanctuary and the nave—and this too is covered with icons. The dome of the sanctuary always depicts an enormous, breathtaking image of Christ the Pantocrator, the ruler of heaven, and the eastern apse always depicts Mary *Theotokos*—the mother of God. This lush, expansive visual experience invites Christians into a particular way of experiencing the Divine, much different from the stark visual simplicity of many Protestant church buildings. One has the vivid sense of being surrounded at all times by the "great cloud of witnesses" described in Hebrews and is therefore reminded that in the body of Christ, one is never alone. Finally, for those who cannot read or cannot hear, this visual feast is a powerful proclamation of the gospel in and of itself, no

9. Ibid., 260.

words needed. This gift of icons—and the craft of iconography—is a blessing to the whole church and enriches the whole body.

Figure 32: A classic icon of Jesus harrowing hell and rescuing Adam and Eve—from the Chora Museum (formerly the Church of the Holy Savior), Istanbul, Turkey (author's photo).

THE SIXTEENTH-CENTURY REFORMATIONS: PRESERVING THE WORD AND THE INDIVIDUAL

In the Western context, arguably the most significant moment in the life of the church was the Protestant Reformation—more properly, Reformations—of the sixteenth century. The time was ripe for reform as various forms of corruption had become rampant at the highest levels of the Catholic Church. In addition, European society was changing as well: Columbus had reached the Americas, Copernicus had reoriented the whole universe, and Gutenberg had revolutionized the dissemination of information with the printing press. The Bible had been translated into the vernacular by John Wycliffe in England more than a century earlier. Erasmus had gained a large following by emphasizing moral behavior for Christians over doctrine; he seemed on the verge of leading a reform of the Catholic Church from within. However, Martin Luther got there first, bringing with him a tornado instead of a gentle breeze, and when the winds finally died down, which did not really happen until the Peace of Westphalia in 1648, little in Europe looked the same.

Figure 33: All Saints' Church (also called the Schlosskirche), Wittenberg, Germany (author's photo).

The beginning of the Reformation is typically dated October 31, 1517, with the publishing of Luther's Ninety-Five Theses on the door of the Wittenberg Castle Church (All Saints' Church). In these theses, Luther challenged, among other things, the prevailing theology of the Catholic Church that demanded anxious (and expensive) participation in a complex penitential system in order to secure the forgiveness of one's sins. Over a period of time, and particularly—though not exclusively—through a reading of Romans, Luther had come to the realization that justification, being made right with God, was a free gift from God through Jesus Christ. Humans were neither able nor obligated to do anything to earn this gift. This was not only a theological challenge but an economic one as well, as Luther's rejection of the sale of indulgences struck the papal purse and imperiled Pope Leo X's plans to build the basilica of St. Peter. (Luther's rejection of the soteriological efficacy of viewing relics and making pilgrimages had the same negative economic effects on a variety of local rulers, including Frederick the Wise in Wittenberg.)

Originally, Luther had hoped to reform the Catholic Church, but it became clear very quickly that this movement was going to result in something else entirely. Luther's vivid and inflammatory language did not help, and once Luther was excommunicated, there was no going back. The reform movement in Germany was echoed by Ulrich Zwingli in Zurich and John Calvin in France (later Geneva). The Anabaptist movement also came out of Reformation theologies and practices. In the meantime, Henry VIII was orchestrating his own reformation in England. Both European society and the church—now the churches, plural—would be forever changed.

The Catholic response to the Reformation was the Council of Trent. It opened on December 13, 1545, and closed on December 4, 1563, and over this long stretch of time, the council fathers met in three different periods for a total of twenty-five sessions. As might well be imagined, one of the main goals of the meeting was to respond to and refute the new teachings of the various Protestant groups; another goal was a reiteration of Catholic teaching and a repristination of Catholic practices. Various condemnations were issued, and official church teachings on salvation and the sacraments were promulgated. It is also worth noting that a few years after the council closed, what has come to be known as the Tridentine Mass was initiated, with a revised Roman Missal being published in 1570.

To be clear, this was not considered a reform of Catholic doctrine. Instead, the council reiterated the unchanging and unerring nature of church doctrine and demanded a reform of the Catholic people, both the clergy and the lay people. Thus the council sought to reform morals and confirm dogmas.[10] The response was a rejection of the new, a reinforcement of defenses, and a raising of walls, walls that would stand for another four hundred years until the sudden announcement of Vatican II.

Justo González notes that "the sixteenth century was one of the most convulsed periods in the entire history of Christianity. In a few decades, the towering edifice of medieval Christianity collapsed."[11] One can imagine, then,

---

10. John W. O'Malley, *Tradition and Transition: Historical Perspectives on Vatican II* (Wilmington, DE: Michael Glazier, 1989), 55–56.

how, from the perspective of the Catholic Church, this whole period and the ecclesial changes it wrought felt like a massive loss and an overwhelmingly negative experience. However, from a twenty-first-century vantage point, we can better see some of the positive results of the Reformation movements, which Christians still enjoy today. Of these I mention only one: the shift to the Word and its subsequent twin emphases on Bible translation and personal engagement with Scripture.

Margaret Miles describes this shift in this way: "Protestant reformations brought a massive paradigm shift within Christianity, a new identification of which sense should be centrally engaged and exercised in Christian worship and devotional practice. In Protestant movements, the ear and hearing assumed new importance, while the eye lost its privileged role in religious practice."[12] This correlated with Luther's emphasis on the Word alone, and even though Luther never rejected the use of religious images (and certainly welcomed them in his printed tracts, especially the images of Lucas Cranach), an enduring hallmark of most Protestant congregations is an elevated pulpit and a relative lack of imagery in the sanctuary. Related to this is Luther's stress on "Scripture alone"—*sola Scriptura*. This was the way he underscored his belief in the authority of Scripture over tradition or human hierarchies. The Bible, not the pope, was the final arbitrator of truth, and if the Bible convinced him of the accuracy of his teaching, no individual or institution could sway him.

Today's church reaps the rewards of this shift in several ways. First, almost all denominations, including the Catholic Church, now encourage individuals to read the Bible for themselves, and there are innumerable programs for reading the entirety of the Bible in the course of a year. Second, many different church bodies continue to sponsor translation projects, with the goal of having Scripture available in as many spoken languages as possible. A wealth of theological insight has come out of these translation projects, and the church as a whole has been greatly enhanced because of them. These twin emphases have resulted in a less hierarchical structure overall for most Protestant denominations, with greater power vested both in local clergy and in the laity in general. This has nurtured the development of different models of the church, which has allowed the church to function differently in different contexts. In general, this is a constructive example of ecclesial diversity that has supported the growth of the church worldwide.

A LONG-AWAITED RESPONSE: VATICAN II

Before Vatican II, there was Vatican I, convened by Pope Pius IX on June 29, 1868. It lasted only about ten months, thanks to the Franco-Prussian War, and was called primarily to combat what was seen as the rising tide of modernism, specifically the threats of Enlightenment rationalism, atheism, and the scientific

11. Justo L. González, *The Story of Christianity*, vol. 2 (San Francisco: HarperSanFrancisco, 1985), 122.
12. Miles, *Word Made Flesh*, 248.

method. It thus reiterated the authority of church teaching and repudiated what were seen as modernist errors. However, what Vatican I is best known for is the doctrine of papal infallibility, which was developed in the context of reiterating the supremacy of the Roman pontiff. The dogmatic constitution *Pastor aeternus* (First Dogmatic Constitution on the Church of Christ) emphasized that the primacy of the pope is supreme over even ecumenical councils, and that the pope has absolute jurisdiction over all individual congregations as well as all individual Catholics. The rationale for papal infallibility is stated this way, in the last chapter of this constitution:

> Faithfully adhering, therefore, to the tradition inherited from the beginning of the Christian Faith, we, with the approbation of the sacred council, for the glory of God our Saviour, for the exaltation of the Catholic religion, and the salvation of Christian peoples, teach and define, as a Divinely revealed dogma, that the Roman pontiff, when he speaks ex cathedra, that is, when he, in the exercise of his office as shepherd and teacher of all Christians, by virtue of his supreme Apostolic authority, decides that a doctrine concerning faith or morals is to be held by the entire Church he possesses, in consequence of the Divine aid promised him in St. Peter, that infallibility with which the Divine Saviour wished to have His Church furnished for the definition of doctrine concerning faith or morals; and that such definitions of the Roman pontiff are of themselves, and not in consequence of the Church's consent, irreformable.[13]

The attitude of thinly veiled hostility toward the modern world continued into the twentieth century, which made the convening of Vatican II such a surprise. It was announced by Pope John XXIII in 1959, just three months after his election as pope. He took full responsibility for the council and really initiated it on his own; part of what he intended in this was that the conference would be pastoral, rather than dogmatic.[14] The word that has come to be associated with Vatican II is *aggiornamento*; this word was used by Pope John XXIII to indicate what he sought from the council: a radical shift in the attitude of the church toward the world. The word literally means "bringing up to date," but it is more

---

13. Charles Herbermann et al., eds., *The Catholic Encyclopedia: An International Work of Reference on the Constitution, Doctrine, Discipline, and History of the Catholic Church* (London: Catholic Way, 2014), 308.

14. Leo Lefebure quotes John O'Malley, who notes the importance of this shift in style: "John O'Malley terms the style of Vatican II 'poetic-rhetorical,' in contrast to the 'legislative-juridical' style that had largely dominated earlier ecumenical councils." Leo Lefebure, "Is There Reason for Hope? The Second Vatican Council and Catholic Interreligious Relations," in *The Long Shadow of Vatican II: Living Faith and Negotiating Authority since the Second Vatican Council*, ed. Lucas von Rompey, Sam Miglarese, and David Morgan (Chapel Hill: University of North Carolina Press, 2015), 21.

often characterized by its more figurative meaning, "opening the windows" of the church to the world to allow for the movement of the Holy Spirit.

The importance of this fundamental orientation cannot be overstated. The pope was optimistic about the work of the Spirit in the world and felt a deep sense of joy in the promise of the Christian faith. Sadly, Pope John XXIII did not live much beyond the first session of the council; he opened the council on October 11, 1962, and he died in June 1963. However, the work he had begun continued under Pope Paul VI, who brought the council to a successful conclusion on December 8, 1965, the Feast of the Immaculate Conception. On December 7, the final public session of the council, the pope removed the excommunication of 1054 against the Ecumenical Patriarch of Constantinople; this action was reciprocated by the patriarch in Istanbul. The waves of liturgical, theological, and ecclesiastical reforms continue to ripple through the church and the world today.

There were a total of sixteen documents issued by the council, including decrees on ecumenism, the media, and non-Christian religions, among other things. Of these, the most important are the four apostolic constitutions. The four are as follows (the titles come from their opening words in Latin): *Lumen Gentium* (On the Church), *Dei Verbum* (Revelation), *Sacrosanctum Concilium* (The Constitution on the Liturgy), and *Gaudium et Spes* (Church in the Modern World). These documents are the tree from which all the fruits of the council grew, and each in their own way broke new ground, opening fresh pathways of conversation, engagement, and transformation with other Christians, other religious traditions, science, and various global contexts.[15]

Certainly, the reforms most typically associated with the council are the liturgical reforms, including the use of the vernacular in the Mass and a more visible and active role for the laity. However, the doctrinal and theological shifts in orientation were no less significant and wide reaching. In his analysis of Vatican II, Adrian Hastings identifies several major areas of lasting significance. First is the conversion in general orientation in the life of the church as a whole. This includes an emphasis on people—the people of God—rather than hierarchies; a renewed focus on Scripture; a celebration of diversity, even theological diversity; and a concern for the larger issues facing the whole world, not just the church. Second, Hastings notes significant shifts in official church teaching, including: the right of religious freedom; the explicit condemnation of anti-Semitism; an emphasis on conjugal love, not merely procreation in a marriage; and finally, the openness to the possibility of salvation outside the church—more specifically, openness to the work of the Holy Spirit and the

15. Also extremely significant in this area, however, are the three documents *Nostra Aetate*, *Dignitatis Humanae*, and *Unitatis Redintegratio*, specifically because of the way they reshaped the relationship between the Catholic Church and other religious communities (Leo Lefebure, personal correspondence with the author, April 26, 2017).

presence of divine grace outside the Catholic Church.[16] Altogether, these shifts were seismic, and the ground still has not fully settled, even fifty years later.

Vatican II thus exemplifies—like perhaps no other moment in the life of the church in the twentieth century—the way in which a specific denomination can reiterate and reemphasize its own unique identity while simultaneously reaching out its hand in fellowship to others. Karl Rahner notes in his assessment of the council that its abiding significance rests on the openness to diversity and plurality in three ways. First, in liturgy and language: "In the long run the liturgy of the Church as a whole will not simply be the liturgy of the Roman church in translation, but a unit in the variety of regional liturgies, each of which will have its own peculiar character which will not consist merely in its language."[17] Second, the theology of the church "will become a world theology: that is, it will exist in the non-European, non-North American countries, but no longer merely as an export from the West."[18] And finally, in ecumenism and interreligious relations: "at this Council, Catholic Christendom adopted expressly a different, a new attitude toward other Christians and their Churches and toward the non-Christian world-religions and ratified it as truly Christian."[19] In Rahner's estimation, Vatican II represents unity in diversity, harmony in multiplicity, and concord even among lingering disagreements. Not only the Catholic Church but the church catholic, too, is still living into the promise of this council today.

In his analysis of the shift from Tridentine Catholicism to the Catholicism of Vatican II, Yves Congar quoted Father Émile Mersch, who said, "Some animals are surrounded by a shell because they have no skeleton."[20] In Vatican II, that shell dissolved and the Catholic Church was able to move forward, trusting in the stability and strength of its skeleton. In this way, Vatican II serves as a model for all churches as they seek to define their own uniqueness and live out of their distinctiveness, but in such a way as to celebrate and welcome the distinctiveness of other churches at the same time.

The Native American Church

Various Native American peoples have their own religious practices, beliefs, and communities, and while some general characteristics of Native American religion can be described, the category itself is somewhat of an artificial one. It is more accurate to describe the religious beliefs of the Lakota people (or the confederation of Sioux tribes), for example, or the Navajo Nation. However,

16. Adrian Hastings, *Modern Catholicism: Vatican II and After* (Oxford: Oxford University Press, 1990).

17. Karl Rahner, "The Abiding Significance of the Second Vatican Council," in *Concern for the Church*, vol. 20 of *Theological Investigations* (New York: Crossroad, 1981), 92.

18. Ibid., 95–96.

19. Ibid., 98.

20. Yves Congar, *Fifty Years of Catholic Theology: Conversations with Yves Congar*, ed. Bernard Lauret (Philadelphia: Fortress Press, 1988), 5.

there is something called the Native American Church, which spans a variety of different Native peoples and is not based in any particular tribe. To be clear, this is not the same as Native American Christianity. Under that umbrella, there are a variety of traditional Protestant and Catholic churches that work on Native American reservations and with specific Native American groups, and whose worship bears a distinctly Native American character.

The Native American Church, however, is something else. It has its origins in what is now the southwest United States and Mexico in the ceremonial use of peyote, which has been going on for centuries. Peyote is a hallucinogenic cactus plant, which was used by a variety of Native peoples in specific spiritual ceremonies. There are many different stories about how peyote came to Native peoples, but in all of them, it comes to the people through the agency of a woman and brings life and health.[21]

Formerly known as American Peyote religion or Peyotism, it began in Western Oklahoma among the various Southern Plains tribes who had been forced onto reservations there in the late nineteenth century. In 1918, ceremonial peyote use was incorporated as an institution named the Native American Church of North America, primarily to offer religious protection to peyote users from various state laws prohibiting drug use. In the Native American Church, peyote use is harmonized with belief in Jesus Christ, and peyote ceremonies are meant to strengthen the bonds among the community and also strengthen the user for an ethical life, which includes abstinence from alcohol.

Today, the Native American Church is also known as the Peyote Road, and it is a confederation of a variety of local and state branches. They have a website,[22] officers, and regular meetings. Some tribes are more explicitly Christian in their beliefs than others, and there is no unifying creed or statement of belief that links all local chapters of the church together. Its estimated membership is roughly 250,000–300,000 individuals, and branches of the church are found in a wide variety of different Native American peoples.

THE UNIQUE GIFTS AND PURPOSE OF THE CHURCH: THE MARKS OF THE CHURCH

One of the most well-known phrases when it comes to the relationship of Christianity and the larger society in which it exists is, "in the world but not of the world." This is not a direct quote from Scripture, but there are a variety of Bible verses that reinforce this basic idea. In John 15, Jesus says, "If you belonged to the world, the world would love you as its own. Because you do not belong the world, but I have chosen you out of the world—therefore the

---

21. See Robert J. Preston and Carl A. Hammerschlag, "The Native American Church," in *Psychodynamic Perspectives on Religion, Sect and Cult*, ed. David A. Halperin (Boston: John Wright, 1983), 93–103.

22. http://nacna.weebly.com/.

world hates you" (John 15:19). Later in John, Jesus prays, "I have given them your word, and the world has hated them because they do not belong to the world, just as I do not belong to the world" (John 17:14). In 1 John 2:15, we read, "Do not love the world or the things of the world. The love of the Father is not in those who love the world"; and finally, James 4:4 admonishes, "Do you not know that friendship with the world is enmity with God? Therefore whoever wishes to be a friend of the world becomes an enemy of God."

The extent and degree of this "mis-belonging" and "enmity" vary from denomination to denomination and from culture to culture, but in general, there are two main conclusions that can be taken from this idea of a church/world disconnect. First, Jesus seems to assume that there is to be some distinction, some separation between the church and the world, and, by analogy, between a Christian and the society in which s/he lives. One of the classic studies on the relationship between the church and the world is H. Richard Niebuhr's *Christ and Culture*.[23] In that text, he analyzes a variety of stances the church has adopted in relationship to the world over time and gives a concrete example of each. Niebuhr describes a range of options, with one extreme being "Christ against Culture," where an antagonistic opposition characterizes the relationship between the two, and the other being "Christ of Culture," where there is fundamental agreement between the two, such that any possible tension between them is eliminated. The vast majority of denominations fall somewhere in the middle, of course, and the point is that at various times in its history—and in various contexts—the church has understood this separation from society in very different ways.

What remains true still today is that one's allegiance to Christ always has the potential to put one in conflict with the demands and standards of a society. This is what Dietrich Bonhoeffer and Martin Niemöller experienced in Germany, what Desmond Tutu experienced in South Africa, and what Óscar Romero experienced in El Salvador. The primary reason for this is that the church, the body of Christ, is not merely another social organization, another self-help group, or even another charitable nonprofit. It gets its identity from Jesus Christ, and it takes its cues from the gospel message that Jesus embodied. When that gospel runs counter to the prevailing societal norms—as it always will, at some point, so goes the church and the Christians who belong to it.

Second, a Christian identity stems from the fact that one "belongs" to Christ, and therefore this identity can only be expressed in the context of a Christian community, the body of Christ into which one is baptized. That is, if it is not technically impossible to be a Christian by oneself, it is highly improbable and impractical. Christians need regular contact with the body, the community, in order to remain healthy and strong in their faith. It is not entirely metaphorical to say that the church is the place where Christians are fed, and without that food, they will slowly starve. This means that even if there

---

23. H. Richard Niebuhr, *Christ and Culture* (New York: Harper & Row, 1951).

are many places in the world where a Christian can meet God—in moments of interpersonal love and grace, in experiences in nature, in daily life with family and friends—none of these can replace the practice of regularly meeting to hear Scripture, pray, ask for and receive forgiveness, receive communion, and be strengthened and sent out for service for the sake of the world.

This runs counter to many ideas about "church" in a twenty-first-century US context, where "church" can be used widely and loosely to refer to almost any group of individuals coming together for almost any reason or for any individual experience that feels particularly spirituality edifying. As an example of the latter, country singer Maren Morris has a catchy song titled "My Church" in which she equates the feeling of driving in her car with the radio on and the windows down with going to church. *My* church: sometimes people act as though "church" is whatever they want it to be, whatever makes them feel good, relaxed, happy, and restored, whether or not it is a solitary or communal experience, diverse or monolithic. There is nothing inherently wrong with desiring uplifting, feel-good experiences, except for calling them church on that basis alone: while "church" can include those kinds of experiences, nothing in those experiences in and of themselves has an explicit, essential connection with what a church is. To suggest otherwise misses a fundamental point of the very nature of church.

Therefore, in light of both these realities, it is clear that some means of recognizing the church is required: both for those insiders who belong to the church and for those on the outside who want to know what the church is and what it does. There are two aspects of any answer to this question, neither of which can or should be separated from the other. First is what happens inside the church walls, that is, the specific things that typically occur during a gathering of the community or directly relate to that gathering. Second is what happens outside the church walls, that is, the things that a congregation or a denomination does in direct relationship to the larger world. Both of these aspects of the church's life can be encompassed under the broad category "marks of the church."

The first set of marks described here come from Martin Luther. These marks directly relate to the liturgical life of a congregation, and are, in that sense, more inwardly focused. The second set of marks are what are often called the "classic" marks of the church, taken from the Nicene Creed: "one, holy, catholic and apostolic." I describe these with the work of Lutheran theologian Craig Nessan, who uses them to explain the outward orientation of the church to the larger society. Together, they point to the unique, dual nature of the church as the body of Christ in the world, where Christians are nurtured and strengthened for the exercise of their baptismal vocation: giving glory to God through service to the neighbor and stranger.

MARTIN LUTHER'S MARKS OF THE CHURCH

It is no surprise that the nature and function of the church were a key consideration for Martin Luther throughout his lifetime. On the one hand, the abuses he had seen in the Roman Catholic Church led him to challenge the hierarchical structure that had lodged itself firmly between the individual and salvation, as well as the salvific importance placed on relics, pilgrimage, and indulgences. On the other hand, he was also very concerned about the "enthusiasts," whom he saw as having denigrated the incarnation by their lack of emphasis on sacraments and the external means of grace. Thus questions of ecclesiology appear frequently in his vast corpus.

At its core, Luther's definition of the church was quite simple: "God be praised, a seven-year-old child knows what the church is: holy believers and 'the little sheep who hear the voice of their shepherd.'"[24] However, this was by no means all he had to say. In 1539, Luther wrote a lengthy treatise titled "On the Councils and the Church." In this work, Luther reiterates his view that first and foremost the church is the people of God, but with an important qualifier regarding its existence: "This is no purely spiritual, invisible church, but a church whose existence may be known by important outward and objective marks."[25] This is a key point and one that is still relevant today. No one should have to guess about the church's existence or go looking for it. Instead, it is recognizable by certain acts that are visible for all to see.

Therefore, after critiquing papal authority in part 1 of the document and discussing the significance of the first four ecumenical councils in part 2, he then turns in part 3 to an explication of what he views as "the seven holy possessions of the church."[26] It is by these marks that "a poor confused person" can tell "where such Christian holy people are to be found in this world."[27] Gerhard Forde helpfully reminds us that all the marks Luther describes share one central characteristic: they are "acts of liberation." That is, they are acts that announce freedom from sin, death, and the devil. "If it is not that, it is no mark of the church. The true church, that is, reveals itself, shows its hand, breaks in upon us, in acts of freedom, not in acts of tyranny. Where the Spirit of the Lord is, there is liberty."[28] The seven marks are as follows:

1. Possession of the holy Word of God
2. The holy sacrament of baptism
3. The holy sacrament of the altar
4. The office of the keys (absolution for sin)
5. The office of ministry (including bishops and pastors)
6. Prayer, public praise, and thanksgiving to God

24. Martin Luther, "The Smalcald Articles," in *The Book of Concord: The Confessions of the Evangelical Lutheran Church*, ed. Robert Kolb and Timothy J. Wengert (Minneapolis: Fortress Press, 2000), 324.

25. Martin Luther, "On the Councils and the Church, 1539," trans. Charles M. Jacobs, in *Church and Ministry III*, ed. Eric Gritsch, vol. 41 of Luther's Works (Philadelphia: Fortress Press, 1966), xiv.

26. Ibid., 166.

27. Ibid., 148.

28. Gerhard O. Forde, "The Word That Kills and Makes Alive," in *Marks of the Body of Christ*, ed. Carl E. Braaten and Robert W. Jenson (Grand Rapids: Eerdmans, 1999), 3.

7. Possession of the sacred cross—that is, the experience of suffering

These are relatively straightforward, and only a brief comment needs to be said about each of them, with perhaps the exception of the last mark, about which more explanation is needed.

Without a doubt, the first three are the most important, and even among the three, the first has priority for Luther. He states the connection plainly: "for God's word cannot be without God's people, and conversely, God's people cannot be without God's word."[29] Therefore, Luther says, "Even if there were no other sign than this alone, it would still suffice to prove that a Christian, holy people must exist there. . . . It is enough for us to know how this chief holy possession purges, sustains, nourishes, strengthens, and protects the church."[30] For any group that gathers together for any reason, anywhere, at any time, if the word of God is not read, recited, and heard, it is not a gathering of the church.

Even so, the Word does not stand alone but is intimately linked to the sacraments of baptism and communion. Again, Luther: "For, as was said above of the word, wherever God's word is, there the church must be; likewise wherever baptism and the sacrament [the 'sacrament of the altar'] are, God's people must be, and vice versa."[31] Luther emphasizes that both these sacraments are to be "rightly administered," but he is also clear that such "rightness" has nothing to do with the holiness of the presider or the worthiness of the recipient. Instead, the sacraments are first and foremost a gift from God to God's beloved people.

Over the centuries, while it is certainly true that among sacramental churches these two rites have always had priority, it is equally true that their interpretation and implementation have been, and continue to be, hotly debated. Some denominations baptize infants, while others wait for a time of decision on the part of the individual. Some denominations welcome all Christians to their communion table, while others require either a specific denominational affiliation or specific theological confession for shared communion. More hopefully, however, this is also a place where there has been much work on the part of ecumenical committees and global church bodies, resulting in some full communion agreements and other memorandums of understanding.[32]

The fourth mark, the "office of the keys," refers to the practice of

29. Luther, "On the Councils," 150.
30. Ibid., 150–51.
31. Ibid., 152.
32. The work of the World Council of Churches is notable here; see their website https://www.oikoumene.org/en/. In addition, in the United States, there are full communion agreements between several mainline denominations: for example, the Episcopal Church is in full communion with the Evangelical Lutheran Church in America, the Moravian Church, and the Philippine Independent Church, among others. The Presbyterian Church USA is in full communion with the Reformed Church in America, the United Church of Christ, and the Evangelical Lutheran Church in America, among

absolution for sin and stems from Christ's declaration to his disciples in Matthew 18 (and to Peter more specifically in Matthew 16): "Truly I tell you, whatever you bind on earth will be bound in heaven, and whatever you loose on earth will be loosed in heaven." The danger here, of course, is to put the emphasis on the one who binds or lets loose—as though this mark was meant to emphasize hierarchical ecclesial authority. However, Luther wants the focus kept on the believer's relationship with God and the way in which the office of the keys nurtures and supports it. So, on the one hand, "There are some people with consciences so tender and despairing that even if they have not been publicly condemned, they cannot find comfort until they have been individually absolved by the pastor."[33] For these people, the office of the keys provides solace, strengthening their belief in a loving God.

On the other hand, there are people who refuse to accept responsibility for their injustice and sinfulness, and for them, they need to be held accountable. In other words, in a Christian community, sin must be named, and those who are "so obdurate that they neither recant in their heart and want their sins forgiven individually by the pastor, nor desist from their sins"[34] must face the consequences. There is no escaping that this is a hard word: Luther says that "those who refuse to be converted or sanctified again shall be cast out from this holy people, that is, bound and excluded by means of the keys."[35] Is it possible, or even advisable, to "cast someone out" from a community? And even more, who can and should make that decision and on what grounds?

The practical definition of sin is always contested and certain behaviors that are deemed sinful by some are not viewed that way at all by others. In light of these challenges, there are perhaps only two things the church can say with absolute certainty. First, the office of the keys should only be exercised with great care and humility, and second, the office of keys should only be exercised under the overarching umbrella of God's infinite grace and mercy, particularly in light of Christ's exhortation to forgive "seventy times seven."

The *Angakkuq*: Religious Leadership in the Inuit

Like many other indigenous peoples, the Inuit rely on shamans for a variety of religious functions. These shamans are called *angakkuit* (this is the plural form). Both men and women can become *angakkuit*, and they are typically identified and trained by other *angakkuit*. They are believed to have great powers, and they can interpret dreams, communicate with the spirits, and travel quickly over long distances. There are a variety of rituals through which

others. In addition, there are robust ecumenical dialogues between most major denominations, including the Catholic Church.

33. Ibid., 153.
34. Ibid.
35. Ibid.

spirit communication takes place, and in these rituals, which usually involve dance, the *angakkuit* typically wear special masks that themselves have the power to facilitate communication with the spirit world. It is believed that each *angakkuq* has a spirit guide, called a *tuurngaq*. This guide accompanies the *angakkuq* and protects them.

The *angakkuit* do not live apart from the rest of their community; on the contrary, they live as others do, sharing traditional roles and responsibilities most of the time. However, when someone becomes sick or needs a dream interpreted, or a misfortune befalls the community, then the *angakkuq* is called upon to act. One major function of an *angakkuq* is to appease Sedna, the goddess of the sea. Sedna is believed to have control over the arctic animals, and therefore, she has the power to either provide or withhold food from the community. Thus in some Inuit communities, the *angakkuq* participates in an annual ceremony designed to placate Sedna and assure a good season of hunting. This is accomplished by traveling down to her realm and combing out the tangles in her hair, which she cannot do for herself (in all the mythological accounts of her, she has lost her fingers; typically it is said that they transformed into the first seals and other marine mammals). The ceremony also involves communal confession and repentance for breaking any taboos over the year, particularly those that govern proper rituals around hunting and the killing/eating of animals.

The fifth mark of the church is its leadership: "bishops, pastors, or preachers, who publicly and privately give, administer, and use the aforementioned four things or holy possessions in behalf of and in the name of the church. . . . The people as a whole cannot do these things, but must entrust or have them entrusted to one person."[36] Luther is very clear that the individuals to whom these possessions are entrusted are not ontologically different than other Christians, nor is their calling higher or better than that of others. There is not a check-off sheet of personal qualifications for a public minister, and minsters are just as sinful as the flocks they tend. However, such offices are needed for the sake of good order and healthy functioning of the church, and therefore Luther commends them. It should be noted, however, that Luther was certain that women could not fulfill this role; he believed the Holy Spirit has "excepted women, children and incompetent people from this function, but chooses (except in emergencies) only competent males to fulfill this office."[37] This debate continues still today among the many denominations and church bodies that continue to exclude women from these roles.

The sixth mark is "prayer, public praise, and thanksgiving to God." By this, Luther means the Lord's Prayer being recited in church, psalms and hymns

36. Ibid., 154.
37. Ibid.

being sung, and the public use of the Creeds and the Catechism. Finally, the seventh mark is possession of the sacred cross, which Luther equates with the experience of suffering. There are two helpful ways to understand this mark and one interpretation that must be avoided at all costs. First is the way Luther himself understood it. For Luther, it was clear: insofar as the body of Christ stands against the world and the demonic powers of evil, those who are members of that body will suffer the consequences. In most contemporary US contexts, this possibility is hardly imaginable; even though there are Christians who feel maligned and persecuted because they are no longer allowed to pray the Lord's Prayer in public schools or because the Ten Commandments are not displayed in public buildings, this hardly counts as persecution. Those in other countries who are imprisoned or even killed for their faith, and those whose churches must meet underground for fear of legal and even physical reprisal—*that* is the kind of suffering Luther had in mind here. One way to interpret this mark, then, is the willingness to suffer as a consequence of proclaiming one's faith.

The other way this mark might be interpreted is more in line with some of the recent pronouncements by Pope Francis, who emphasizes that the church must be down in the trenches with the people who are suffering poverty, oppression, and discrimination, and stand with them and suffer with them. In Pope Francis's recent book, *The Church of Mercy*, part two is titled "A Poor Church for the Poor," and in these chapters, he emphasizes that "we are called to find Christ in [the poor], to lend our voice to their causes, but also to be their friends, to listen to them, to speak for them, and to embrace the mysterious wisdom that God wishes to share with us through them."[38]

By contrast, the interpretation that must be strenuously and vociferously rejected is the idea that all suffering, regardless of its source, is somehow Christ-like and must be accepted as part of one's Christian duty to carry one's cross and follow Christ. Again, Luther is clear about what kind of suffering he is talking about here: "the only reason [Christians] must suffer is that they steadfastly adhere to Christ and God's word, enduring this for the sake of Christ."[39] So, the suffering that one endures in an abusive marriage, an exploitative job, or an unjust legal system, or the suffering that comes from hunger, homelessness, or illness—these explicitly are *not* examples of Christian suffering. These kinds of suffering are the result of human sinfulness and must be resisted both by individual Christians and by the church as a whole.

While today's context is in multiple and significant ways unlike sixteenth-century Germany, these seven marks of Martin Luther still can function as a means by which to determine what kinds of gatherings and what kinds of institutions can properly bear the name "church." While certainly different denominations might disagree on the number and/or ranking of these seven

---

38. Pope Francis, *The Church of Mercy: A Vision for the Church* (Chicago: Loyola Press, 2014), 25.
39. Luther, "On the Councils," 165.

marks, at the same time, in their complete absence one could rightly wonder if the name "church" is perhaps not being misused. At their core, Luther's marks keep the focus on God and remind the congregation/institution in whose name it is gathered and, indeed, how it is able to gather at all.

Ancestral Rites in Confucianism

There is no institutional comparison in Confucianism to the Christian church. In its early growth in China, it was a "sociopolitical vision" that over the centuries played out in different ways in all spheres of society: the government, domestic life and gender roles, ritual practice, and the education of both peasants and the elite.[40] Thus the idea of a separation between Confucianism and society as a whole was never operative. Instead, the question was how and to what degree society was characterized by Confucian ideals. Beginning in the second century BCE and culminating in the tenth century CE, Confucianism established itself as the overwhelmingly dominant ideology of the Chinese state.

One of the key markers of Confucianism (and the Chinese society in which it developed) is filial piety, and a primary way in which this piety is expressed religiously is in the practice of ancestral rites. These rites can be performed at home or in a larger public temple, but their purpose in either place is the same: to express a family's gratitude to the ancestors for their continued blessing and protection, to sustain the presence of the ancestors in the current world in order to maintain the connection between this world and the next, to ask for relief from misfortune, and to ask for continued assistance in the future. These rites strengthen the bonds of family over time and space and remind the living family members that one day they too will be ancestors, and they will continue to live on in the lives of their descendants.

The belief in ancestors, and the remembrance of them in the rites, also has a way of demystifying the afterlife. Unlike in Christianity, where heaven is often best understood and described apophatically—that is, by what it is not, and by how *unlike* it is to what exists now—in Chinese society and in Confucianism, the similarity between this world and the afterworld is emphasized. "In the Chinese tradition, it is Second Uncle Feng and Grandpa Feng who reside in the other world. There is little about Second Uncle and Grandpa that is unfamiliar—or immaterial—to the younger generations of Fengs. . . . This is to say that in China the 'other-world' was not very 'otherly' or remote. It is perhaps best, then, to understand the Chinese spirit world not as an 'other' world but rather as part of a continuum in the world of the family."[41] The ancestral rites help cement this understanding and the bond between family members over generations.

---

40. Gardner, *Confucianism*, 87.
41. Ibid., 103–4.

THE CLASSIC MARKS OF THE CHURCH:
ONE, HOLY, CATHOLIC, AND APOSTOLIC

Luther's marks do not tell the full story of the church's existence, in no small part because the church is not only concerned with those "within" but also those "without"; not only with what happens in the chancel but also what happens on the street. For this, we turn to the third article of the Nicene Creed, where Christians confess their faith in the "one, holy, catholic and apostolic" church. Jürgen Moltmann describes these classic marks of the church as statements of faith, hope, and action,[42] and Cheryl Peterson calls them "dimensions of the Spirit's activity in and amidst this 'holy community.'"[43] These descriptions point to the fact that these marks are not so much adjectives of classification as they are adverbs of engagement: that is, they herald a way of being in the world to which the church is inspired to embrace through the ongoing empowerment of the Holy Spirit.

The different ways of interpreting and describing these marks are legion, but one interesting and helpful analysis can be found in Craig Nessan's book *Shalom Church*. Here, he uses them in the service of offering a concrete strategy for both understanding and undergirding the life of the church in today's world. Nessan writes, "The four classical marks of the church provide a constructive agenda delineating what the church is 'for' in its corporate life,"[44] specifically in the face of twin "spiritual maladies" facing the church: "the disease of rampant individualism that conceives religiosity primarily as a matter of personal preferences rather than communal responsibility"; and the "increasing gravitational pull toward construing [the church's] mission most ardently in relationship to those things it 'opposes.'"[45] In light of these maladies, Nessan argues that the church is called to be a "shalom church," a church of peace, justice, care, and respect for all people and the whole world. Using the Jewish concept of *tikkun olam* (repairing the world), Nessan writes, "God is calling the church as the body of Christ to act as a servant for the minding of creation. By giving itself away to nourish a world in need, the church discovers its vocation as a ministering community."[46]

With this goal in mind, then, the marks of the church are explicitly turned outward, defined not primarily with a description of what happens inside the sanctuary walls but how the church orients itself ethically toward the rest of the world. The "oneness" of the church, then, is seen not first and foremost in a creedal confession but in the practice of reconciliation and peacemaking:

---

42. Jürgen Moltmann, *The Church in the Power of the Spirit: A Contribution to Messianic Ecclesiology,* trans. Margaret Kohl (Minneapolis: Fortress Press, 1993), 337–61.

43. Cheryl M. Peterson, *Who Is the Church? An Ecclesiology for the Twenty-First Century* (Minneapolis: Fortress Press, 2013), 131.

44. Craig L. Nessan, *Shalom Church: The Body of Christ as Ministering Community* (Minneapolis: Fortress Press, 2010), 2.

45. Ibid., 1.

46. Ibid., 7.

"The members of the body of Christ are formed by the biblical narrative to be the people of peace."[47] The "holiness" of the church is not manifest primarily in the personal piety of individuals or congregations but rather in the practice of justice, in "the vocation to be a holy people who demonstrate justice to the poor and powerless."[48] The catholicity of the church is not merely the sum of its disparate parts, emphasizing the unity of the whole ecclesial body around the world. Instead, catholicity points to something even more universal, a wholeness that "entails the incorporation of all creation into Christ"[49] and calls for faithful care of the whole creation. Finally, the apostolic character of the church serves as a reminder that the church is called to conform its teaching to the gospel message as first proclaimed by the apostles; what that looks like today is embodying "the vital affirmation that every human person has been created in the image of God (*imago Dei*) and for that reason alone is deserving of infinite respect."[50]

This interpretation of the marks of the church serves as a helpful reminder that the church's unique identity is not meant to isolate and segregate the church away from the rest of the world, nor is it meant to nurture a relationship of judgment, antagonism, or even indifference to the rest of the world. Instead, the church's identity is a tool of empowerment, a way to draw strength from its connection to Christ, the apostles, and its global manifestations in order to be a presence of *shalom* wherever it finds itself, to all those—human and non-human—with whom it comes in contact. None of this is possible without the gift of the Holy Spirit, of course, and first and foremost, the church is something we receive through the power of God. Yet, at the same time, Christians are called to work with the Spirit as they seek to actively and faithfully embody the body of Christ in all its manifestations in all corners of the world.

THE POWER OF THE HOLY SPIRIT: THE DYNAMIC GLOBAL CHURCH

A chapter on ecclesiology in the twenty-first century cannot but end on a global note, with a discussion of the rapid and dynamic growth of the church in the Global South. The demographic shift in the "statistical center of gravity" of the church from the Global North to the Global South,[51] which has occurred rapidly over the past half century, is indisputable. Even though the relative population of Christians worldwide has stayed mostly flat in the last century—roughly 34 percent in 1900 and 33 percent in 2010[52]—the location of those Christians has changed dramatically. Some statistics help tell the story.

47. Ibid., 69.
48. Ibid., 87.
49. Ibid., 114.
50. Ibid., 143.
51. Albert W. Hickman, "Christianity's Shift from the Global North to the Global South," *Review and Expositor* 111, no. 1 (2014): 42.
52. Ibid.

In 1900, almost 70 percent of all Christians lived in Europe; by 2010, only roughly 25 percent of Christians were European. By contrast, in 1900 less than 2 percent of all Christians lived in Africa; by 2010, that number had grown to just under 22 percent.[53] Within Africa, it is the middle section of the continent that has seen the most dramatic change: in 1910, only 1 percent of that population was Christian; by 2010, that number reached 80 percent.[54] In addition, in 1910, nine of the ten countries with the largest Christian population were in the Global North (Brazil, at number nine, was the only exception). In 2010, seven of the top ten countries were in the Global South; only the United States, Russia, and Germany were left representing the North.[55] What this means is obvious: "The typical late twentieth-century Christian was no longer a European man, but a Latin American or African woman."[56] (And, I would add, a *young* woman.) At the same time, it should be noted that the shift in numbers has not been matched by a shift in material wealth. Although over 60 percent of all Christians live in the Global South today, the Global North still holds roughly 80 percent of Christian wealth.[57]

In addition to Christianity, Islam is also growing. In fact, Islam is the fastest-growing religion in the world. If current growth patterns hold, by 2050 there will be nearly as many Muslims worldwide as Christians.[58] This is related to a greater trend: the past few decades have continued to see overall growth in religious affiliation in general, in no small part because of the growth of religious adherents in China. In 1970, 80 percent of the world's population was religious. By 2010, that number was 88 percent, and by 2020, the percentage is expected to rise to 90 percent.[59]

The growth is not uniform among the various Christian denominations, however, and the most rapid growth has been seen in Pentecostal and Charismatic churches; between 1970 and 2010, they grew at almost four times the rate of Christianity in general. In 2010, they made up roughly 26 percent of all Christians worldwide, and if their growth continues as expected, by 2020 they will comprise almost 28 percent of global Christians.[60] One more point is worth mentioning here and that is the decline of Christians in the Middle East. Thanks to years of violent conflict, entire communities of Christians in

53. Ibid.

54. Todd M. Johnson et al., "Christianity 2010: A View from the New *Atlas of Global Christianity*," *International Bulletin of Missionary Research* 34, no. 1 (2010): 29.

55. Hickman, "Christianity's Shift," 43.

56. Dana L. Robert, "Shifting Southward: Global Christianity Since 1945," *International Bulletin of Missionary Research* 24, no. 2 (April 2000): 50.

57. Hickman, "Christianity's Shift," 45–46.

58. "The Future of World Religions: Population Growth Projections, 2010–2050," *Religion and Public Life*, Pew Research Center, published April 2, 2015, http://tinyurl.com/zk2qwre.

59. Gina A. Bellofatto and Todd M. Johnson, "Key Findings of *Christianity in Its Global Context, 1970–2020*," *International Bulletin of Missionary Research* 37, no. 3 (July 2013): 157.

60. Ibid., 158.

Syria, Lebanon, and Iraq have fled those countries: in 1970, the population of Christians in Western Asia was 7.3 percent; by 2020, it is predicted to be only 5.4 percent Christian.[61]

The situation in China is worth noting in particular, given the large population there and the fact that the church in China is expected to grow rapidly in the next decades. However, what form this growth will take is not entirely clear. Christianity has existed in China for millennia—at least since the eighth century—but following the rise of the Communist Party in 1949, all Christian missionaries were expelled and the Christian church in general was criticized as a manifestation of Western powers. The attempts to eradicate religion from China proved ineffective, however, such that one can say that today "what we see in China is an increasingly religious society, even though the communist party is still in power."[62] This includes a relaxing of the ban on Christianity. In 2005, China published its "Regulations on Religious Affairs," which many hoped would facilitate the possibility of registration for a wider variety of Chinese Christian congregations. The promise is still there, but more than ten years later, it has not yet been fully realized.[63]

In addition to a great number of Protestant churches in China, there also exists a form of Chinese Catholicism. However, the "Chinese Patriotic Catholic Association" does not accept the authority of the pope and elects its own bishops independently. One of the most significant, and controversial, churches in China is what is known as the "Three-Self Patriotic Movement," a government-sanctioned Protestant Church and one of the largest Christian organizations in the country. The three "selves" of the movement are self-governance, self-support, and self-propagation—all of which are meant to affirm complete independence from Western churches, missionaries, and dollars. The controversy is around how "pro-Party" this church (as well as its members) is and how much it is controlled by the government. It will be interesting in the years to come to see if a gulf continues to widen between the TSPM Church and what is called the "house church," or "underground church," which is unregistered and subject to persecution, or if China will demonstrate a greater willingness to tolerate—and perhaps even sanction—more diversity in Chinese Christianity.

CONCLUSION: CHALLENGES AND OPPORTUNITIES

For the churches in the Global South, the challenge of true indigenization remains. Even though, as Dana Robert writes, "the Second World War revealed

---

61. Ibid., 160.

62. Kevin Xiyi Yao, "Religion and Church in China: Trends and Dynamics," *Africanus Journal* 6, no. 1 (2014): 23.

63. For more detailed information, see Lauren B. Homer, "Registration of Chinese Protestant House Churches Under China's 2005 Regulation on Religious Affairs: Resolving the Implementation Impasse," *Journal of Church and State* 52, no. 1 (2010): 50–73.

the rotten underbelly of European imperialism,"[64] in many places in the Global South, churches still suffer from acute "Northernization" and are still working to throw off the vestiges of colonialism and grow into their own indigenous identities. Albert Hickman writes, "Despite Christianity's inherent linguistic and cultural translatability, however, Southern Christianity was formed with and still retains many Northern trappings, so that it often appears foreign to non-Christians (and even, at times, to Southern Christians)."[65] In addition, Hickman quotes Daniel Daesoon Kim, Director of Chiang Mai Theological Seminary in Thailand, who says, "The biggest issue the Church in Asia is facing is a severe violation of the incarnational principle. . . . Contextualization has been very poor, making Christianity so foreign to local people."[66]

One place, however, where this contextualization is happening is in Africa, with the work of the African Independent Churches or African Initiated Churches (AICs): "churches founded in Africa, by Africans, primarily for Africans."[67] Robert notes that by 1984, there were over seven thousand of these churches, located in forty-three countries across Africa.[68] Many of these churches are known as "Spirit churches," also called *Aladura* churches in Western Africa, and as such, they emphasize dramatic manifestations of the Holy Spirit, such as speaking in tongues, exorcisms, and miraculous healings. Surely in the decades to come, the church catholic will see more examples like this occurring all around the world.

Finally, for the churches in the Global North, one of the main challenges is to break out of traditional European patterns and develop a more welcoming, relevant presence for non-European Christian immigrants. Hickman notes that "the United States will likely continue to have the largest Christian population of any country well into the twenty-first century, largely owing to the high numbers of Christian immigrants (many from the Global South) who continue to arrive in the county."[69] In fact, almost half of all people living in diaspora worldwide are Christian, and most of these are individuals moving from the Global South to the Global North; Mexico has sent the most Christians into other countries and most of them have ended up in the United States.[70]

Yet, many traditional denominational churches still represent the white European backgrounds out of which they developed. As of 2014, the National Baptist Convention, the Evangelical Lutheran Church in America, the United Methodist Church, and the Episcopal Church were at the very bottom of the diversity spectrum of Christian denominations in the United States.[71] Much more intentional work must be done here so that what Martin Luther King Jr.

---

64. Robert, "Shifting Southward," 50.
65. Hickman, "Christianity's Shift," 41.
66. Ibid., 44.
67. Robert, "Shifting Southward," 53.
68. Ibid.
69. Hickman, "Christianity's Shift," 43.
70. Bellofatto and Johnson, "Key Findings," 163.

observed in 1960 does not remain true in 2016: the most segregated hour of Christian America is 11:00 a.m. on Sunday morning.

At this point in the long arc of the church's existence, living as it does in this "in-between" time, looking back toward the resurrection and forward toward the in-breaking reign of God, perhaps what we can say with the greatest confidence going forward is that which we do not yet know. Surely, the church will look very different in ten, twenty, and certainly fifty years, but what that look will be is as yet unclear. However, amidst that uncertainty, there is room for hope: hope for more communion in diversity, more understanding in differences, and more shared action in the face of injustice. "For mortals it is impossible, but for God all things are possible" (Matt 19:26). For the church everywhere, in all times and places, may it be so.

QUESTIONS FOR FURTHER DISCUSSION AND REFLECTION:

1. If a Sikh *gurdwara* is centered around the Guru Granth Sahib, what is your congregation's center? What are the important components of your congregation's sanctuary? What are the strengths/weaknesses that you see?

2. In some descriptions of peyote use, it is called "sacramental." Is that a helpful way to characterize it? How do you understand a sacrament? Does it make sense to talk about sacraments in other religious traditions? On what grounds?

3. Is there a relationship between the "cloud of witnesses" described in Christianity and the veneration of ancestors in Confucianism? What is the same? What is different?

4. What are the characteristics of leadership in your church? What kinds of things disqualify one for leadership? Do you agree with those standards?

5. What does it mean to be able to communicate with the spirit world, like the *angakkuq* does in Inuit communities? Do Christian religious leaders have a special ability to do this? Does everyone? *Is* there a spirit world in Christianity?

71. Michael Lipka, "The Most and Least Racially Diverse U.S. Religious Groups," *Fact Tank: News in the Numbers*, Pew Research Center, July 27, 2015, http://tinyurl.com/j4mfrwk.

Conclusion: An Ending Is Always a Beginning

Here, at the end of the second volume of a two-volume work, it seems appropriate to offer a short conclusion to the whole. To that end, there are three final points I want to emphasize, particularly in light of the core assumptions about comparative theology that stand at the heart of both volumes.

The first point involves ends and beginnings. One of the realities that is both terribly frustrating and also terribly exciting about the work of systematic theology is that every ending is always and simultaneously a new beginning. Every theological conclusion about God, humanity, and the universe—and all the myriad complex relationships between them—is only provisional, awaiting modification, confirmation, or even rejection. It simply cannot be otherwise. God is still and always at work, moving in and among God's creation, such that every new interlocutor, every new scientific discovery, every new cultural shift calls the theologian back to the writing desk, demanding a response, an answer to what it all means for Christian doctrine and practice.

This is terribly frustrating, because it means that no sooner is a book or article published, full of wise, creative theological thinking, than its argument is challenged, revised, and perhaps even repudiated altogether. As soon as we think the decisive, ultimate word has been said on a topic, another scholar or practitioner comes out with a fresh perspective or new idea that shakes that word to its core and calls into question its validity and veracity. Or, equally likely, an event occurs, or a discovery—9/11, the Holocaust, the theory of evolution, the big bang theory—that causes us to step back and rethink everything, our very existence, and the stories we tell to make sense of it. If theology is unwilling to engage in this discipline of reimagining, it ossifies and quickly becomes irrelevant, telling a story that no one cares about or understands, a story that has no relationship to the world around it. Theology is a marathon, not a sprint.

However, there is another way to interpret this theological fluidity, a way that could be terribly exciting. Another thing that often happens once a book or article is published is that someone sees something new in the argument that the author herself did not see—some new ramification or conclusion—and the conversation quickly grows and expands, including new voices and new perspectives. In this way, the great theological chorus goes on, carrying forward the work from earlier mothers and fathers and creating space for daughters and sons yet to come. New levels of theological thinking need foundations on which to build, and every presentation, every dialogue, every argument contributes to that foundation. (Including, of course, the lived praxis of theology, the embodiment of Christian thought.) So, an important aspect of any theological conclusion is the invitation to see in it a new beginning and a summons to pick up the pen yet again.

The second point emphasizes the relevance and necessity of Christian theology in the twenty-first century. One of the principal theological commitments on which this two-volume work is founded is the belief that theology matters: that is, doing the difficult and necessary work of making sense of God's presence and role in the world, and the interrelatedness of all creation in God, has a critical role to play in human life. The work of Christian theology in general, and comparative theology in particular, facilitates meaning-making, relationship-building, and community formation in radical, creative ways, and is desperately needed in times of fragmentation, hopelessness, and division.

Too often, Christian theology is mute in the face of social unrest, racial injustice, and economic exploitation. Too often, Christian theology fails to consider real-world bodies in its reflection. Too often, Christian theology seeks only to confirm the beliefs of an in-group and reassure the faithful. We cannot be content with that. Instead, Christian theology can and must step out with both feet into today's world, with all its complexities, its messiness, its violence, and its suffering, in order to speak a word of hope and embody a gospel of promise. The world is a terrible, brutal place, but it is also breathtakingly lovely. The world bears the scars of hate and cruelty, but it also swells with love and gentleness. The world is threatened by darkness on all sides, and yet light still shines—persistently, insistently, ceaselessly. And if the light still shines, so must we, but we cannot do this alone. Instead, as I have said repeatedly and adamantly, to challenge the powers of death and destruction in the world, Christian theology needs the strength and wisdom of other theological voices as well, those from Islam and Sikhism, from Confucianism and Buddhism, in order to offer the most faithful witness and the most compelling response. This leads to my third and last point.

The final and most important point to emphasize here is that Christian theology can and should be inherently interreligious. This is the foundational conviction of this entire work, a conviction that only grows with time and experience. The fact is that if the Christian theological silo ever existed, it most certainly does not exist anymore. And, to be clear, by "silo," I mean the presumption that Christian theologians can keep to themselves as they go about their work, without recognition or consideration of other religious traditions or, even worse, with only a sweeping dismissal or condemnation of them. A good argument can be made that this silo never really existed, not even in the earliest moments of the life of the Christian church when the first Christian theologians were constructing their arguments squarely within the arena of Judaism and Jewish thought (as well as other religious influences). However, in spite of these solidly interreligious beginnings, throughout its history, Christianity often has acted like it is the only religion that exists or, at the very least, the only religion that matters. Over and over it has paid little attention to the wisdom of others and the manifestations of the Divine in others, and it has not brought into its sphere of discourse the wise voices of Hindus and Buddhists, for example. Now, however, in the twenty-first century, given what we know about God, given the dynamic global interrelatedness of the human family, and given the desperate ecological crises we face, all Christians, including Christian theologians, cannot but think, talk, and work with, not apart from, our interreligious brothers and sisters. There simply is no other fruitful way forward.

And, perhaps even more to the point, even if we could go it alone, why would we want to? We are stronger together than we are apart: stronger in wisdom, stronger in friendship, stronger in work, and stronger in witness. The religions of the world, and the theological thinking that grounds them, can be and do so much more together than they can be and do individually. To be clear, this commitment to togetherness does not in any way demand a diluting of differences. On the contrary, dialogue often sharpens an understanding and appreciation of differences and makes them clearer, and this, too, is a strength. The point of interreligious dialogue is not conformity or agreement but mutual learning and respect, mutual growth and transformation. Diversity is better than uniformity; each religion brings different gifts to the table, and each gift is a treasure, desperately needed.

Confidence in the joy of ongoing theological reflection, enthusiasm for the increasing relevance and necessity of Christian theology for life in the world, and appreciation for the bountiful riches that result from the inherently interreligious nature of Christian theology: these are the convictions I have attempted to persuade the reader to share. Overall, then, I hope to have created for the Christian reader in particular not only an openness and eagerness for receiving fresh insights, but equally the invitation to live out of those insights: for the church, for the whole human family, and for the flourishing of the entire creation, which God, and we, cherish so dearly.

Bibliography

Abelard, Peter. *Commentary on the Epistle to the Romans*. Translated by Steven R. Cartwright. Washington, DC: The Catholic University of America Press, 2011.

Abimbola, Wande. "Aspects of Yoruba Images of the Divine: Ifa Divination Artifacts." *Dialogue & Alliance* 3, no. 2 (Summer 1989): 24–29.

Aftandilian, Dave. "Toward a Native American Theology of Animals: Creek and Cherokee Perspectives." *Cross Currents* 61, no. 2 (June 2011): 191–207.

Akino, Shigeki. "Spirit-Sending Ceremonies." In *Ainu: Spirit of a Northern People*. Edited by William W. Fitzhugh and Chisato O. Dubreuil, 248–55. Washington, DC: Arctic Studies Center, National Museum of Natural History, 1999.

Anselm of Canterbury. *Cur Deus Homo*. Translated by Joseph M. Colleran. Albany, NY: Magi Books, 1969.

Augustine. *The Trinity (De Trinitate)*. Edited by John E. Rotelle, OSA. Translated by Edmund Hill, OP. Hyde Park, NY: New City Press, 1991.

Awolalu, J. Omosade. "A Review of Scholars' Views on the Yoruba Concept of God." *Journal of Religious Thought* 31, no. 2 (Fall–Winter 1974–75): 5–15.

Balthasar, Hans Urs von. *Dare We Hope "That All Men Be Saved"?: With a Short Discourse on Hell*. Translated by David Kipp and Lothar Krauth. San Francisco: Ignatius Press, 1988.

Bellofatto, Gina A., and Todd M. Johnson. "Key Findings of *Christianity in Its Global Context, 1970–2020*," *International Bulletin of Missionary Research* 37, no. 3 (July 2013): 157–64.

Berling, Judith A. *A Pilgrim in Chinese Culture: Negotiating Religious Diversity*. Maryknoll, NY: Orbis Books, 1997.

Berthrong, John. "Confucian Formulas for Peace: Harmony." *Society* 51, no. 6 (2014): 645–55.

Berthrong, John, and Evelyn Nagai Berthrong. *Confucianism: A Short Introduction*. Oxford: Oneworld, 2014.

Birch, Bruce C., Walter Brueggemann, Terence E. Fretheim, and David L. Petersen, eds. *A Theological Introduction to the Old Testament*. 2nd ed. Nashville: Abingdon Press, 2005.

Boff, Leonardo. *Holy Trinity, Perfect Community*. Maryknoll, NY: Orbis Books, 2000.

Bowker, John. *World Religions*. London: DK Publications, 2006.

Braaten, Carl. "The Christian Doctrine of Salvation." *Interpretation* 35, no. 2 (April 1981): 117–31.

Brass, Paul. "Victims, Heroes or Martyrs? Partition and the Problem of

Memorialization in Contemporary Sikh History." *Sikh Formations* 2, no. 1 (June 2006): 17–31.

Brock, Rita Nakashima, and Rebecca Ann Parker. *Proverbs of Ashes: Violence, Redemptive Suffering, and the Search for What Saves Us.* Boston: Beacon Press, 2001.

Brown, Joanne Carlson, and Carole R. Bohn, eds. *Christianity, Patriarchy and Abuse: A Feminist Critique.* New York: Pilgrim, 1989.

Brown, Peter. *Augustine of Hippo: A Biography.* Berkeley: University of California Press, 1969.

Buckley, Anthony D. "The God of Smallpox: Aspects of Yoruba Religious Knowledge." *Africa* 55, no. 2 (1985): 187–200.

Budden, Chris. "Exploring Contextual Theology in Australia in Dialogue with Indigenous People." *International Journal of Public Theology* 2, no. 3 (2008): 292–312.

Charlesworth, Max, Françoise Dussart, and Howard Morphy, eds. *Aboriginal Religions in Australia: An Anthology of Recent Writings.* Aldershot, UK: Ashgate, 2005.

Chuang Tzu. *Chuang Tzu: Basic Writings.* Translated by Burton Watson. New York: Columbia University Press, 1996.

Clooney, Francis X. *Comparative Theology: Deep Learning Across Religious Borders.* Malden, MA: Wiley-Blackwell, 2010.

Cole, W. Owen. *Understanding Sikhism.* Edinburgh: Dunedin Academic Press, 2004.

Coleman, Monica A. "Sacrifice, Surrogacy and Salvation: Womanist Reflections on Motherhood and Work." *Black Theology* 12, no. 3 (November 2014): 200–212.

Confucius. *The Analects.* Translated by D. C. Lau. London: Penguin Books, 1979.

Congar, Yves. *Fifty Years of Catholic Theology: Conversations with Yves Congar.* Edited by Bernard Lauret. Philadelphia: Fortress Press, 1988.

Dada, Adekunle Oyinloye. "Old Wine in New Bottle: Elements of Yoruba Culture in Aladura Christianity." *Black Theology* 12, no. 1 (April 2014): 19–32.

Daley, Brian E. *Gregory of Nazianzus.* London: Routledge, 2006.

Dass, Nirmal, trans. *Songs of the Saints from the Adi Granth.* Albany: State University of New York Press, 2000.

De La Torre, Miguel. *Santería: The Beliefs and Rituals of a Growing Religion in America.* Grand Rapids: Eerdmans, 2004.

Despeux, Catherine, and Livia Kohn. *Women in Daoism.* Cambridge, MA: Three Pines Press, 2003.

Dietz, Kelly L. "Ainu in the International Arena." In *Ainu: Spirit of a Northern People.* Edited by William W. Fitzhugh and Chisato O. Dubreuil, 359–65.

Washington, DC: Arctic Studies Center, National Museum of Natural History, 1999.

Engelhardt, Ute. "Longevity Techniques and Chinese Medicine." In *Daoism Handbook*. Edited by Livia Kohn, 74–108. Leiden: Brill, 2000.

Evangelical Lutheran Church in American and Evangelical Lutheran Church in Canada. *Evangelical Lutheran Worship*. Minneapolis: Augsburg Fortress, 2006.

Fenech, Louis E. "Martyrdom and the Execution of Guru Arjan in Early Sikh Sources." *Journal of the American Oriental Society* 121, no. 1 (January/March 2001): 20–31.

Fitzhugh, William W. "Ainu Ethnicity: A History." In *Ainu: Spirit of a Northern People*. Edited by William W. Fitzhugh and Chisato O. Dubreuil, 9–26. Washington, DC: Arctic Studies Center, National Museum of Natural History, 1999.

Forde, Gerhard O. "The Word That Kills and Makes Alive." In *Marks of the Body of Christ*. Edited by Carl E. Braaten and Robert W. Jenson, 1–12. Grand Rapids: Eerdmans, 1999.

Foster, Richard J. *Celebration of Discipline: The Path to Spiritual Growth*. London: Hodder & Stoughton, 1989.

Francis. *The Church of Mercy: A Vision for the Church*. Chicago: Loyola Press, 2014.

Fujimura, Hisakazu. "*Kamuy*: Gods You Can Argue With." In *Ainu: Spirit of a Northern People*. Edited by William W. Fitzhugh and Chisato O. Dubreuil, 193–97. Washington, DC: Arctic Studies Center, National Museum of Natural History, 1999.

Gao, Xiongya. "Women Existing for Men: Confucianism and Social Injustice against Women in China." *Race, Gender & Class* 10, no. 3 (2003): 114–25.

Gardner, Daniel K. *Confucianism: A Very Short Introduction*. Oxford: Oxford University Press, 2014.

González, Justo, L. *The Story of Christianity*. 2 vols. San Francisco: HarperSanFrancisco, 1984–85.

Gorman, Michael J. "Romans: The First Christian Treatise on Theosis." *Journal of Theological Interpretation* 5, no. 1 (2011): 13–34.

Gregersen, Niels Henrik. "The Extended Body of Christ: Three Dimensions of Deep Incarnation." In *Incarnation: On the Scope and Depth of Christology*. Edited by Niels Henrik Gregersen, 225–54. Minneapolis: Fortress Press, 2015.

Haight, Roger. "Holy Spirit and the Religions." In *The Lord and Giver of Life: Perspectives on Constructive Pneumatology*. Edited by David H. Jensen, 55–70. Louisville: Westminster John Knox, 2008.

Hang, Lin. "Traditional Confucianism and Its Contemporary Relevance." *Asian Philosophy* 21, no. 4 (November 2011): 437–45.

Hans, Surjit, ed. *B-40 Janamsakhi Guru Baba Nanak Paintings*. Amritsar: Guru Nanak Dev University, 1987.

Harrison, Nonna Verna. "Theosis as Salvation: An Orthodox Perspective." *Pro Ecclesia* 6, no. 4 (Fall 1997): 429–43.

Harvey, Graham, ed. *Indigenous Religions: A Companion*. London: Cassell, 2000.

Hastings, Adrian. *Modern Catholicism: Vatican II and After*. New York: Oxford University Press, 1990.

Herbermann, Charles G., Edward A. Pace, Condé B. Fallen, Thomas J. Shahan, John J. Wynne, eds. *The Catholic Encyclopedia: An International Work of Reference on the Constitution, Doctrine, Discipline, and History of the Catholic Church*. London: Catholic Way, 2014.

Hickman, Albert W. "Christianity's Shift from the Global North to the Global South." *Review and Expositor* 111, no. 1 (2014): 41–47.

Homer, Lauren B. "Registration of Chinese Protestant House Churches Under China's 2005 Regulation on Religious Affairs: Resolving the Implementation Impasse." *Journal of Church and State* 52, no. 1 (2010): 50–73.

Huang, Yong. "Confucianism." In *Religions of the World: An Introduction to Culture and Meaning*. Edited by Lawrence E. Sullivan, 143–58. Minneapolis: Fortress Press, 2013.

Hume, Lynne. "Accessing the Eternal: Dreaming 'The Dreaming' and Ceremonial Performance." *Zygon* 39, no. 1 (March 2004): 237–58.

Hut, Janneke. "In Search of Affirmed Aboriginality as Christian: 'If you do not walk on the tracks of your grandparents, you will get lost . . .'" *Exchange* 41, no. 1 (2012): 19–43.

Imasogie, Osadolor. *Guidelines for Christian Theology in Africa*. Achimota, Ghana: African Christian Press, 1993.

Jantzen, Grace. "Human Diversity and Salvation in Christ." *Religious Studies* 20, no. 4 (1984): 579–92.

Jegede, Charles Obafemi. "An Exploration into Soteriology in Ifa: Oral and Intangible Heritage for Humanity." *Black Theology* 11, no. 2 (2013): 201–18.

Jensen, David H. "Discerning the Spirit: A Historical Introduction." In *The Lord and Giver of Life: Perspectives on Constructive Pneumatology*. Edited by David H. Jensen, 1–24. Louisville: Westminster John Knox, 2008.

Jenson, Robert. "The Triune God." In *Christian Dogmatics: Volume 1*. Edited by Carl E. Braaten and Robert W. Jenson, 87–98. Philadelphia: Fortress Press, 2011.

Johnson, Elizabeth A. *Ask the Beasts: Darwin and the God of Love*. London: Bloomsbury, 2014.

———. *Women, Earth, and Creator Spirit*. New York: Paulist Press, 1993.

Johnson, Todd M., David Barrett, and Peter F. Crossing. "Christianity 2010: A View from the New *Atlas of Global Christianity*." *International Bulletin of Missionary Research* 34, no. 1 (2010): 29–36.

Kärkkäinen, Veli-Matti. *The Holy Spirit: A Guide to Christian Theology*. Louisville: Westminster John Knox, 2012.

_____, ed. *Holy Spirit and Salvation*. Louisville: Westminster John Knox, 2010.

Katsuichi, Honda. *Harukor: An Ainu Woman's Tale*. Translated by Kyoko Selden. Berkeley: University of California Press, 2000.

Kelly, J. N. D. *Early Christian Doctrines*. San Francisco: HarperSanFrancisco, 1978.

Kim, Kirsteen. *The Holy Spirit in the World: A Global Conversation*. Maryknoll, NY: Orbis Books, 2007.

Knitter, Paul F. *No Other Name? A Critical Survey of Christian Attitudes Toward the World Religions*. Maryknoll, NY: Orbis Books, 1996.

Ko, Dorothy, JaHyun Kim Haboush, and Joan R. Piggott, eds. *Women and Confucian Cultures in Premodern China, Korea, and Japan*. Berkeley: University of California Press, 2003.

Kohn, Livia. *Daoist Dietetics: Food for Immortality*. Dunedin, FL: Three Pines Press, 2010.

_____. "Laozi: Ancient Philosopher, Master of Immortality, and God." In *Religions of China in Practice*. Edited by Donald S. Lopez Jr., 52–63. Princeton, NJ: Princeton University Press, 1996.

Komjathy, Louis. *The Daoist Tradition: An Introduction*. London: Bloomsbury, 2013.

_____. "Tracing the Contours of Daoism in North America." *Nova Religio: The Journal of Alternative and Emergent Religions* 8, no. 2 (2004): 5–27.

Krupat, Arnold. "Chief Seattle's Speech Revisited." *American Indian Quarterly* 35, no. 2 (Spring 2011): 192–214.

Kunnie, Julian E. and Nomalungelo I. Goduka, eds. *Indigenous Peoples' Wisdom and Power: Affirming Our Knowledge Through Narratives*. Aldershot, UK: Ashgate, 2006.

Kupperman, Joel. *Classic Asian Philosophy: A Guide to the Essential Texts*. Oxford: Oxford University Press, 2001.

Langton, Marcia. "Sacred Geography." In *Aboriginal Religions in Australia: An Anthology of Recent Writings*. Edited by Max Charlesworth, Françoise Dussart, and Howard Morphy, 131–40. Aldershot, UK: Ashgate, 2005.

Lao-Tzu. *Tao Te Ching*. Translated by Stephen Addiss and Stanley Lombardo. Indianapolis: Hackett, 1993.

Laozi. *Daodejing*. Translated by Hans-Georg Moeller. Chicago: Open Court, 2007.

_____. *Daodejing*. Translated by Edmund Ryden. Oxford: Oxford University Press, 2008.

_____. *Tao Te Ching*. Translated by Stephen Mitchell. New York: HarperCollins, 1988.

Lawson, E. Thomas. *Religions of Africa: Traditions in Transformation.* San Francisco: Harper & Row, 1984.

Lefebure, Leo. "Is There Reason for Hope? The Second Vatican Council and Catholic Interreligious Relations." In *The Long Shadow of Vatican II: Living Faith and Negotiating Authority since the Second Vatican Council.* Edited by Lucas van Rompay, Sam Miglarese, and David Morgan, 8–36. Chapel Hill: University of North Carolina Press, 2015.

Li, Chenyang, ed. *The Sage and the Second Sex: Confucianism, Ethics, and Gender.* Chicago: Open Court, 2000.

Liu, Zehau, and Quan Ge. "On the 'Human' in Confucianism." *Journal of Ecumenical Studies* 26, no. 2 (Spring 1989): 313–35.

Louth, Andrew. *Maximus the Confessor.* London: Routledge, 1999.

Lovejoy, Paul E. *Transformations in Slavery: A History of Slavery in Africa.* Cambridge: Cambridge University Press, 1983.

Low, Denise. "Contemporary Reinvention of Chief Seattle: Variant Texts of Chief Seattle's 1854 Speech." *American Indian Quarterly* 19, no. 3 (Summer 1995): 407–21.

Luther, Martin. *Lectures on Genesis, Chapters 1-5.* Vol. 1 of Luther's Works. Edited by Jaroslav Pelikan. St. Louis: Concordia, 1958.

_____. "On the Councils and the Church, 1539." Translated by Charles M. Jacobs. In *Church and Ministry III.* Edited by Eric Gritsch, 9–178. Vol. 41 of Luther's Works. Philadelphia: Fortress Press, 1966.

_____. "The Smalcald Articles." In *The Book of Concord: The Confessions of the Evangelical Lutheran Church.* Edited by Robert Kolb and Timothy J. Wengert, 295–328. Minneapolis: Fortress Press, 2000.

_____. *A Treatise on Christian Liberty.* Translated by W. A. Lambert. Philadelphia: Fortress Press, 1957.

MacDonald, Mary. "The Primitive, the Primal, and the Indigenous in the Study of Religion." *Journal of the American Academy of Religion* 79, no. 4 (December 2011): 814–26.

Mair, Victor. "The *Zhuangzi* and Its Impact." In *Daoism Handbook.* Edited by Livia Kohn, 30–52. Leiden: Brill, 2000.

Mann, Susan, and Yu-Yin Cheng, eds. *Under Confucian Eyes: Writings on Gender in Chinese History.* Berkeley: University of California Press, 2001.

Mannermaa, Tuomo. *Christ Present in Faith: Luther's View of Justification.* Translated by Kirsi I. Stjerna. Minneapolis: Fortress Press, 2005.

Masuzawa, Tomoko. *The Invention of World Religions: Or, How European Universalism Was Preserved in the Language of Pluralism.* Chicago: University of Chicago Press, 2005.

Maximus the Confessor. *Maximus Confessor: Selected Writings.* Translation by George C. Berthold. New York: Paulist Press, 1985.

Mbiti, John S. *African Religions and Philosophy.* New York: Praeger, 1969.

McCall, John C. "Rethinking Ancestors in Africa." *Africa* 65, no. 2 (1995): 256–70.

McCarthy, Rory G. "Martyrdom and Violence in Sikhism." In *Religious Innovation in a Global Age: Essays on the Construction of Spirituality*. Edited by George N. Lundskow, 258–69. Jefferson, NC: McFarland, 2005.

McGrath, Alister E., ed. *The Blackwell Encyclopedia of Modern Christian Thought*. Malden, MA: Blackwell, 1998.

_____. *Iustitia Dei: A History of Christian Doctrine of Justification*. Vol. 1, *From the Beginnings to 1500*. Cambridge: Cambridge University Press, 1986.

McLeod, Hew. "The Five Ks of the Khalsa Sikhs." *Journal of the American Oriental Society* 128, no. 2 (2008): 325–31.

McNiven, Ian J. "Saltwater People: Spiritscapes, Maritime Rituals and the Archaeology of Australian Indigenous Seascapes." *World Archaeology* 35, no. 3 (December 2003): 329–49.

Mencius. *Mencius*. Translated by D. C. Lau. London: Penguin Books, 2003.

Mercadante, Linda A. *Belief without Borders: Inside the Minds of the Spiritual but not Religious*. Oxford: Oxford University Press, 2014.

Meredith, Anthony. *Gregory of Nyssa*. London: Routledge, 1999.

Miles, Margaret R. *The Word Made Flesh: A History of Christian Thought*. Malden, MA: Blackwell, 2005.

Miller, Amy Lynn. "Hell." In *The Encyclopedia of Taoism*. Vol. 1. Edited by Fabrizio Pregadio, 69–71. London: Routledge, 2008.

_____. "Otherworldly Bureaucracy." In *The Encyclopedia of Taoism*. Vol. 1. Edited by Fabrizio Pregadio, 67–68. London: Routledge, 2008.

Miller, James. *Daoism: A Short Introduction*. Oxford: Oneworld, 2003.

Moltmann, Jürgen. *The Church in the Power of the Spirit: A Contribution to Messianic Ecclesiology*. Translated by Margaret Kohl. Minneapolis: Fortress Press, 1993.

_____. *The Spirit of Life: A Universal Affirmation*. Translated by Margaret Kohl. Minneapolis: Fortress Press, 1992.

Morton, John. "Aboriginal Religion Today." In *Aboriginal Religions in Australia: An Anthology of Recent Writings*. Edited by Max Charlesworth, Françoise Dussart, and Howard Morphy, 195–204. Aldershot, UK: Ashgate, 2005.

Musser, Donald W., and Joseph L. Price, eds. *A New Handbook of Christian Theologians*. Nashville: Abingdon Press, 1996.

Myrvold, Kristina. "Making the Scripture a Person: Reinventing Death Rituals of Guru Granth Sahib in Sikhism." In *The Death of Sacred Texts: Ritual Disposal and Renovation of Texts in World Religions*. Edited by Kristina Myrvold, 125–46. Burlington, VT: Ashgate, 2010.

_____. "Sikhism and Death." In *Death and Religion in a Changing World*. Edited by Kathleen Garces-Foley, 178–206. New York: Routledge, 2006.

Need, Stephen W. *Truly Divine and Truly Human: The Story of Christ and the Seven Ecumenical Councils.* Peabody, MA: Hendrickson, 2008.

Nesbitt, Eleanor. "Issues in Writing 'Introductions' to 'Sikhism.'" *Religions of South Asia* 1, no. 1 (2007): 47–63.

Nessan, Craig L. *Shalom Church: The Body of Christ as Ministering Community.* Minneapolis: Fortress Press, 2010.

Niebuhr, H. Richard. *Christ and Culture.* New York: Harper & Row, 1951.

Norris, Frederick W. *Faith Gives Fullness to Reasoning: The Five Theological Orations of Gregory Nazianzen.* Translated by Lionel R. Wickham and Frederick Williams. Leiden: E. J. Brill, 1991.

Nyitray, Vivian-Lee. "The Real Trouble with Confucianism." In *Love, Sex and Gender in the World Religions.* Edited by Joseph Runzo and Nancy M. Martin, 181–202. Oxford: Oneworld, 2000.

———. "Treacherous Terrain: Mapping Feminine Spirituality in Confucian Worlds." In *Confucian Spirituality.* Vol. 2. Edited by Tu Weming and Mary Evelyn Tucker, 463–79. New York: Crossroad, 2004.

Ojo, Olatunji. "'Heepa' (Hail) Òrìṣà: The Òrìṣà Factor in the Birth of Yoruba Identity." *Journal of Religion in Africa* 39, no. 1 (2009): 30–59.

Ölschlieger, Hans Dieter. "Technology, Settlement, and Hunting Ritual." In *Ainu: Spirit of a Northern People.* Edited by William W. Fitzhugh and Chisato O. Dubreuil, 219–21. Washington, DC: Arctic Studies Center, National Museum of Natural History, 1999.

Olupọna, Jacob K. *African Religions: A Very Short Introduction.* Oxford: Oxford University Press, 2014.

O'Malley, John W. *Tradition and Transition: Historical Perspectives on Vatican II.* Wilmington, DE: Michael Glazier, 1989.

Ono, Yugo. "Ainu Homelands: Natural History from Ice Age to Modern Times." In *Ainu: Spirit of a Northern People.* Edited by William W. Fitzhugh and Chisato O. Dubreuil, 32–38. Washington, DC: Arctic Studies Center, National Museum of Natural History, 1999.

Otto, Rudolf. *The Idea of the Holy: An Inquiry into the Non-Rational Factor in the Idea of the Divine and Its Relation to the Rational.* Translated by John W. Harvey. Oxford: Oxford University Press, 1967.

Pannenberg, Wolfhart. *The Apostles' Creed in the Light of Today's Questions.* Translated by Margaret Kohl. Philadelphia: Westminster Press, 1972.

———. *Systematic Theology.* Vol. 2. Translated by Geoffrey W. Bromiley. Grand Rapids: Eerdmans, 1994.

———. *Theology and the Kingdom of God.* Philadelphia: Westminster Press, 1969.

Pauw, Amy Plantinga. "The Holy Spirit and Scripture." In *The Lord and Giver of Life: Perspectives on Constructive Pneumatology.* Edited by David H. Jensen, 25–40. Louisville: Westminster John Knox, 2008.

Pelikan, Jaroslav. *The Emergence of the Catholic Tradition (100–600)*. Vol. 1 of *The Christian Tradition: A History of the Development of Doctrine*. Chicago: University of Chicago Press, 1975.

———. *The Growth of Medieval Theology (600–1300)*. Vol. 3 of *The Christian Tradition: A History of the Development of Doctrine*. Chicago: University of Chicago Press, 1978.

Penny, Benjamin. "Immortality and Transcendence." In *Daoism Handbook*. Edited by Livia Kohn, 109–33. Leiden: Brill, 2000.

Peterson, Cheryl M. *Who Is the Church? An Ecclesiology for the Twenty-First Century*. Minneapolis: Fortress Press, 2013.

Placher, William C. *The Triune God: An Essay in Postliberal Theology*. Louisville: Westminster John Knox, 2007.

Poceski, Mario. *Introducing Chinese Religions*. New York: Routledge, 2009.

Porter, Crystal. "After the Ainu Shinpō: The United Nations and the Indigenous People of Japan." *New Voices* 2 (December 2008): 201–19.

Powell, Mark Allan. *Introducing the New Testament: A Historical, Literary, and Theological Survey*. Grand Rapids: Baker Academic, 2009.

Pregadio, Fabrizio. "Elixirs and Alchemy." In *Daoism Handbook*. Edited by Livia Kohn, 165–95. Leiden: Brill, 2000.

Preston, Robert J., and Carl A. Hammerschlag. "The Native American Church." In *Psychodynamic Perspectives on Religion, Sect and Cult*. Edited by David A. Halperin, 93–103. Boston: John Wright, 1983.

Rahner, Karl. "The Abiding Significance of the Second Vatican Council." In *Concern for the Church*, 90–102. Vol. 20 of *Theological Investigations*. New York: Crossroad, 1981.

Raphals, Lisa. "A Woman Who Understood the Rites." In *Confucius and the Analects: New Essays*. Edited by Bryan W. Van Norden, 275–302. New York: Oxford University Press, 2002.

Reed, Barbara. "Women and Chinese Religion in Contemporary Taiwan." In *Today's Woman in World Religions*. Edited by Arvind Sharma, 225–44. Albany: State University of New York Press, 1994.

Robert, Dana L. "Shifting Southward: Global Christianity Since 1945." *International Bulletin of Missionary Research* 24, no. 2 (April 2000): 50–58.

Rolston, Holmes, III. "Does Nature Need to Be Redeemed?" *Zygon* 29, no. 2 (June 1994): 205–29.

Roth, Harold D. "The Inner Cultivation Tradition of Early Daoism." In *Religions of China in Practice*. Edited by Donald S. Lopez Jr., 123–48. Princeton, NJ: Princeton University Press, 1996.

Sanders, John. "Raising Hell about Razing Hell: Evangelical Debates on Universal Salvation." *Perspectives in Religious Studies* 40, no. 3 (Fall 2013): 267–82.

Sasamura, Jiro. "Beyond the Ainu Shinpo: An Ainu View." In *Ainu: Spirit of a*

Northern People. Edited by William W. Fitzhugh and Chisato O. Dubreuil, 369–70. Washington, DC: Arctic Studies Center, National Museum of Natural History, 1999.

Schipper, Kristofer. *The Taoist Body.* Berkeley: University of California Press, 1993.

Shackle, Christopher, and Arvind-pal Singh Mandair. *Teachings of the Sikh Gurus: Selections from the Sikh Scriptures.* London: Routledge, 2005.

Shih, Fang-Long. "Chinese 'Bad Death' Practices in Taiwan: Maidens and Modernity." *Mortality* 15, no. 2 (May 2010): 122–37.

Shorty, Lawrence, and Ulrike Wiethaus. "Diné (Navajo) Narratives of Death and Bereavement." In *Bereavement and Death Rituals*, vol. 3 of *Religion, Death, and Dying.* Edited by Lucy Bregman, 171–90. Santa Barbara, CA: Praeger, 2010.

Siddle, Richard. "Ainu History: An Overview." In *Ainu: Spirit of a Northern People.* Edited by William W. Fitzhugh and Chisato O. Dubreuil, 67–73. Washington, DC: Arctic Studies Center, National Museum of Natural History, 1999.

Singh, Nikky-Guninder Kaur. *The Birth of the Khalsa: A Feminist Re-Memory of Sikh Identity.* Albany: State University of New York Press, 2005.

_____. "Female Feticide in the Punjab and Fetus Imagery in Sikhism." In *Imagining the Fetus: The Unborn in Myth, Religion and Culture.* Edited by Vanessa R. Sasson and Jane Marie Law, 121–36. New York: Oxford University Press, 2009.

_____, trans. *The Name of My Beloved: Verses of the Sikh Gurus.* San Francisco: HarperSanFrancisco, 1995.

_____. "The Sikh Bridal Symbol: An Epiphany of Interconnections." *Journal of Feminist Studies in Religion* 8, no. 2 (Fall 1992): 41–64.

Singh, Nikky-Guninder Kaur, and Todd Curcuru. "Sikhism." In *Religions of the World: An Introduction to Culture and Meaning.* Edited by Lawrence E. Sullivan, 109–28. Minneapolis: Fortress Press, 2013.

Singh, Pashaura. "The Guru Granth Sahib." In *The Oxford Handbook of Sikh Studies.* Edited by Pashaura Singh and Louis E. Fenech, 125–35. Oxford: Oxford University Press, 2014.

_____. "New Directions in Sikh Studies." In *The Oxford Handbook of Sikh Studies.* Edited by Pashaura Singh and Louis E. Fenech, 625–44. Oxford: Oxford University Press, 2014.

Southern, R. W. *Saint Anselm and His Biographer.* Cambridge: Cambridge University Press, 1963.

Streufert, Mary. "Maternal Sacrifice as a Hermeneutics of the Cross." In *Cross Examinations: Readings on the Meaning of the Cross.* Edited by Marit Trelstad, 63–75. Minneapolis: Fortress Press, 2006.

Swain, Tony. *Aboriginal Religions in Australia: A Bibliographic Survey*. New York: Greenwood Press, 1991.

Swidler, Leonard. "Confucianism for Modern Persons in Dialogue with Christianity and Modernity." *Journal of Ecumenical Studies* 40, no. 1–2 (Winter–Spring 2003): 12–25.

Tatla, Darshan Singh. "The Sikh Diaspora." In *The Oxford Handbook of Sikh Studies*. Edited by Pashaura Singh and Louis E. Fenech, 495–512. Oxford: Oxford University Press, 2014.

Thompson, Marjorie J. *Soul Feast: An Invitation to the Christian Spiritual Life*. Louisville: Westminster John Knox, 2005.

Tucker, Mary Evelyn, and John Berthrong, eds. *Confucianism and Ecology: The Interrelation of Heaven, Earth, and Humans*. Cambridge, MA: Harvard University Center for the Study of World Religions, 1998.

Turner, Alice. *The History of Hell*. New York: Harcourt Brace, 1993.

Utagawa, Hiroshui. "The Archaeology of *Iyomante*." In *Ainu: Spirit of a Northern People*. Edited by William W. Fitzhugh and Chisato O. Dubreuil, 256–60. Washington, DC: Arctic Studies Center, National Museum of Natural History, 1999.

Venbrux, Eric. "Social Life and the Dreamtime: Clues to Creation Myths as Rhetorical Devices in Tiwi Mortuary Ritual." *Religion and the Arts* 13, no. 4 (2009): 464–76.

Wada, Kan. "Ainu Shamanism." In *Ainu: Spirit of a Northern People*. Edited by William W. Fitzhugh and Chisato O. Dubreuil, 261–67. Washington, DC: Arctic Studies Center, National Museum of Natural History, 1999.

Wallace, Mark I. *Finding God in the Singing River: Christianity, Spirit, Nature*. Minneapolis: Fortress Press, 2005.

Weingart, Richard E. *The Logic of Divine Love: A Critical Analysis of the Soteriology of Peter Abailard*. Oxford: Clarendon Press, 1970.

Williams, Delores S. "Black Women's Surrogacy Experience and the Christian Notion of Redemption." In *Cross Examinations: Readings on the Meaning of the Cross*. Edited by Marit Trelstad, 19–32. Minneapolis: Fortress Press, 2006.

Winslow, Donald F. *The Dynamics of Salvation: A Study in Gregory of Nazianzus*. Cambridge, MA: Philadelphia Patristic Foundation, 1979.

Witt, Joseph, and David Wiles. "Nature in Asian Indigenous Traditions: A Survey Article." *Worldviews* 10, no. 1 (2006): 40–68.

Woo, Terry. "Confucianism and Feminism." In *Feminism and World Religions*. Edited by Arvind Sharma and Katherine K. Young, 110–47. Albany: State University of New York Press, 1999.

Yao, Kevin Xiyi. "Religion and Church in China: Trends and Dynamics." *Africanus Journal* 6, no. 1 (2014): 23–28.

Yao, Xinzhong. *An Introduction to Confucianism*. Cambridge: Cambridge University Press, 2000.

Index

Abelard, Peter, 128, 135–37, 223
Aborigines, 5, 6, 16, 18–19
AdiGranth (see Guru Granth Sahib),
    38–39, 43–45, 45n20, 183, 224, xi,
    33, 35, 37–38, 38n9, 39–41, 41n12,
    44, 9, 51, 55–58, 60, 180, 192, 217,
    229, 232
African Initiated Churches, 216
Ainu, 5, 19, 19n51, 20, 20n52,
    20nn53–54, 21–24, 165, 183,
    223–25, 227, 230–33
alchemy, 92, 104–5, 105n33, 231
amrit, 37, 53, 56
Analects, 71–73, 75, 75n30, 76, 76n35,
    77, 78n42, 79–80, 80n48, 53,
    81n56, 224, 231
Anandpur Sahib, 52
ancestors, 7–8, 10–12, 12n29, 13, 16–19,
    77, 65, 79n45, 81, 82, 101, 124, 165,
    211, 217, 229
ancestral rites (Confucianism), 211, xii,
    61–64, 64n5, 66–68, 68n10, 69–72,
    72n19, 22, 73–74, 75n29, 76, 76n33,
    77, 77n38, 39, 78, 78n73, 79, 79n45,
    47, 80, 80n52, 54, 81, 81n57, 58, 82,
    82n59, 84n63, 85, 85n66, 86,
    86n67–69, 71, 87, 87n72, 73, 89n1,
    90, 93–94, 100–101, 114, 124, 156,
    211, 211n40, 217, 220, 223, 225,
    226, 228, 230, 233
angakkuq, 208, 209, 217
animal spirits, 22, 165
Anselm, 128, 135, 137, 138n98, 139,
    139n55, 140, 140n58, 223, 232
apokatastasis, 154
Athanasius, 129
atonement, 106, 120, 126, 134–37,139
Augustine, 155, 168, 179, 179n60, 182,
    189, 190, 191, 191n6, 223, 224

Babalawo, 28–29
Balthasar, Hansurs von, 155, 223
Bandi Chhor Divas, 55

Bernard of Clairvaux, 168, 168n29,
    202n20, 224
Boston Confucianism, 86
Braaten, Carl, 117, 117n1, 223
breathing (Daoism), 90, 103, 104, 168
bureaucracy (Daoism), 120, 121n3, 156,
    229

Catherine of Sienna, 168, 168n28, 170,
    171n39, 224
Celestial Masters, 91, 92
Chief Seattle, 2, 3, 3n3, 4, 227–28
Chinese Christianity, 215
Chinese popular religion, 93
Christus victor, 120, 126–27, 129
Chrysostom, John, 127, 129, 129n25
Chuang Tzu (see *Zhuangzi*), 69n15, 91,
    105, 105n37, 108, 111, 112n64, 113,
    113n68, 114, 114n70, 224
church, Global South, 4, 185, 213,
    213n51, 214–16
Classical Daoism, 91
communicatio idiomatum, 134
Confucius (*Kongzi*), 63–64, 66, 69–75,
    75n30, 76, 76n35, 77, 78, 78n72,
    79–80, 80n48, 80n53, 81, 81n56, 82,
    94, 108, 112, 124, 224, 231
Council of Trent, 198
Cultural Revolution, 92
Cur Deus Homo, 137, 139n55, 140n58,
    223

Dao, 74, 78, 89, 91–92, 99, 102, 106,
    109, 110, 112–13, 115–16
Daodejing, 90–91, 98–99, 108–9,
    109n53, 110, 110n56–58, 111, 115,
    227
Daozang, 107
Darwin, 149, 149n84, 226
De, 179, 179n60, 223
death (Christianity), vii,11–12, 23, 31,
    36–38, 38n9, 39, 42, 46, 48, 51, 56,
    56n39, 59, 75–76, 79, 92, 105–6,

110–13, 117, 119–20, 122–24, 125n9, 126–27, 129, 131–32, 134–36, 139–44, 146–51, 151n88, 152–53, 153n91, 154–57, 160, 162, 171–72, 174, 183
death (Confucianism), 75–76, 79, 105–6, 110
deep incarnation, 148–49, 149n83, 225
deification (see *theosis*), 120, 126, 129, 131, 131n27, 133, 133n41, 134, 136, 225–26
diet (Daoism), 22, 104, 105
Diné, 150–51, 157
divination, Africa, 25, 27n84, 28, 29–31
divination, China, 67, 70, 94–95, 97
divine child abuse, 140–41
Donatist, 186, 189–91
Dreamtime (also The Dreaming), 16, 18, 18n47, 233

Eastern Orthodoxy, 193
Ecumenical Patriarch, 193, 201
ek onkar (also *ik oankar*), 49–50
Esu, 29, 30
Ethiopian eunuch, 176–77
evolution, 73, 86, 148–50, 219

filioque, 195
finitude, 147–49
Finnish School, 133
Foster, Richard, 181, 182n68, 225
four virtues, 73

Gandhi, Indira, 48–49
Gehenna, 125
Gongfu (Kung Fu), 103
González, Justo, 193n8, 198, 199n11, 225
Gospel of Luke, 143
granthi, 56–57, 180
Gregersen, Niels, 148, 149n83, 225
Gregory of Nazianzus, 128, 131, 131n29, 132n32, 224, 230, 233
Gregory of Nyssa, 127, 127nn17–18, 129, 172, 229
gurdwara, 33–34, 41–42, 56–57, 59, 192, 217
gurpurb, 55

Guru Arjan, 38–41, 43–44, 48, 55, 58, 146, 146n72, 225
Guru Gobind Singh, 35, 39–40, 52–53, 55, 146, 180
Guru Granth Sahib, xi, 33, 35, 37–38, 38n9, 39–41, 41n12, 44, 49, 51, 55–57, 60, 180, 192, 217, 229, 232
Guru Nanak, 35–37, 37n5, 38–39, 44, 50–51, 55, 57, 60, 146, 225
Gurumukh, 33, 51

Haight, Roger, 165, 166n19, 172, 172n43, 225
Han dynasty, 63–64, 67, 69–71, 91
happy exchange, 133
Har Krishnan, 33
Harmandir Sahib, 38–39, 41, 48, 57–58, 58n41
harmony, 24, 36, 64n5, 75, 77–78, 81–82, 100–101, 106, 111–14, 140, 157, 202, 223
Heaven, 12, 30, 65–67, 69, 72, 75–76, 78–82, 89n1, 99, 101–2, 106, 108–9, 119–20, 129, 133, 141–43, 146, 151–52, 155–56, 171, 175, 177, 195, 208, 211, 233
Hola Maholla, 55
holiness, 57, 188, 190–91, 207, 213
Holy Ghost, 169
hózhò, 150–51
hukamnama, 41, 192

I-Ching (see *Yijing*), 67–68, 70
icons, 194–96
Ifa, 26, 27n84, 27n86, 28
Ikin, 29–31
immortality/immortals (Daoism), xi, 23, 35, 51, 56, 65, 81, 101, 104, 104n30, 105, 105n34, 39, 106, 108n48, 109n51, 115–16, 147–49, 152, 171, 227, 231
Inuit, 208–9, 217
Irenaeus, 168
Iyomante, 22n65, 23–24, 24n71, 25, 233

Jap, 41, 43
Jensen, David, 176–77
Jesus, 117, 119–23, 125–29, 131–37, 141–45, 148–49, 152, 154–55, 169,

174, 177, 185, 187–89, 195–96, 198, 203–4
jiao, 106–7
John of the Cross, 168, 169n30
Johnson, Elizabeth, 149, 149n84, 170, 170n35, 177, 177n52, 214n54,59, 216n70, 223, 226
junzi, 80

kaccha, 53–54
kamuy, 22, 22n63, 23n67, 24, 225
kangha, 53–54
kara, 53–54, 57
Kärkkäinen, Veli-Matti, 168n25, 172n42, 174, 192, 209, 227
Kau Cim, 95
kesha, 53
Khalsa, 33, 39–40, 47–48, 51–52, 52n30, 53–54, 54n32, 55–56, 59, 59n46, 146, 229, 232
Khalistan, 48
Khanda, 39, 52
Kim, Kirsteen, 174, 174n46, 227
kingdom of heaven, 152
kirpan, 53–54
kirtan, 33, 41, 57, 192
Knitter, Paul, 125, 126n14, 171, 227
Kumarajiva, 63

langar, 33, 56–57, 192
Laozi, 66, 90, 99n17, 107–8, 108n48, 109, 109n51, 53, 110n56–58, 111, 115, 227
Luther, Martin, 35, 133, 134n43, 170, 170n38, 178n56, 196, 205–6, 206n24–25, 207, 207n29, 228

manmukh, 51
Mannermaa, Tuomo, 133, 134n42, 228
marks of the church, 203, 205–6, 212–13
Mao Zedong, 64, 92
martyrdom, 48, 55, 146, 146n72, 147nn76–77, 156, 225, 229
Maximus the Confessor, 132, 132n36, 132n38, 228
mela, 55

Mencius, 63–64, 66, 82–84, 84n64, 112, 229
Mercadante, Linda, 162–63, 229
Miles, Margaret, 190, 190n4, 199, 229
Moltmann, Jürgen, 174, 177n51, 212, 212n42, 229
moral example, 120, 135
Mountbatten, Louis, 48
mysterium tremendum, 161

Native American, 1, 3, 6, 13, 13n32, 14, 151, 202–3, 203n21, 223, 231
Native American Church, 151, 202–3, 203n21, 231
Navajo (see Diné), 150–51, 151n88, 157, 202, 232
Neo-Confucianism, xii, 61–64, 64n5, 66–68, 68n10, 69–72, 72nn19–22, 73, 73nn23–26, 74, 75n29, 76, 76n33, 77, 77nn38–39, 78, 78n43, 79, 79nn45–47, 80, 80nn52–54, 81, 81nn57–58, 82, 82n59, 84n63, 85, 85n66, 86, 86nn67–71, 87, 87nn72–73, 89n1, 90, 93–94, 100–101, 114, 124, 156, 211, 211n40, 217, 220, 223, 225–26, 228, 230, 233
Nessan, Craig, 205, 212, 212n44, 230
New Confucianism, 64, 85–86
New Testament, 120, 122, 125, 129, 143n63, 167, 179, 186–87, 231
Niebuhr, H. Richard, 204, 204n23, 230
Ninety-Five Theses, 197
Noah's Ark, 118–19
nones, 159, 162

Odu, 28–29, 31
Oliver, Mary, 152–53, 153n91, 154
Olodumare, 27–28, 162
Operation Blue Star, 48–49, 172
Opon, 30
oracle bones, 64–65, 67, 95–96
ori, 161–62
orisha, 26–27, 162
Orunmila, 27–28, 30–31
Otto, Rudolph, 160, 161n5, 230
outer darkness, 125

panj pyare, 52, 59
Pannenberg, Wolfhart, 143–44, 144nn66–69, 145n70, 147, 147n79, 148, 230
Panth, 35
parshad, 57, 192
partition of India, 48, 58
Pauw, Amy Plantinga, 175–76, 230
Pelikan, Jaroslav, 126n16, 128, 129n24, 132, 137, 167, 167n22, 170n38, 228, 231
penal substitution (see satisfaction), 126, 137
Peyotism, 203
pinyin, 61, 89n1
Pope Francis, 189, 210, 210n38
Pope John XXIII, 200–201
Pope Pius VI, 199
prolepsis, 143–44
Protestant reformations, 196, 199
purity, 33, 123–24, 190–91

qi, 62, 102–3, 115
Qigong, 103, 116
Qing Dynasty, 63–64, 91

Ravidas, 45
reformation (see Protestant reformations), 186, 196–99
religion, definition, ix, 5n8–9, 6, 6nn10–11, 7, 7n15, 8, 8n21, 11, 12n28, 14–16, 16n37, 18nn43–44, 18n47, 25–26, 26n77, 27, 27n85, 28, 31, 31n96, 32–33, 33n1, 35n2, 37, 37n6, 38n8–9, 46, 50, 56, 56n39, 59, 59n49, 60n50, 61–63, 63n4, 64n6, 69, 69n12, 70n16, 71–72, 72n21, 73, 73n24, 74n26, 86, 89, 90n5, 92–96, 98, 101–2, 102n27, 109, 115–16, 120, 146, 150, 156–57, 159, 159n1, 160, 160nn3–4, 161–62, 162n7, 163–64, 166, 166n19, 200–203, 203n21, 214, 214n58, 215, 215n62, 220, 221, 223–24, 232
religion, indigenous, xii, 1, 4–5, 5nn8–9, 6–8, 12, 14, 26, 32, 98n15, 226, 228
resurrection, 122, 126–27, 131, 133, 135, 142, 152, 188, 217

Romans, 129, 131, 131n27, 133, 135, 135n46, 136, 188, 198, 223, 225

Santeria, 26, 161, 183, 224
satisfaction, 120, 137, 139–40
Second Vatican Council (See Vatican II), 186, 195, 198, 198n10, 199–200, 200n14, 201–2, 202nn16–17, 226, 228, 230–31
Seventh Ecumenical Council, 194
shamans, 115, 165, 208
Shang Dynasty, 63–65, 70, 90, 108
Shangdi (or *Di*), 65
Sima Qian, 108, 111
Singh, Ranjit, 46
Smalcald Articles, 178, 178n56, 206n24, 228
spiritual body, 152
spiritual but not religious, 162–64, 177, 183
Song Dynasty, 63–64, 70, 91
Spring and Autumn Period, 66, 70, 74
spirit-sending ceremonies, 19, 22n66, 24, 24n72, 24n75, 223
spiritual disciplines, 181–82
surrogacy, 141, 141n60, 141n62, 224, 233

Taijiquan, 103, 116
Tang Dynasty, 63, 70–71, 91–92
Tao Te Ching (see Daodejing), 90–91, 98, 99n17, 108–9, 109n53, 110, 110nn56–58, 111, 115, 227
temples, Chinese, 69, 92–95, 106
terra nullius, 14
Tertullian, 173
theosis, 120, 126, 129, 131, 131n27, 133, 133n41, 134, 136, 225–26
Thompson, Marjorie, 181, 181n65, 233
three obediences, 73
Tian, 65, 89n1
Tin Hau Temple, 95–96
Trinity, 167, 171n40, 172, 179, 179n60, 223
Torres Strait Islanders, 9–10

Vatican II, 186, 198, 198n10, 199–200, 200n14, 201–2, 202n16, 226, 228, 230 vivifier, 169

Wade-Giles, 61, 67, 77, 89n1
Ware, Kallistos, 167, 168n25, 181,
    181n64
Warring States Period, 66, 82, 90, 99
"When Death Comes", 152–53, 153n91
Williams, Delores, 141, 141n62, 233
women in Confucianism, 72–73
women in Daoism, 103n28, 114–15,
    115n73, 224
women in the church, 187
Wong Tai Sin Temple, 94–95, 97
wuwei, 101, 104

xiaoren, 80
xin, 77
Xunzi, 61–64, 66, 82, 84–85

Yijing (*Book of Changes*), 67–68, 70
yin/yang, 63–64, 67–68, 90, 100–101,
    103–4, 115
Yoruba, xii, 4n6, 12, 25–26, 26n77,
    26n79, 26n83, 27, 27n84, 28, 29n93,
    31, 161, 223–24, 230

Zacchaeus, 122, 143
Zhai, 106
zhi, 77
Zhou Dynasty, 62–63, 65–66, 70, 74,
    82, 90–91, 108, 112
Zhu Xi, 70–71
Zhuang Zhou, 91
Zhuangzi, 67, 90–91, 98, 105, 108,
    111–12, 112n61, 113, 113n69, 114,
    228